GLOBAL BUSINESS

As the world gets ever smaller, all serious businesses must understand the influences and complexities of international trade. Those who don't risk being left behind, or worse, being outmaneuvered by their competitors Global Business: From Theory to Practice offers an insightful way to gain the critical knowledge needed to navigate global business. I highly recommend this book for anyone in business today.

Brian Dearing
Vice President Business Development, Government Relations
Hunter Defense Technologies

This book presents a long experience of actual successful business techniques that bridges culture and commercial know-how for both the Mid-East and US business community. I recommend this helpful book for all who are interested in doing practical business between these two great global regions.

Saud M. Al-Suwaileh, Riyadh Officer Manager
U. S. - Saudi Arabian Business Council

From a marketing and sales point of view I find this book very informative, not only the technical details of international trade, but the real life and practical situations and solutions that are really needed to make the sale. I wish I had this information when I started in international sales, I know I would have had greater success.

Sam Sahouri Ghanem, President,
AFG International Inc.

As the world of international business spins through the 21st century and internet based communications methodologies reduce transaction times to mere microseconds, products and services are provided more and more frequently from sources around the globe with little regard for distances, country of origin or language. The objective of this book is to provide the reader with a thorough grounding in the bases of these realities and GLOBAL TRADE: FROM THEORY TO PRACTICE achieves its objective very nicely.

James R. Loux, President
Allegheny Brokerage Company, Inc.

A 'must read' for those wanting to succeed in the evolving global economy.

Joe W. Meredith, Ph.D.
President
Virginia Tech Corporate Research Center, Inc.

GLOBAL BUSINESS
From Theory to Practice

Brian C. Satterlee
Joseph A. Robinson

SYNERGISTICS
Roanoke, Virginia 24024

GLOBAL BUSINESS: FROM THEORY TO PRACTICE

Between the time website information is gathered and published, some sites may have changed or closed. In addition, the transcription or URLs can result in typographical errors. The publisher would appreciate notification where these occur so they may be corrected in subsequent editions.

ISBN 13: 978-0-9788748-6-5 (CLOTH)
ISBN 10: 0-9788748-6-2 (CLOTH)

Published by Synergistics Inc.,
Roanoke, VA 24024
info@synpub.com
First Edition: January 2008

Typeface: 11/15 Garamond LT
Printer: Edwards Brothers, Inc.
Editorial Director: Kerry Hogan
Designer: Kelly Pittman

Library of Congress Cataloging-in-Publication Data

Satterlee, Brian C., 1956-
  Global business : from theory to practice / Brian C. Satterlee and Joseph A. Robinson. -- 1st ed.
     p. cm.
  Includes index.
  ISBN-13: 978-0-9788748-6-5 (hardcover : alk. paper)
  ISBN-10: 0-9788748-6-2 (hardcover : alk. paper) 1. International trade. 2. International business enterprises. 3. Globalization. I. Robinson, Joseph A., 1942- II. Title.

HF1379.S258 2008
658'.049--dc22

                    2007040205

Printed in the United States of America
12 11 10 09 08   1 2 3 4 5

To Brian Satterlee without whose foresight, direction and facilitating this book would not exist for the benefit of students of international commerce and global road warriors alike. Thanks. Joe Robinson.

ABOUT THE AUTHORS

Brian Satterlee holds earned doctorates in both Business Administration and in Higher Education. He has been teaching college-level courses since 1980 and currently serves as Professor of Business Administration at Liberty University, where he teaches the MBA courses International Business, Global Financial Markets, and Developing Global Markets. In 2004 he was recognized with the Liberty University Chancellor's Award for Teaching Excellence.

In addition to his academic career, he is experienced in business and industry. During the 1970s and early 1980s, Dr. Satterlee worked in the construction industry, experiencing increasing levels of responsibility and authority in both technical and managerial positions. He has been a successful entrepreneur and engaged in various small business enterprises over the years. During the mid-1990s, he was invited to the Caribbean islands of Grenada and Dominica and to the Central American nation of Belize, where he was instrumental in assisting non-governmental organizations create and sustain economic development activity.

Dr. Satterlee has served as consultant to numerous organizations and government agencies in areas such as productivity improvement, leadership, technology, and innovation. Other executive-level positions include serving as business school dean, graduate school dean, and dean of continuing education.

A member of the Oxford Round Table, he has authored books in the areas of Strategic Management, Knowledge Management, E-Commerce, and International Business. He has published 23 scholarly papers nationally within his disciplines and has been invited to speak at 25 professional conferences, both national and international.

Joe Robinson's 41 years of experience in global commerce include living abroad 4 times, travel to 67 countries, and exporting to 105 countries. In addition to being a graduate of Virginia Tech and Thunderbird School of Global Management, he was one of five Americans to receive a Japanese government post graduate scholarship to study International Industrial Market Research at Keio University in Tokyo.

As International Trade Manager for the State of Virginia, Mr. Robinson provided counseling on export management and successful best practices and procedures—in addition to leading numerous overseas trade missions. His highly acclaimed "Export Management and Marketing Procedures, Documents and Compliance" workshop has been attended by over 1000 exporters representing 310 companies, some of which are in the global top 100 manufacturers.

He held managerial positions at a Fortune 500 chemical company, was country manager for a major American pharmaceutical firm in Japan, and was vice president and board of directors member of a leading American-Japanese joint venture. He managed his own international business: Robinson Engineering Products.

Joe was president of three international trade associations, one of which he founded. He authored numerous export marketing articles for International Business Training (www.i-b-t.net). One highlight of Joe's career was providing White House Executive Briefing to the President of the United States on NAFTA.

CONTENTS

PREFACE

For the first half of the twentieth century, collegiate business education courses were considered primarily skill-intensive—deficient in the application of scientific research methodology. Such practical courses were taught by faculty who had business experience and demonstrated expertise in the specific skill being taught. During the 1960s, the emphasis on a specific-skills business curriculum was abandoned in favor of the management science approach, taught by faculty who were trained in the scientific method of research. These faculty members possessed little or no business experience. Critics of the management-science-only method believed that the specific skills were abandoned in favor of teaching critical thinking, though many believed students had nothing to think about that they could use beyond the ivory tower of academia. Business students, though well versed in theoretical constructs, were not being equipped to confront the realities of the business world.

This shift in the approach to teaching business courses was reflected in the type of textbooks published for use in the class. The new business textbooks, typically written by career academics, were essentially being published more for the benefit of the professors than students—as more institutions of higher learning instituted faculty polices, such as "publish or perish." This policy stimulated textbook publishers to flood the market with book packages that had added features and ancillary teaching materials to make the teaching process easier—as the ancillary materials provided lecture outlines, test banks, videos, and CDs—all of which greatly added to student textbook costs. These "extra materials" were used as incentives for faculty to adopt the textbooks. In addition, the instructor could now devote the time normally spent on class preparation to other activities that contributed to earning tenure and career promotion. Tenure and career promotion was based on publication—an end result of "publish or perish" policies. It is interesting to note that many institutions of higher learning view books written by non-academics or practitioners as not fitting the "publish or perish" paradigm. The erroneous presupposition is that these books are perceived by some in the academy as deficient in academic rigor, due to the so called "lack of scientific research" methodology. Thus, the typical business textbook of the late twentieth century was written by those motivated more by research than teaching—for the primary benefit of the author who possessed little or no business experience. The student was a secondary consideration and "paid the price" as textbook prices escalated at very high levels each year.

The twentieth century collegiate teaching model was based on the proposition that the teacher was the purveyor of knowledge and was the one responsible for student learning; transmitting course knowledge via passive learning methods required little or no interaction on the part of the student. The development of the Internet during the last decade of the twentieth century ushered the twenty-first century model of collegiate learning: online education. In contrast to the twentieth century emphasis on the role of the teacher, the twenty-first century model places at least equal emphasis on the role of the learner. Students have become more involved (active) in the new learning model, as the role of the faculty has shifted from an emphasis on "teaching the student what is to be learned" to "being a mentor and facilitator of the learning process." Mentoring and facilitating is a more empowering approach to teaching, as the student essentially learns how to learn, thus moving away from being dependent on the need for a teacher to explain everything to becoming a more independent learner.

Synergistics Publishing was established in response to the growing concern that the typical textbook used in college classes today, based on the old twentieth century model, is obsolete in light of the realities of the twenty-first century. Textbooks should be written and published, first and foremost, with the student needs in mind. Obviously, there is nothing inherently wrong with the author enjoying the fruits of the labor of publishing, yet the primary purpose of publishing textbooks for student use must uphold the needs of the student—high-quality academic content that is usable in a timely manner and low cost.

The twenty-first century student rarely has the leisure time that was available to the Twentieth century student. Today's typical college student balances a full time schedule of classes, demands of a job, socialization with family and friends, and church/community volunteer activities. The student is always connected to someone or some organization via e-mail, instant messaging, cellular telephone, personal digital assistant, corporate intranets and extranets, and so forth. Time is a precious commodity to the twenty-first century student. Hence, a textbook needs to provide the essentials of high-quality academic content in an easy-to-read format—one that does not require exhaustive hours of reading for comprehension. Synergistics Publishing authors are scholar/practitioners, who combine academic knowledge with real-world experience in developing a textbook that delivers the essential high-quality subject matter in a reader-friendly format.

The second student need is low cost. The typical business textbook is sold by college bookstores well in excess of $150, and many exceed $200. Synergistics Publishing textbooks are intended to be sold by college bookstores for approximately half the price of traditional publishing houses. This is the result of an innovative business model using the latest in management processes and information technologies. Our scholar/practitioners develop high-quality textbooks that are relevant to Internet-Age learners and contemporary in coverage of essential core concepts. Our publishing processes engender the development of a personalized approach to instruction, allowing professors who adopt our textbooks to add value to their courses, whether online or in the physical classroom.

This textbook—developed to provide essential core concept body of knowledge to business students that meets the dual objectives of high quality and low cost—is suitable for use in both undergraduate and graduate classes. While the body of knowledge at both academic levels remains the same, the level of learning and application is higher at the graduate level than at the undergraduate level. This concept is supported in the literature concerning Learning Theory.

In 1956, Benjamin Bloom led a team of educational psychologists who developed a classification of levels of intellectual behavior important in learning. Bloom's team found that over 95 percent of the test questions students encountered required them to think only at the lowest possible level—the recall of information. Bloom identified six levels within the cognitive domain— from the simple recall or recognition of facts, as the lowest level, through increasingly more complex and abstract mental levels—to the highest order which is classified as evaluation.*

Thus, in the undergraduate course, the concepts of this book would be dealt with at the Bloom lower-domain levels of knowledge, comprehension, and application. In the graduate course, the higher learning domain levels of analysis, synthesis, and evaluation would be emphasized.

The Publisher is committed to helping professor's who teach business courses by providing both a Student Guide and an Instructor's Resource Manual to accompany this textbook. The Student Guide is appropriate for use at the undergraduate level, and is a proven resource for enhancing student learning. Recent surveys reveal that those students who completed the exercises in the Study Guide scored at least one letter-grade higher on objective tests than those who did not complete the exercises. The Instructor's Resource Manual contains PowerPoint® presentation slides, a test bank, answers to Student Guide questions, and suggested resources for enhancing the teaching-learning process (including current IB-events video clips) for use in teaching the course in both online and residential format. Faculty who adopt this textbook for use in their courses may contact the Publisher by e-mail to request the Instructor's Resource Manual.

* Bloom's Taxonomy. Retrieved January 1, 2007 from http://www.officeport.com/edu/blooms.htm

INTRODUCTION

Global Business: From Theory to Practice was written with two specific learning audiences in mind: learners and business professionals.

This book provides learners from diverse academic backgrounds an overview of the theoretical knowledge and practical experiences needed to be literate and competent in the field of global business and management. While the book assumes that learners will have limited knowledge in the area of global business and management prior to enrolling in their course, the content provides exit learning and competencies comparable to those experienced in courses which require prerequisite knowledge or prior coursework in the field. Thus, this book is suitable for undergraduate and graduate courses in International Business, Global Business, and Global Management—in which no prerequisite knowledge or prior coursework is required for enrollment.

Global Business: From Theory to Practice serves as an excellent resource for professionals who wish to supplement their work experience with a clear and comprehensive understanding of global business theory. Additionally, the authors provide practical wisdom and advice through the application of real world examples and scenarios. Each chapter concludes with a section that discusses how the business professional can apply the knowledge gained to enhance their global businesses and careers. Thus, this book is suitable for business professionals seeking to gain a competitive edge by adding to their knowledge base.

Chapters 1 through 4 cover the major theoretical foundations for the study of global commerce, such as globalization, impacts of culture, the environments of international business, international trade theory, global trading systems, and foreign direct investment. Chapters 5 through 8 are designed for the reader to build on these foundations and develop the ability to create and sustain competency in the implementation of global business activities. Specific competencies include interface with global financial markets, regional economic integration, entering global markets, and global operations management.

Chapter 1, "Globalization and Global Business," provides the foundational concepts necessary for the study and practice of international commerce. It begins by defining globalization and its importance to nations. After comparing and contrasting domestic business with global business, it provides a brief discussion of the historical developments of global trade, from Pax Romana to Pax Americana. In addition to describing the forces driving the globalization of business, it illustrates the impact of globalization on nations, business, employees, and citizens. The chapter concludes by delineating the differences and similarities between managing domestic and global businesses, with the implications of globalization for the business manager.

Chapter 2, "The Impact of Culture on Global Business," builds upon the foundation provided in Chapter 1 with extended coverage of the major implications of culture on global business. It begins with a discussion of managerial-cultural paradigms and the communication dimensions of culture. The chapter delineates the major beliefs of world religions— which form the foundation for differences in values and ethical behavior across cultures—and includes the importance of understanding business manners and customs across cultures. The chapter concludes by outlining theoretical frameworks concerning understanding the dimensions of culture, with implications of culture for the business manager.

Armed with a thorough understanding of globalization and the cultural aspects of conducting global commerce, the reader is introduced to the political, legal, and economic environments of global business. Chapter 3, "Global Business Environments and Risk: Political, Legal, Economic Systems," provides coverage which enables the reader to navigate these environments. The political and legal competencies allow the reader to interpret the political issues impacting global business, list government actions that promote and restrict trade, and classify global legal systems. Chapter 3 discusses the important issues of standardization, property rights, and copyrights, and describes global economic systems and their basic elements. The chapter concludes by identifying the sources and causes of risk for global businesses, with implications of political and legal environments for the business manager.

Chapter 4, "International Trade, Global Trading Systems, and Foreign Direct Investment," continues the systematic coverage of global business by building on the concepts covered in Chapters 1 through 3.

This chapter explores the benefits of international trade further, beginning with the historical development of international trade theory. Modern global trading systems are presented, including foreign direct investment and the importance of balance of payments. The chapter concludes with ways in which governments intervene in international trade, as well as implications of international trade and investment for the business manager.

Chapter 5, "Global Financial Markets and Monetary Systems," provides essentials regarding the importance of global financial markets to international trade. The chapter begins with coverage of the functions of foreign exchange markets, quotations and the terminology of foreign exchange markets, purchasing power parity, and the effects of exchange rates on global business. Next, chapter 5 analyzes the historical development of the modern global monetary system, including an examination of the European monetary system. The chapter concludes with implications of global financial markets and monetary systems for the business manager.

"Regional Economic Integration" is the focus of Chapter 6. The chapter begins by defining the topic and discussing the levels of regional economic integration. Arguments for and against regional economic integration are presented. The major regional trade agreements are covered, categorized by world region. International organizations that influence trade agreements, such as OPEC on international business and OECD in global economic development are covered. The chapter concludes with the implications of regional economic integration for the business manager.

Chapter 7, "Entering Global Markets," begins with the discussion of why domestic firms expand into global markets, and evaluates the conditions necessary for expansion into global markets. Chapter 7 presents basic questions managers must ask prior to entering global markets, as well as the key factors that influence the decision mode selection. The chapter concludes with an analysis of the modes of entry into global markets and implications of entering global markets for the business manager.

Chapter 8, "Global Operations Management," defines and states the importance of global operations management. Coverage includes planning issues such as capacity, facilities location, processes, facilities layout, make or buy decisions, selection and acquisition of raw materials and fixed assets. Chapter 8 also discusses production issues, such as quality and continuous improvement, just-in-time systems, and inventory control. The chapter concludes with the concepts of global logistics and the implications of global operations management for the business manager.

We hope that after reading this book you will agree with David I Bowen (Manager, Hardware Development Engineering ME/A-COM, Inc. Tyco Electronics), when he states,

> *Global Business: From Theory to Practice is an excellent handbook for today's business professional environment. Having worked in global product development for 20 years, I have observed fellow managers who did not fare well with our international partners. They could have benefited greatly from this book's message. By making the professional aware of global business framework, this book provides a concise guide for those interested in succeeding in international business.*

GLOBAL BUSINESS
From Theory to Practice

Brian C. Satterlee
Joseph A. Robinson

Chapter 1   GLOBALIZATION AND GLOBAL BUSINESS

Global Business in Practice
Global Mindset: Innate or Created?

Success in the competitive, ever-changing arena of international business requires a global mindset. Researchers generally agree that a global mindset is one that combines an openness to and awareness of cultural diversity, coupled with the ability to sustain this mindset through the knowledge and skills of international business practices.[*]

A study of the typical mindsets of managers in the business world today produces some interesting findings. The findings of this study prove that many managers do not have a suitable mindset for global or international business success. Four types of managerial mindsets can be found in the business world today:

- The Defender—The defender mindset is the most traditional of the four, focusing almost exclusively on the domestic market. Defenders do acknowledge that international markets exist, but they consider them dangerous, insisting upon trader barriers, government protection, etc. An example of the defender mindset would be the complaints of the steel producers of the 1960s and 1980s, which resulted in a truce with the United Steel Workers Union and subsequent government intercession concerning foreign steel imports.

- The Explorer—The explorer mindset has a lot in common with the defender, but the explorer does recognize that opportunities do exist in foreign markets. However, managers with the explorer mindset will only navigate foreign waters with trepidation. The strategy behind the explorer mindset is to explore foreign markets to evaluate "competition, threats, and political changes," before retreating back to the domestic office. An example of the explorer mindset would be Seiko's early attempts of internationalization. Seiko made several trips to the U.S. and Europe to investigate efficient ways to produce their product, eventually becoming an electronics mogul.

- The Controller—The controller mindset, unlike the defender and explorer, is more international in focus, with a considerable proportion of commerce directed towards foreign markets. The primary weakness of the controller mindset is that it includes an ethnocentric approach

[*] Gupta, Anil K., and Vijay Govindarajan. "Cultivating a Global Mindset." *Academy of Management Executive* 16:1 (February 2002): 116-126.

to business, imposing one's culture and methods on foreign practices. An example of the controller mindset would be how Coke relied upon its successful, global-American image in advertising to India. Pepsi tailored its advertising to India and nudged Coke in overall sales.

- The Integrator—The researchers behind this study consider the integrator the only true, global mindset. The integrator combines the openness and awareness of cultural diversity with the acute knowledge and skills necessary to function successfully in today's global business market. The integrator educates himself or herself about the cultural world and becomes saturated with the complexities of the global environment. One should note that the integrator more often assumes the task of coordination than control, seeking cooperation among the manifold components of the international system. Perhaps Toyota is the best example of the integrator mindset because of its effective network of relationships and firms worldwide. This solid global network reveals an open and culturally diverse outlook, although Toyota does appear guilty of selling its culture overseas.[*]

But what is the source of a global mindset? Is one's global mindset a result of innate hardwiring—static and unchanged over time—or can the "integrator" mindset be developed over time. A certain group of researchers would suggest the latter. These researchers have made four proposals, attempting to prove that market characteristics and international experience are the primary factors that drive the manager to develop a global mindset: The proposals are as follows:

1. A positive relationship exists between the manager's international experience and a global mindset.
2. A positive relationship exists between market characteristics and a global mindset.
3. A positive relationship exists between a global mindset and the manager's perception of the international performance of the firm (subjective performance).
4. A positive relationship exists between a global mindset and the financial indicators of the international performance of the firm (objective performance).

* Kedia, Ben L., and Ananda Mukherji "Global Managers: Developing a Mindset for Global Competitiveness.". *Journal of World Business* 34:3 (Fall 1999): 230-251.

The subjects for this research project were a small group of Finnish companies in the field of information and communications technology (ICT). The results revealed that international business experience (Proposal 1), existing market conditions (Proposal 2), and the objective predictability of success when entering into international commerce (depending upon the marketability of one's product) (Proposal 4) encourages the development of a global mindset. However, a manager's subjective predictions of the international success of his or her product(s) (Proposal 3) had little correlation with the development of a global mindset.[*]

Current marketing trends place a high premium on those managers who can think and perform with a global mindset. For those managers who believe that they do not have the natural "aptitude" to perform at the global level, research encourages that international business experience, cultural education, and market demands can create within the manager a global mindset. Therefore, the less competent or experienced "defender," "explorer," and "controller" has the opportunity to progress to the level of "integrator," competing with a global mindset, at a global level.

---

[*] Nummela, Nina, Kaisu Puumalainen, and Sami Saarenketo. "A global mindset—A Prerequisite for Successful Internationalization?" *Canadian Journal of Administrative Sciences, 21:1* (March 2004): 51-64.

What is Globalization?

Globalization, the growing integration of economies and societies worldwide, has been one of the most important topics in international business over the past few years. The pendulum of opinion swings from approval on one side to disapproval on the other. On the positive side, rapid economic growth and poverty reduction in some developing nations have been perceived as a positive aspect of globalization. From the negative end, significant international opposition exists over concerns that it has increased inequality and environmental degradation.[1]

No precise, widely agreed-upon definition exists for such an extensively used term as globalization. The array of definitions seems to be increasing rather than narrowing over time, taking on cultural, political, and other connotations—in addition to the economic. However, the most prevalent thinking on globalization refers to the observation that in recent years a quickly rising share of economic activity in the world is taking place between people who live in different nations, rather than in the same country.[2]

Globalization is not a new phenomenon but has been an aspect of humanity from earliest times, as widely scattered populations gradually became involved in more extensive and complicated economic relations. The growth of modern globalization began towards the end of the nineteenth century, mainly among the nations that are today developed or prosperous. The growth of globalization slowed considerably during the first half of the twentieth century. This slowdown was caused by many factors, including a worldwide sense of growing protectionism in a context of bitter national and Great Power strife, world wars, revolutions, rising authoritarian ideologies, and massive economic and political instability.

Since World War II (WWII), the pace of globalization has been steadily increasing. International relations have continually improved since the end of WWII. The improved post-war relations were brought about in part by the creation of institutions such as the General Agreement on Tariffs and Trade (GATT)—known today as the World Trade Organization (WTO)—which provides the enforceable agreement for signatory member nations to conduct global business. Additionally, developing nations were invited to become engaged on a wide range of multilateral international trade issues for the first time in history.

The pace of globalization continued to accelerate during the last decade of the twentieth century, as nations, in their desire to capitalize on the new economic realities of the twenty-first century, eliminated or reduced barriers to international trade and investment. Opening to the outside world has been part of a more general shift towards greater reliance on markets and private enterprise, especially as many developing and communist countries realized that high levels of government planning and intervention were failing to deliver the desired development outcomes.[3]

Prime Characteristics and Outcomes of Globalization

Some believe that globalization amounts to the selling of America to the world. While the U.S. is the largest worldwide exporter of culture, these exports are, in reality, "bringing a kind of market masala* to everyone in the world. Despite the embrace of polyethnic imagery, market-driven globalization doesn't want diversity; quite the opposite. Its enemies are national habits, local brands and distinctive regional tastes."[4] Thus, the term *"glocalization"* has been coined to explain the phenomenon that the globalization of a product or service is more likely to succeed when that product or service is adapted specifically to each locality or culture to which it is marketed. More specifically, the term describes the tempering effects of local conditions on global pressures.

What, then, are the prime characteristics and outcomes of globalization?

- Globalization creates interdependencies among nations. As nations rely increasingly on global trade, they become more dependent upon the functioning of a global economy. A nation with a strong international trade presence has a much higher dependency profile than that of a nation with limited (or little to no) participation in the global marketplace. Consequently, critics argue that dependency reduces a nation's strength and dilutes its ability to be self-sufficient. Proponents, on the other hand, argue that self-sufficiency is not the best measure of a nation's strengths and weaknesses and that dependency can actually foster a more contributive and harmonious society.

- Globalization requires transparency. In the well-integrated global economy, a consumer might be oblivious to the origin of the product he or she is consuming. This oblivion is especially true when the origin is immaterial to the purchasing decision, as in the case of commodities. Transparency is less effective for products with brand recognition or differentiation. For example, consider the U.S. consumer who prefers to purchase a Japanese-manufactured automobile for its perceived superiority in reliability or a German-engineered automobile for its distinctive design. Whether transparent or not, the impact of globalization affords this consumer the option of deciding between locally produced goods or foreign imports. In another example, a consumer product such as a digital camera might

---

* Masala - a mixture of many spices in Indian cooking.

contain components manufactured in Taiwan, assembled in Thailand, marketed by a French firm, and ultimately distributed in Canada. Globalization is demarcated by the way it transparently integrates all of these separate activities to form a single, seemingly inconsequential purchasing decision for the local consumer.

- Globalization requires that business people understand the seamless international marketplace. Financial professionals must be aware of the monetary impact of globalization, including its affect on macroeconomic and microeconomic models, accounting regulations and differences in legislation, and foreign exchange considerations. The economic environment is worldwide. Marketing professionals must be aware of the broad competitive landscape, including the negotiation protocols peculiar to each nation in which business is conducted. They must favorably negotiate pricing models to capture each local market because the product territory is worldwide. As a result, the consumer should benefit from the increased number of product alternatives made available in this global marketplace. Overall, the competitive environment is more competitive, but it becomes more integrated than ever.

- Globalization involves the blending and merging of various cultures; however, it is not the same as assimilation. Assimilation historically resulted from situations where immigrants were isolated from their home cultures.[5] Globalization is an integrative model that is contrary to the results of isolation produced by arcane immigration models. Integration of cultures is more desirable than assimilation, as the integration allows the better elements of that culture to remain intact. Assimilation requires the rejection of the old culture, with total acceptance of the new.

Figure 1.1

Characteristics of Globalization

- Interdependencies among nations

- Transparency

- Desire for seamless international marketplace

- Blending and merging of cultures

Globalization and its impact on international commerce is one of the most discussed topics in the world of business today. Likewise, the decisions and actions made by business professionals impact the future directions and perspectives of globalization. At the same time, no one doubts that globalization has led to the growth of world trade and output. The following sections of this chapter cover these growth patterns, both worldwide and in the USA.

Growth of World Trade and Output (1992—Present)

The World Trade Organization (WTO) was established in the early 1990s to help foster international trade and resolve disputes.[6] Many question the necessity of the WTO, but it was originally created in order to provide uniform standards and rules of engagement to a growing international trade market. International trade growth was also fueled in the 1990s by government legislation that created a more favorable trading environment. The North American Free Trade Agreement (NAFTA) was enacted in order to facilitate the importation and exportation of goods and services among the signatory nations (United States, Canada, and Mexico) by reducing trade tariffs and restrictions. NAFTA was originally projected to create two hundred thousand jobs per year in the U.S. alone, although the results show that in actuality, the job mix has simply changed.[7] Mexico emerged as a viable location for manufacturing facilities due to its low wage costs and close proximity. Canada is also a viable location for production facilities and service industries, due to its highly skilled labor force and close cultural similarities. Today, this manufacturing emergence is increasingly shifting to Asia—especially China, Taiwan, Thailand, and Malaysia.

In the United States, the gross domestic product (GDP) has steadily increased every year since 1992.[8] GDP is the official measure of total output of goods and services in a nation's economy. The average GDP growth rate per annum was 3.22 percent, taking into account a positive growth rate in every year above 2 percent, with the exception of 2001 at 0.8 percent and 2002 at 1.6 percent. The highest growth rates occurred in 1997 and 1999 at 4.5 percent each. A major driver for this growth was the demand for technology-based products and services. The U.S. is home to some of the world's leading hardware and software manufacturers. For example, Microsoft—the world's largest software company—is headquartered in the state of Washington. Windows® is the predominant operating system used in personal computers around the world. The increase in demand for technology-based products and services has created a job market for highly-skilled workers who demand higher salaries, which results in increased consumer purchasing power. These increases have all attributed to the growth rates witnessed in the United States over the past decade.

The GDP of nations outside of the U.S. has also risen steadily. China, the most populous country in the world, has emerged as a cost-leading manufacturer of products ranging from consumer goods to industrial equipment. China's GDP annual growth rate is currently in excess of 9 percent.[9] Elsewhere, Vietnam—a country fraught with devastation and crippling sanctions after the Vietnam War—has emerged as a major exporter of furniture. Thailand has emerged as a leading manufacturer of semiconductors.

Middle Eastern nations have also experienced GDP growth. In oil-producing nations such as Saudi Arabia and Kuwait, an increase in global energy demand has been a financial windfall. Nearby, India's growth has also topped expectations. India is particularly attractive as a U.S. trade partner because of its highly educated, English-speaking workforce. Services that can be easily contracted to third parties, known as outsourcing, make up a large portion of foreign direct investment in India.

Brief Summary of Current U.S. International Trade Competitive Situation

The United States is a major consumer and producer in the international marketplace. As reported by the U.S. government in 2006, the GDP purchasing power parity of the United States ranked first in comparison to other economies, with the European Union coming in at a close second.[10] The U.S.' top five export partners were the following countries:

- Canada at 23.4%,
- Mexico at 13.3%,
- Japan at 6.1%,
- China at 4.6%, and the
- United Kingdom at 4.3%.

United States' imports primarily came from the following countries:

- Canada at 16.9%,
- China at 15%,
- Mexico at 10%,
- Japan at 8.2%, and
- Germany at 5%.[11]

Canada consistently ranks as one of the leading suppliers to the United States. NAFTA was a major contributor to continental trade growth between the United States, Mexico, and Canada because it eased quotas, tariffs, and customs procedures.

Why Global Business and International Trade is Important to the U.S.A.

Figure 1.2

Reasons International Trade is Important to the United States

1. Maximizing production and efficiency.

2. Increasing market audience.

3. Receiving foreign direct investment.

First, the international market allows for domestic vendors to optimize production through the use of foreign vendors under potentially more favorable economic conditions. Production is efficient when any increase or decrease in output would cause a disproportionate increase in the cost of production and when there is no alternative that would lead to a more profitable production of a given product. In international trade, these alternatives include outsourcing production to foreign firms. Nations with lower wage costs can often produce more efficiently; therefore, United States firms rely heavily on operations in lower wage cost nations for tasks such as manufacturing, which can be easily reassigned. Through outsourcing, the domestic firm is able to focus its resources on areas in which it maintains a distinct competitive advantage, such as service offerings or research and development. In a recent survey of financial executives, 73 percent of the respondents consider outsourcing to be an important component of their long-term growth strategies.[12] Overall, outsourcing usually results in lower consumer prices, which would rise considerably if domestic firms were forced to procure similar items locally.

Second, the international market removes the boundaries of local market territories, thereby increasing the potential market audience. In other words, territorial boundaries that define potential markets are removed. This redefines a global business market as representing the entire world. When a domestic firm expands its market to include the entire world, the potential is a much larger revenue base. Additionally, firms that are losing domestic business can recapture and often expand sales by strategically pursuing customers overseas. This global view can be particularly useful to a firm that competes through product differentiation. For example, the U.S. international trade involvement can be seen in its export of coal.[13] The U.S. holds one of the largest coal reserves in the world. Many nations rely on U.S. exports of coal to service their own national infrastructure needs. U.S. firms could not recognize most of this revenue in the absence of an international trade market.

Third, foreign direct investment allows domestic firms to receive capital financing from foreign entities. It also provides financing to international markets as part of a diversified investment vehicle. The funds from foreign direct investment make up a sizable amount of capital expenditure in the U.S. Japanese-based Honda Motor Company and Toyota Motors have built automobile manufacturing facilities in the Midwest and Southern United States, which have infused billions of dollars of capital into the U.S. economy. Other examples include foreign firms that maintain corporate operations in different global locations. For example, Schlumberger—a company with 2005 earnings revenue of 14.31 billion USD—is incorporated in the Netherlands Antilles, traded on the New York Stock Exchange, and maintains its headquarters in Houston, TX.[14] A portion of its income is still subject to taxation within the United States. The healthy international business environment enables the U.S. to attract foreign firms and add jobs, taxes, and technology to its economy. Just as the U.S. receives foreign capital, it also invests heavily in other nations. Without a positive international trade environment, foreign investment of any type would not be possible.

Globalization has created a thriving market for international trade and can be classified as a narrower focus on this trade activity. In addition, global business can be examined in an individual or collective context and can be compared and contrasted with domestic business.

Global Business

Global business can be considered, in a broad context, as business without boundaries. As a collective term, global business includes all domestic businesses with transactions in the international market. Additionally, global business includes all transnational or multinational businesses, which are enterprises that manage production establishments or deliver services in at least two nations. Multinational corporations (MNCs) are often divided into three broad groups:

1. Horizontally integrated multinational corporations manage production establishments, located in different countries to produce the same or similar products.

2. Vertically integrated multinational corporations manage production establishment in certain country/countries to produce products that serve as input to its production establishments in other country/countries.

3. Diversified multinational corporations manage production establishments located in different countries that are neither horizontally nor vertically integrated.[15]

Global business can also be examined as it relates to individual business entities. When a firm in one nation exchanges products, services, resources, or capital with a firm located in another nation, this exchange constitutes an international transaction. The frequency of international transactions can help determine whether an individual business also qualifies as a global business.

A business with frequent international transactions is a global business. In congruence with globalization principles, the entire world is one large market. The astute global business professional discerns between domestic and international customers. Firms pursuing international commerce consider differences between domestic and international standards, languages, cultural preferences, and government regulations. A well-known saying in global business circles is, "Think globally; act locally." What then are some of the major differences and similarities between domestic and international business?

Differences and Similarities with Domestic Business

A global business has considerable operational differences from that of a strictly domestic business. First, a global business must consider the broader geographical scope in which it operates. Second, it must understand that each market contains different cultural influences that will affect the product marketing mix. Third, it must take into account market factors, such as foreign exchange rates, which can materially alter operating conditions. Finally, the management of a global business requires carefully selected and trained leadership, salesmanship, and support staff.

Figure 1.3

Global Business Differences

- Scope
- Cultural influences
- Market factors
- Management practices

The scope of a domestic business is specific. A domestic business' scope is generally confined to a local marketing territory. The territory can be made up of a single city, county, state, or even multi-state area. In a global business, this scope is expanded to include other countries over a far greater geographical area. A global business must carefully consider the nations in which it can compete, giving special attention to each nation's unique blend of challenges, competitive landscape, and environmental factors. To illustrate, a winter clothing manufacturer concludes that consumers located in tropical regions have little interest in their winter clothing line. To be profitable, the firm either has to exclude this region from its target audience or find another product that will be suitable to the tropical region.

The second difference between global and domestic business management is observed in a nation's culture. Culture is defined as the set of shared attitudes, values, goals, and practices that characterize a particular category. In this business context, the category is the particular region or nation that is foreign to the domestic firm that is closely correlated to consumer spending patterns. A domestic business operates in the "comfort of its own backyard," whereas a global enterprise operates within foreign cultures that may be entirely different from the well-known domestic market. Even the most subtle differences require thorough evaluation before an appropriate product marketing mix can be determined. A study of the correlation between advertising effectiveness and ritual concludes that "the notion of advertising as simply transferring ritual meaning to a product through straightforward association . . . does not adequately describe the complex interaction between the two institutions."[16] For example, an alcoholic beverage manufacturer could face great difficulty in trying to market its product in a country where a strongly influential religious community discourages the consumption of alcohol.

The third difference between global and domestic business management takes into consideration market factors. Market factors are the demographic, sociologic, and economic forces that vary from one region to another. One area of particular concern is the exchange of foreign currencies. Countries have their own unique currency systems, complete with different denominations. In order to translate the domestic country's currency into the foreign country's currency, an intermediary—typically a foreign exchange market—is often required. This foreign exchange market adds overhead to the cost of buying and selling in almost all foreign markets. To make matters worse, some governments impose artificially inflated or fixed currency exchange rates. For European nations, the introduction of the Euro has significantly reduced the burdens previously associated with foreign currency exchange in this region.

The fourth difference between global and domestic business management is the need for global business leaders to be equipped with special management skills. The global business manager must have a wide perspective of foreign affairs. General world market knowledge, in addition to knowledge specific to each target country, is necessary in order to make decisions about which markets would best complement the firm's competitive strategy. Another difficulty often faced by the global business manager is the encounter with customs, which can vary greatly from one country to another. For example, the use of government bribery is a routine part of business operations in a number of nations, but the U.S. considers this practice illegal. The global business manager must be equipped to respond to such challenges in ways that best perpetuates the firm's interests and maintains the integrity of the individual. One of the greatest challenges of working in this environment is doing so without sacrificing corporate or personal integrity.

The old adage says that, "those who fail to learn from history are doomed to repeat it." This saying is especially true for those engaged in global business. Armed with a good understanding of the impact of globalization on business, as well as knowledge of similarities and differences between global and domestic business, we now turn our attention to a brief discussion of the historical developments in global business.

Brief Historical Examples of Global Business and Trade— from Pax Romana to Pax Americana

International exchange is often thought of as a recent concept; however, there is evidence to suggest that the first international trade took place as early as 2500 BC. Starting in Phoenicia, historical records indicate a steady progression of trade throughout the Middle East, Africa, Europe, and Asia. Global trade was greatly enhanced during the second millennium AD with the widespread use of vessels, rail, and air transportation options. Improvement in transportation, advances in communications technology, and trade-friendly legislation have all contributed to the desire to produce a seamless global economy.

To the Time of Christ

Phoenicia was one of the oldest examples of an international trading community, dating back to 1100 BC.[17] The Phoenicians made up for their lack of arable land by trading precious metals and textiles with surrounding communities. Another early trading civilization was found in Africa, where the Berbers would cross the Saharan desert to trade salt. International trade was involved in the building of Solomon's Temple, completed in the tenth century BC. Solomon, king of Israel, entered into a trade agreement with Hiram I, king of Tyre, for the supply of timber from the forests of Lebanon. The timber was brought in great rafts by the sea to Joppa and dragged to Jerusalem to be used in the construction of the temple. Hiram also provided labor for the task. In return, Solomon provided food for Hiram's royal household. The entire pact was recorded in the Old Testament book of I Kings: 5:

When Hiram king of Tyre heard that Solomon had been anointed king to succeed his father, David, he sent his envoys to Solomon, because he had always been on friendly terms with David. Solomon sent back this message to Hiram: "You know that because of the wars waged against my father David from all sides, he could not build a temple for the Name of the LORD his God until the LORD put his enemies under his feet. But now the LORD my God has given me rest on every side, and there is no adversary or disaster. I intend, therefore, to build a temple for the Name of the LORD my God, as the LORD told my father David, when he said, 'Your son whom I will put on the throne in your place will build the temple for my Name.' So give orders that cedars of Lebanon be cut for me. My men will work with yours, and I will pay you for your men whatever wages you set. You know that we have no one so skilled in felling timber as the Sidonians." When Hiram heard Solomon's message, he was greatly pleased and said, "Praise be to the LORD today, for he has given David a wise son to rule over this great nation."

So Hiram sent word to Solomon: "I have received the message you sent me and will do all you want in providing the cedar and pine logs. My men will haul them down from Lebanon to the sea, and I will float them in rafts by sea to the place you specify. There I will separate them and you can take them away. And you are to grant my wish by providing food for my royal household." In this way Hiram kept Solomon supplied with all the cedar and pine logs he wanted, and Solomon gave Hiram twenty thousand cors of wheat as food for his household, in addition to twenty thousand baths of pressed olive oil.* Solomon continued to do this for Hiram year after year. The LORD gave Solomon wisdom, just as he had promised him. There were peaceful relations between Hiram and Solomon, and the two of them made a treaty.

King Solomon conscripted laborers from all Israel—thirty thousand men. He sent them off to Lebanon in shifts of ten thousand a month, so that they spent one month in Lebanon and two months at home. Adoniram was in charge of the forced labor. Solomon had seventy thousand carriers and eighty thousand stonecutters in the hills, as well as thirty-three hundred foremen who supervised the project and directed the workmen. At the king's command they removed from the quarry large blocks of quality stone to provide a foundation of dressed stone for

---

* One hundred twenty thousand "cors" of wheat amounts to approximately 125,000 bushels. Twenty thousand "baths" of pressed olive oil amounts to approximately 115,000 gallons (about 440 kiloliters).

the temple. The craftsmen of Solomon and Hiram and the men of Gebal cut and prepared the timber and stone for the building of the temple.[18]

Perhaps the most well-known example of international trade in this era was the *Pax Romana* or Roman Peace. This Latin term refers to the Empire in its glorified prime. From the end of the Republican civil wars, beginning with the accession of Augustus in 27 BC, this era in Roman history lasted until 180 AD and the death of Marcus Aurelius. Though the use of the word "peace" may be a bit misleading, this period refers mainly to the great Romanization of the western world. The Roman legal system, which forms the basis of many western court systems today, brought law and order to the provinces. The Legions patrolled the borders with success; and though many foreign wars still existed, the internal empire was free from major invasion, piracy, or social disorder on any grand scale.[19]

Through the Middle Ages to the Renaissance

International trade continued to develop through the Middle Ages. Stone roads started to appear throughout Europe, and regular trade networks extended all the way to Africa and Asia. Travel was a time consuming and hazardous activity. The upper class, an elite concentration of wealthy individuals, often of noble heritage, only traveled by horse-drawn carriages and enjoyed lavishing lifestyles. Peasants and slaves were not so fortunate, traveling without the benefit of even horses or camels and often left to perform manual labor.

In 1215, *Magna Carta Liberatum* was chartered as a way to formally recognize the legal limitations of a king's power. This charter is sometimes credited with stimulating the growth of free trade during this time period. Even today, modern democratic societies refer to the *Magna Carta* as a key legal baseline. Elsewhere, the Ming Dynasty in China built a powerful naval fleet with high hopes of exploration and expansion. Some scholars assert that these Chinese expeditions were the first successful voyages to America.

Modern trade history began with the exploration of the Western Hemisphere by Christopher Columbus in 1492. Once discovered, the Americas were quickly colonized by European nations to become critical provincial trading resources. Transatlantic trade flourished, but not without peril. The sea vessels of this time were slow and dangerous, relying exclusively on wind power for propulsion. Most manufacturing methods were still manual-labor intensive.

Western history records numerous periods of trade growth, from the discovery of America by Spanish traders to the establishment of the Dutch East India Trading Company. One interesting example of global trade from that period of time involves the processing of cocoa into chocolate. Chocolate is processed from the seeds (or beans) of the Cacao tree, which grows in South America and other equatorial and tropical climate regions.

The Mayans, an indigenous people of Central America, introduced Spanish explorers of the early sixteenth century to Xocatl, a chocolate-type drink based on the cocoa bean. The Mayans enjoyed Xocatl for at least two-thousand years before their encounter with Spanish explorers. Soon after the first taste of this delicious beverage, Spanish traders imported cocoa to various European ports, where sugar was eventually added to process hot chocolate. Originally, the Spanish processed the imported cocoa beans into various powder, butter, and liquor modalities. Later, with the rise and development of the West India Trading Company, the Netherlands became the prime processors of cocoa. Demand for the product grew in dramatic fashion, and investors expanded cocoa tree plantations into other tropical climate regions, such as Africa, the Caribbean, Hawaii, South America, and Southeast Asia.

To the Industrial Revolution

The Industrial Revolution heralded the introduction of mass production, improved transportation, technological progress, and the industrial factory system. Social and economic changes during this period enabled the transition from a stable agricultural and commercial society to a modern industrial society that relied on complex machinery rather than hand tools. Exploration and trade from Western European nations during the Renaissance led to an increased supply of precious metals from the New World, which in turn, resulted in rising prices, which in turn stimulated the growth of industry and fostered an international economy, based on money rather than barter. Expansion of trade and the money economy stimulated the development of new institutions of finance and credit. During the eighteenth century, an expanding and wealthier population demanded more and better goods.

In the productive process, coal came to replace wood. The Industrial Revolution was characterized by a marked surge in manufacturing techniques that included mass assembly, electricity, and new forms of propulsion. One such innovation was the steam engine—an economical form of self-propulsion. The steam engine brought about the first efficient forms of mass transportation using machine power. As a result, transatlantic and transpacific transit times were greatly reduced.[20] The steam engine was also used to create manufacturing systems capable of mass production. Developed nations, such as the United States and Britain, used mass production as a competitive advantage to increase their dominance in the world's marketplace.

Consequently, the focus of trade shifted from Mediterranean to Atlantic ports, chartered companies were organized, and continued improvements in navigation and ship construction sped long voyages. As a worldwide trade evolved, local trade barriers were reduced, stimulating global trade. Modern credit facilities also appeared, such as the state bank, the bourse (the European term for stock exchange), and the futures market. Additionally, the promissory note and other new media of exchange were created.

To the Information Age

The Information Age is the era where information is considered to be a valuable resource, and its capture and distribution generates competitive advantage to organizations. While the era technically could be traced to the invention of the telephone and the telegraph in the late 1800s, it rose to the forefront in the early 1970s with the advent of the microprocessor. Modern increases in trade activity can be attributed to the improvements in communications networks.

In 1866, the telegraph opened the first transatlantic communications channel to facilitate real-time communication over long distances. By the early 1900s, radio and telephone networks were widespread in developed nations, followed by televisions several decades later. *Pax Americana*, Latin for "American peace," is the period of relative peace in the Western world since the end of World War II in 1945, coinciding with the dominant military and economic position of the U.S. *Pax Americana* places the U.S. in the military and diplomatic role of a modern-day Roman Empire. During this period, no armed conflict has emerged among major Western nations themselves, and no nuclear weapons have been used, although the U.S. and its allies have been involved in various regional wars.

In 1957, the launch of the Sputnik 1 satellite paved the way for orbital electronic devices. Finally, in the 1980s, the personal desktop computer became a commonplace household fixture. These technologies converged towards the close of the twentieth century to form the basis of the Internet, a distributed communications network that connects computers and electronic devices around the world in real time. In a trade context, the Internet is used for E-commerce, which enables millions of consumers each day to buy and sell products. Common ways that businesses use the Internet include managing field-based operations, employing workers in remote locations, monitoring inventories, and knowledge management. The Information Age has connected the world and greatly expanded the opportunities for true global businesses.

The preceding section presented a concise description of advances in global trade throughout select periods of recorded history. Early globalization efforts clearly were driven by the desire to increase wealth of the ruling class, and later to increase standards of living for the general populace. The modern globalization movement is driven by a complex array of issues and interventions. The following section discusses these driving forces of contemporary globalization.

Driving Forces for Globalization

A number of forces are driving the trend towards globalization. First, reductions in barriers to trade have allowed goods to more easily pass between international borders. Second, reductions in barriers to foreign investment have allowed foreign investors to benefit from growing markets outside of their own. Third, advances in communication and transportation technologies have greatly improved the speed at which international parties can communicate and move goods across borders. Finally, the rise in prominence of multinational corporations has greatly impacted the pace of globalization.

Figure 1.4

Driving Forces

- Reductions in barriers to trade

- Reductions in barriers to foreign investments

- Advances in communications and transportation technologies

- Rise of the multinational corporation

Reduction in Barriers to Trade

Barriers to trade can affect the ease with which a country can import and export goods. Barriers to trade include the following:

- Tariffs or taxes on imported goods.

- Quotas or the restriction of the import of something to a specific quantity.

- Embargoes or the prohibition of commerce and trade with a certain nation.

- Sanctions or economic actions of one nation, or group of nations, against another group as part of a trade dispute.

Cooperative trading agreements have significantly reduced these barriers. In North America, the most notable example is NAFTA, a cooperative agreement between the United States, Canada, and Mexico, which ensures the smooth passage of goods between these countries. An example of similar reduction in certain European countries can be observed in the European Free Trade Association (EFTA).

Reduction in Barriers to Foreign Investment

Foreign investment includes the direct financial investments of foreign entities into the host economy. This is a type of inbound foreign investment. Foreign investment also includes the outbound investment of host country capital into foreign economies. Example of inbound foreign direct investment includes the 2002 acquisition of Equilon Enterprises by Royal Dutch/Shell of the Netherlands and Saudi Aramco of Saudi Arabia. The Energy Information Administration reported the following:

> U.S. petroleum refining and marketing saw two major foreign direct acquisitions in 2002. The largest was a three-way transaction that resulted from an agreement that allowed Chevron and Texaco to merge in 2000. At that time, the U.S. Federal Trade Commission and several State commissions would only consent to the merger if Texaco divested all of its U.S. refining and marketing assets, which it held through Equilon Enterprises and Motiva Enterprises. These two companies were joint ventures of Texaco, Royal Dutch/Shell (Netherlands and United Kingdom), and, for Motiva only, Saudi Aramco (Saudi Arabia). In a three-way deal, the other joint owners purchased Texaco's shares of Equilon and Motiva in a transaction valued at $4.1 billion. After the acquisition, Royal Dutch/Shell owned 100 percent of Equilon, and Royal Dutch/Shell and Saudi Aramco each owned 50 percent of Motiva. The two joint ventures marketed petroleum products through 23 thousand branded service stations in the United States and owned 8 refineries, 30 thousand miles of pipeline, and a trading enterprise. The other major downstream petroleum foreign direct acquisition in 2002 was made.[21]

Foreign direct investment is an attractive option for firms looking to diversify their investment portfolios, creating opportunities for firms looking to enter emerging markets.

Risks to foreign investment vary. One risk can occur when a foreign government limits the ability of foreign investors to expatriate funds in order to mitigate economic uncertainties. Emerging market economies can also be highly volatile. The recognition of the impact of such barriers led countries to form the independent Organization for Economic Co-operation and Development (OECD). OECD provides a cooperative venue for establishing guidelines and cooperation in free-trade markets.[22] Participation in such organizations instills confidence in investors looking to make foreign investments and reduces an important barrier to foreign investment. Additionally, legislative bodies are now highly sensitive to the criticality of international trade and have enacted legislation designed to expedite and stimulate foreign investment.

Communication Technology

Communication technologies are used by the global business professional in the processing and transfer of messages and information. The technologies are used in various applications:

- Television and radio broadcasting

- Multimedia applications

- Internet

- Graphic design

- Digital and analogue audiovisual communication

- Networked communication

- Advertising

- Journalism

- Mass media

- Instructional design

Innovation in networking technologies has significantly reduced the barriers of communication between distant operating locations. Local area networks are now used within most retail operations to network point-of-sale registers to inventory systems.[23] Wide area networks are commonly implemented across operating locations so that each location can access real-time inventory information from other locations. Finally, the Internet has allowed companies to commercialize access to their product offerings in the form of electronic commerce systems. E-commerce has exploded into a multi-billion dollar industry since its widespread adoption in the late 1990s.

Advances in Transportation Technology

Transportation technologies now include a full range of ocean, rail, automotive, and aerial options. Ocean vessels evolved from slow, labor-intensive ships into modern diesel-driven vessels that can survive even the harshest climates with minimal crews. Most countries also use extensive rail networks to move heavier items within a continent. Diesel-powered trucks traveling through elaborate highway systems are used to deliver freight to even more specific destinations. Each of these transportation options have benefited heavily with the introduction of the ISO standard cargo container.[24] The International Standards Organization (ISO) is the world's leading developer of International Standards. ISO standards specify the requirements for state-of-the-art products, services, processes, materials and systems, and for good conformity assessment, managerial and organizational practice. ISO standards are designed to be implemented worldwide.[25] Standard ISO cargo containers, also known as *isotainers*, can be loaded and sealed intact onto container ships, railroad cars, planes, and trucks.

Alternatively, commercial aircraft can be used to move more sensitive freight quickly over long distances. Finally, integrated communications networks are used to link ocean, rail, automotive, and air transportation together and allow real-time freight movement optimization. Despite record high energy costs, the options for moving freight are more efficient than ever.

Multinational Corporations

The final driving force for globalization is the multinational corporation (MNC). Any corporation or enterprise that manages production establishments or delivers services in at least two countries may be considered a MNC. Very large MNCs have budgets that exceed those of many nations. Thus, the largest MNCs operate with a considerable amount of purchasing power. Forbes Inc. has compiled a list of the top 2000 multinational firms, as determined by their sales, profits, assets, and market value. Table 1.1 lists the top twenty-five companies of Forbes' 2000 Rank.[26]

Table 1.1

Forbes 2000 Rank	Name	Country	Category
1	Citigroup	United States	Banking
2	General Electric	United States	Conglomerates
3	American Intl Group	United States	Insurance
4	Bank of America	United States	Banking
5	HSBC Group	United Kingdom	Banking
6	ExxonMobil	United States	Oil & gas operations
7	Royal Dutch/ Shell Group	Netherlands/United Kingdom	Oil & gas operations
8	BP	United Kingdom	Oil & gas operations
9	ING Group	Netherlands	Diversified financials
10	Toyota Motor	Japan	Consumer durables
11	UBS	Switzerland	Diversified financials
12	Wal-Mart Stores	United States	Retailing
13	Royal Bank of Scotland	United Kingdom	Banking
14	JPMorgan Chase	United States	Banking
15	Berkshire Hathaway	United States	Insurance
16	BNP Paribas	France	Banking
17	IBM	United States	Technology hardware & equipment
18	Total	France	Oil & gas operations
18	Verizon Commun	United States	Telecommunications services
20	ChevronTexaco	United States	Oil & gas operations
21	Barclays	United Kingdom	Banking
21	Fannie Mae	United States	Diversified financials
23	Nippon Tel & Tel	Japan	Telecommunications services
24	Pfizer	United States	Drugs & biotechnology
25	Altria Group	United States	Food, drink & tobacco

A study examining the largest economic entities between 1983 and 1999 reveals that fifty one of the world's largest economic entities are in fact corporations, where only forty nine are countries.[27] This finding is significant because there can be a notable difference in the way a nation conducts business versus the way a large corporation conducts business. A nation typically is most interested, ideally, in serving its citizens without bias or qualification. A corporation, on the other hand, has the primary goal of maximizing the wealth of its shareholders. As multinational corporations continue to grow at a rate that outpaces many countries' entire economies, careful consideration must be given to the role of each in the global economic environment.

Having discussed the driving forces of globalization, we now turn our attention to the impact of globalization in terms of political, economic, social, and cultural aspects of doing business across borders.

Impacts of Globalization

Globalization has impacted the political, economic, social, and cultural aspects of international community members. Political and cultural environments of some nations have become more polarized. While most become more subdued, a few become more extreme. Economic health varies in moderate correlation with the amount of international trade activity in each host country. Social systems have been forced to adapt to a new composition of workers and ethnicities— some without success. Finally, cultural impact has emerged as a focal point in international debate concerning the toll of globalization.

Political Impacts of Globalization

Much debate continues over the political effects of globalization. Opponents of globalization claim that globalization has led to widespread government corruption, as indicated through the extensive use of bribery. However, one could argue that globalization is not to blame for this political corruption; rather, these practices were likely preexisting and have only recently gained exposure in the arena of public debate. The results of a recent study reveal that nations such as Finland, Austria, and the United States are far less accommodating to corrupt practices, whereas Vietnam, Saudi Arabia, and China are far more tolerant.[28] U.S. managers routinely rank bribery as being an unethical practice. Respondents in other nations find the use of bribes as a critical leveraging tool that facilitates necessary compromise in business exchange.

Proponents of globalization point out the positive influences upon the political environment. An increasing importance of international trade has led nations to establish specific policy departments that deal exclusively with maintaining favorable foreign relations. Overall, this has brought about a much higher increase in global awareness, as well as legislation to ensure minimum standards in a given level of economic participation. U.S. labor laws have been constructed to prevent domestic companies from employing underage workers—even in foreign countries—which have been estimated to be in excess of 186 million child workers between the ages of five and fourteen.[29]

The multinational company typically views the political landscape in terms of political risks. Political risks can be classified three ways: transfer, operational, and ownership control risks.

- Transfer risk includes the risk of debt consolidation—the debt of a country in a critical financial situation will be rescheduled for repayment over an extended period as a result of an agreement between the countries concerned. This can impair the ability to exchange capital and other real products between countries.

- Operational risk can be defined as the risk of monetary losses resulting from inadequate or failed internal processes, people, and systems—or from external events. Losses from external events, such as a natural disaster, which damages a firm's physical assets, or electrical or telecommunications failures, which disrupt business, are relatively easier to define than losses from internal problems, such as employee fraud and product flaws. These internal and external events can disrupt the day-to-day operations and production of the business.

- Ownership control risk includes government policies or actions that inhibit ownership or control of foreign operations. This governmental interference can disrupt the actual ownership of an entity.

Each of these variables requires constant monitoring on the part of the firm to ensure that governmental disruptions are kept to a minimum.

Economic Impacts of Globalization

The health of a given economy can be measured in part by the number of exports it has relative to the number and economic value of its imports. Economic health is considered negative when a country imports considerably more than it exports. Imported and exported goods must also take into account services provided, such as consulting, which are provided with the physical product. Generally, globalization has increased the market opportunity for countries to undertake both importing and exporting activities, allowing for an infusion of capital from foreign investors. New foreign sources of capital help to create new businesses and increase spending in research and development activities. However, foreign capital can be unsettling in a market with great volatility—either from political or socioeconomic forces. Significant fluctuations in currency exchange rates can reduce the actual value of each dollar that a foreign investor has vested in his or her foreign portfolio, potentially prompting the investor to withdraw from a market entirely. Withdrawals bring negative consequences, such as closures and layoffs, leading some to question the appropriate amount of foreign investment leverage required to maintain a healthy economy, while mitigating disruption to domestic ownership.

Social Impacts of Globalization

Social implications of globalization are generally integrative. New jobs created by international demand have led to growing populations in urban areas, known as urban sprawl. Each new wave of economic activity brings about the inclusion of communities further and further from the city's center. In many modern economies, businesses focus on greater social responsibility, leading to more investments in benevolent or humanitarian efforts. The world economy's purchasing power and its benefits can be seen in the international relief provided to victims of the 2004 tsunami in Indonesia. This almost automatic reaction of benevolence has caused some critics to question the excessiveness of such benevolence.[30] A nation would most likely suffer severe backlash if it were to shun commonly accepted social expectations, whether or not they harmonize with local expectations.

Cultural Impacts of Globalization

A nation's culture consists of the behaviors and characteristics that are unique to its citizens. Globalization has created what critics refer to as a melting pot or clash of various cultural identities. Sometimes this clash becomes violent, especially as a result of religious tensions and riots in some nations. For the most part, however, globalization is a unifying act that requires people to work together. The heightened exposure that ensues usually fosters greater appreciation for diversity. As globalization becomes more embedded in daily life, tolerance must continue to increase in order to avoid unnecessary polarization—again reinforcing the notion that globalization is not assimilation.

The astute global business professional understands the driving forces and impacts of globalization on trade. Additionally, he or she has the ability to translate this knowledge into practice. As many have said, "knowledge is power." In reality, knowledge is potential power; only applied knowledge is power. The following section discusses the application of this knowledge by the global business manager.

The Global Business Manager

The global business manager is responsible for many different types of management and leadership activities: operations, procurement, accounting, marketing, industry-specific technologies, staffing—just to name a few. In addition to standard management qualifications, the complexities of the international operating environment require additional qualities that few candidates fully possess. The global business manager must possess a strong international awareness and must understand the unique factors that contribute to the success of a global business, including formal education. The global business manager also must have an appropriate mix of relevant experience in global business ventures.

Global Mindset vs. the Provincial Mindset

Global businesses transcend physical borders; therefore, the global business manager must possess proficiency in managing a business in any location in which a firm is operating, since the manager is the key coordinator of activities between disconnected operating locations. In addition, the global business manager must be able to juggle the issues that affect each country individually, without accentuating the issues of any one country. Managers sometimes use the input of their subordinates concerning decisions about a firm's direction. However, a global business manager in an international setting must consider that line managers probably lack the contextual awareness to suggest the most optimal change. Therefore, the global business manager must resist any urge to instinctively trust line managers and instead apply his or her discipline and critical thinking capacity to formulate decisions that are most conducive to the international operating environment. Maintaining a global perspective is critical because each provincial market will contain issues that are unique to its region.

Knowledge, Skills, and Attributes needed for Success

A common set of knowledge, skills, and attributes—a human resources concept known as KSA—has been identified as that which best expresses the ideal global business manager's qualifications. KSA are usually outlined in a job requisition. No one formula exists for the perfect global business manager, so KSAs will not by themselves ensure success; however, each KSA that a candidate holds will improve his or her chances for contributing effectively to an international venture's success. The most successful venture is likely to be the one where all of its participants are contributing most effectively.

The first component of KSA is knowledge. Knowledge is the information that a candidate possesses in the area of given disciplines. In business, such disciplines will include accounting, controlling, operations, and staffing. In international business, these disciplines are expanded to contain a contextual facet for each country under consideration. The ideal candidate possesses knowledge in areas pertinent to each country in which the firm operates. For example, staffing practices in socialist France vary from the unregulated labor market in China: a manager of a French multinational corporation with a manufacturing facility in China would require first-hand knowledge of which practices are most effective in each of these two countries in order to prevent failure. Other disciplines that are beneficial, regardless of countries, include knowledge in areas of outsourcing, international law, and global economic principles.

The second component of KSA is skill. Skills are much more narrowly defined than knowledge areas in that they represent quantifiable measures. One example is computer literacy. A minimum standard of proficiency in Microsoft Office® might be required, as the candidate will be responsible for preparing contracts in Microsoft Word or making presentations using Microsoft PowerPoint. Another skill is proficiency in foreign language. Fluency in a foreign language can be especially beneficial in multinational firms in which several different languages are spoken. Recent polls indicate that the demand for Arabic-speaking U.S. citizens has surged as a result of the War on Terror.[31]

The final component of KSA is attributes. Attributes are the characteristics that are unique to an individual's learning experiences or character. Unlike formal knowledge or skills, these characteristics and personality traits are less likely to be taught. However, these can be acquired through understanding and experience. A desirable attribute in a global manager is the ability to manage cross-cultural relationships. An individual who possesses diplomatic traits will naturally be more likely to be successful when dealing with conflicting personalities—often present in cross-cultural relations. Another desirable attribute is the ability to multitask and work efficiently and effectively under pressure. The international business involves a far greater number of variables than that of domestic business, so the ability to adapt to change while managing stress is of critical importance. General management attributes such as friendliness, written and oral communication style, and soft-skills involving leadership qualities are as relevant and desirable in international management as they are in general domestic management.

How These May be Obtained

Knowledge, skills, and attributes are obtained principally through education and experience. Education includes formal learning that often results in a certificate or degree. A highly desirable degree in the current marketplace is the Master of Business Administration (MBA). MBA program offerings have grown substantially over the past decade as a result of this high demand. In addition, professional training is used to complement formal classroom learning. Professional training, such as Six Sigma certification, is especially effective at keeping managers abreast of the latest technologies and business practices.

A growing professional development trend among global business professionals involves the use of independent training firms, such as International Business Training (IBT). IBT offers a variety of resources for exporters to continue to learn more about international trade and the tools to do their jobs. In addition to providing tools for restricted party screen, export license determination, and export document determination, IBT offers one-on-one reviews of companies' import, export, and NAFTA procedures.

Every week, IBT publishes articles written by well-respected industry consultants on topics ranging from export marketing and sales to export and import documentation and procedures to letters of credit and other forms of international payments. IBT also sponsors a free e-mail discussion list that allows international trade practitioners to post questions and answers to other international traders from around the world. And they offer a variety of reference books, online classes, and one-day seminars, which give importers and exporters the chance to learn more about the various aspects of their jobs.

Managers gain experience by the actual hands-on encounters with KSAs in a real, working environment. While education is typically the starting point of a manager's career, past performance (experience) is arguably the most important predictor of a manager's ability to handle a given situation. Education and experience are both necessary components in handling the complex tasks of managing a global business. Staffing is similar for a domestic business manager and a global business manager. The major difference between the two is that in global business, failure is compounded.

Brief Summary of Major Points

Although not entirely new concepts, global business and global business management have evolved considerably over the past century. The effects of globalization are now evident in nearly every aspect of life. From political to socioeconomic, these effects have changed the landscape of international trade. Operating a successful global business requires careful consideration of a broad range of topics:

- A qualified global business manager is a necessary component of running a successful global business.

- International trade has been taking place for several hundred years; however, the most recent centuries have brought about significant technological and communications advancements, which have more tightly integrated this environment to form the global economy.

- Governments have recognized the importance of this global business activity and have responded by enacting legislation that facilitates international trade transactions.

- Trade between different nations has become an integral part of everyday life. In its entirety, this trading is known as globalization.

- Globalization has been a controversial trend but is irrespectively regarded as inevitable.

- Globalization is not assimilation but an integrative system where each country participates out of its respective position of strength to form a global economy.

- Challenges and stakes are much higher in the international environment; therefore, a proficient global business manager is of utmost importance.

- The global manager must possess all of the skills required for managing a domestic business, along with a deep understanding of the international marketplace. The manager must be well versed in the various economies in which his or her firm operates.

- The global business manager must also be able to handle unique human resources challenges presented by workforces with converging cultures.

- The global business manager is forced to see beyond the immediacy of local issues and into the broader global landscape.

Moving from Theory into Practice

The following summarizes a question and answer session with coauthor Joe Robinson. His answers are useful in contemplating how the global business professional can translate the theories and concepts covered in this chapter via practical answers to the questions from real life experiences.

What is the greatest attribute of successful global managers?

It has been said by the most successful and seasoned global managers that empathy for other individuals from other diverse cultures and backgrounds is the number one recurring attribute of the most successful international manager. This applies whether the manager is in sales and marketing, corporate policy, or joint venture supervision. Being able to maintain one's own identity, and at the same time understand and conduct business in other cultures and environments, is essential for long-term and optimum commercial success of any global organization. Such empathy skills can be developed by striving to understand that international differences have evolved historically, and what works for one country may or may not work for another country. Another example is that successful managers do not judge from a stand point of good and bad but must be willing to simply acknowledge that what others do or do not do is what may work best for that particular environment. I am not speaking about moral values of right and wrong but rather methodology. It is recommended that the new global manager be willing to observe before making a value judgment and then proceed accordingly.

What is the most recurring issue or problem of global managers?

When I was in graduate school many years ago, three of my four professors told us that identifying, appointing, training, and motivating overseas partners was the number one concern that we would be faced with when we went to work for our respective companies. Today, this continues to hold true. I see the major "disconnect" and unnecessary problems occurring in the international commercial arena, because the export company appointed the wrong partner, representative, or agent in the first place or does not properly support, train, inform or adequately motivate their overseas partners in the markets they are targeting. The best way to motivate a representative is to keep him intimately and immediately informed about new products, advertisements and company business that will impact his ability to perform his job. Training is another good motivator. Visiting him and inviting him to the corporate headquarters is another good way to motivate the rep. The worst thing to do is to appoint a representative and then ignore him.

What has changed in past forty years in global business management?

Two major changes are transportation and communications. Forty years ago, it was necessary to make a refueling stop in Alaska or Hawaii when traveling to the Far East. I remember well the discretionary "overnighter" in both Anchorage and Honolulu during my frequent travels to Korea, Hong Kong, Manila, and Japan. I miss those days as a bit of nostalgia, but I do appreciate today's more convenient non-stop flights from the East Coast of the U.S. to the Far East. As manager for the regional applications lab in Osaka during the early 1970s, I wrote chemical equations by hand and sent my letters by airmail with my questions to the main lab in the States. Telex machines were generally not conducive to chemical formula writing. Then we began to use the fax machine in the 1980s. This was as major improvement that enabled us to send and receive replies overnight. Then in the 1990s we began to use computers that developed into the e-mail system we all enjoy today. In 2001, I sat in an office in Jeddah, Saudi Arabia and participated in a live teleconference between the exporter in Arlington, Virginia and the agent in the Middle East. We even videoed writing chemical formulas on the white board for clarification on both sides to view and communicate in virtual real time. Today, cell phones are the norm worldwide. Both voice and message communication is instantaneous. Today I frequently call a friend who is truly a global business traveler and am no longer surprised when he says he is in India or Mexico or Australia or in his office nearby from where I am placing my call. Consider the advancement we have made in communications by using overseas call centers from telemarketing, customer service, and medical diagnostics using digital imaging communicating techniques. Surely, we have made a quantum leap in both transportation and communications in the past forty years.

A point of qualification is necessary, though. Many U.S. citizens erroneously believe that the USA is the most technologically sophisticated nation in the world. This may be a true statement in some areas, but is not universally true. According to the Communications Workers of American Union survey in 2007,[32] the downloading of files off the internet rates the U. S. average at 1.97 megabits. However this is far lower than Japan at 61.00 megabits, South Korea at 45.60 megabits and Finland at 21.70 megabits. This means you are able to download a full length movie in two minutes in Japan that will takes two hours in the U. S. The result is that faster downloading speeds could offer a competitive advantage for those firms who depend on internet global communications in responding to their operations abroad and to communicate in high volumes with their customers abroad.[33]

What has not changed in the global business arena in the past 25 years?

Sales, marketing, and negotiating are still contact intensive endeavors. Relationships are and will remain vital in many overseas business cultures. The need for personal contact is constantly reiterated when I see global road warriors penetrating new markets and expanding existing markets—sometimes at the expense of their competitors— simply because they were the only ones who showed up. Young global managers today need to understand that the digital age will never completely eliminate nor negate personal relationship building.

What is the distinction between the global business executive and global business policy maker and how does this impact corporate success?

The term executive has become watered down and diluted. Too many so called executives have the title in name only with out the ability to implement the activities required to move forward in international transactions. The policy maker does indeed have the authority to analyze, commit, and execute the actions required to move international transactions forward. The technique here is to be sure you know who you are dealing with in negotiating your global business arrangements. I strive to negotiate with policy makers whenever possible.

What countries are America's top trading partners today and which are perceived to be the top trading partners in the foreseeable future?

Canada, Mexico, Japan, UK, and the EU have been the major trading partners of the U.S. In the near future, China, India, Korea, and the Middle East will be added to this list. The Office of the U. S. Trade Representative (USTR) is diligently pursuing increasing American exports by government-to-government negotiations, particularly through bilateral and regional Free Trade Agreements (FTAs) that specifically help SMEs (Small- and Medium-sized Enterprises) employing under five-hundred people. Tiffany M. Moore, Assistant U. S. Trade Representative, in a presentation before the House Committee on Small Business on June 13, 2007 stated that, "Ninety-five percent of potential customers reside outside our borders. For small business, our key task is to break down trade barriers abroad through government-to-government negotiations so that we open the door to new markets. Small businesses drive U. S. exports. Ninety-seven percent of all U. S. exporters are small businesses, accounting for more than a quarter of U. S. goods exports. More than two-thirds of U.S. exporters have fewer than twenty employees. Since 95 percent of potential customers reside outside our borders, American small businesses benefit when we expand U.S. access to consumers and households abroad who want to buy and enjoy our products."

How does the successful global manager "follow" his customers who shift manufacturing operations to a foreign country?

Many traditional manufacturers have gone abroad. Witness the migration of manufactures from America, Japan, England, and Germany. Those manufacturers who passively stand by and watch their long term and traditional customers move offshore will eventually lose their major source of revenue as their business will dwindle and in some cases disappear altogether. The clever global manager will follow his customers. When a U.S. company moves its factory to another country such as Mexico or China, the vendors for that company need to visit the new factory and meet the new local managers to first reestablish a relationship and then begin the selling process all over again: this is the meaning of *"it is necessary to follow"* your customer. Those who do not do this will lose the customer altogether in the long run, and those who do this may even increase their business to this type of customer as their production increases.

With travel and communication advancements today, it is desirable that managers follow their customers as they set up shop in overseas locations. I know of several manufacturing firms who have followed their customers overseas and are actually selling and growing their business more, as a result of their traditional customers producing more and needing greater quantities of supplies in their manufacturing process. A few companies I work with actually have shifted form a low percentage of exports a few years ago to earning the major share of their revenue from exports in this manner.

What training does the successful export manager give to his support staff?

Training in skills to deal daily with regulations, documents, and compliance is becoming increasingly important. Export documents provide multiple purpose usages. They need to be handled by different parties to the transaction, and therefore need to be not only accurate, but complete in the information they provide. I have heard from numerous presentations of government officials that half of the paper work, or more professionally stated, export documents, have one or more errors. Training and work shops in this area will save global companies time, money, and in some cases, fines that lack of training could have prevented.

<u>Where does the successful global manager find, hire, and motivate the most productive individuals to be on his global business and sales team?</u>

Employees who thrive on adventure, change, and challenge make the best team members. Add empathy and communication skills and most likely the employee will develop into a productive international player. You can find these players by seeking out those who have lived abroad as youngsters, those who have traveled abroad as youngsters, or those who simply like adventure and travel and have a high degree of self-motivated energy. Another type of individual who fits this description is the one who is married to a "foreign" person. The very nature of this act implies a willingness to reach out and have empathy for other cultures and a global outlook that can be transitioned into a successful global manager.

<u>What are some of the more successful negotiating techniques that even junior managers can use to their benefit?</u>

Setting the stage for a successful negotiating session requires the traditional but meaningful cliché: "Think globally but act locally." Whenever possible, you might try to bond or establish rapport with your potential customer. In Japan, for example, begin by talking about the weather and then move into the business negotiations. Each country and culture has its favorite topics and subjects they like to talk about. Become familiar with these and proceed accordingly.

Another technique that is helpful and impressive in face-to-face negotiating is to make a color copy of the other party's home page and discretely display it as you begin the negotiating session. I have used this technique often with success, even though I could not read the language of the home page, whether it be ion Chinese, Arabic, or German.

Another essential technique is to ask questions up front to ascertain the mood, degree of motivation, and direction of your potential customer. Listen carefully to the meaning of the words rather than the literal translation of words. Watch the body language carefully and understand its significance as you proceed.

In serious negotiations, always use your own interpreter. This is essential for obtaining factual information; it establishes you as a global professional.

Successful global business managers require the same set of skills and attributes that domestic managers require. However, additional abilities are needed to cope with different cultures, languages, time-zone considerations, and procedures for conducting daily business transactions. A talent for communicating and an aspiration for travel typically are found in successful managers in the global market place.

Key Concepts

- Globalization pros
- Globalization cons
- Glocalization
- Interdependencies among nations
- Transparency among nations
- World Trade Organization
- Gross domestic product
- Top U.S.A. global trading partners
- Importance of global trade
- Global business
- Historical examples of international trade
- Driving forces: reduction in barriers to trade
- Driving forces: advances in transportation technology
- Driving forces: advances in communications technologies
- Impacts of globalization: political, economic, social, cultural
- Characteristics of the successful global business professional

Chapter 2

THE IMPACT OF CULTURE ON GLOBAL BUSINESS

Global Business in Practice
Business Etiquette Across Cultures

The mission of the International Trade Administration (ITA) of the Department of Commerce is to create prosperity by strengthening the competitiveness of U.S. industry, promoting trade and investment, and ensuring fair trade and compliance with trade laws and agreements. The organization also provides assistance in the business area of understanding cross cultural communication, including what to do and what not to do while conducting business.

According to Margaret Kammeyer, ITA Office of Public Affairs, doing business with international clients requires more than just an understanding of the myriad of international rules and regulations. A lack of knowledge about a customer's culture can lead to misunderstanding, frustration, potential embarrassment, and even loss of business. Savvy exporters are now not only expected to be familiar with country marketing reports but should also conduct research on their clients' culture and regional etiquette when preparing to enter new markets.

Ms. Kammeyer offers some interesting observations:

- In the People's Republic of China, don't write notes using red ink. This suggests that the writer will die soon. Avoid using the number four at all costs because this, too, signifies death.
- In India, the significance of a business arrangement is often determined by the amount of time spent in negotiations.
- In Thailand, it is considered offensive to show the sole of the shoe or foot to another. Therefore, it is necessary to take care when crossing your legs.
- In Saudi Arabia, the law prohibits the wearing of neck jewelry by men, and westerners have been arrested for neglecting to observe this rule.
- In Argentina, do not be offended if your business associate arrives thirty to forty minutes late to a meeting.
- In Costa Rica, if you are invited for dinner to a home, bring flowers, chocolates, scotch, or wine. Do not bring calla lilies, which are associated with funerals.

- In Germany, first names are reserved for family members and close friends. Moreover, in German business culture, colleagues who have worked together for years often do not know each other's first names.

The building of successful business relationships is a vital part of any venture, and such relationships rely heavily on an understanding of each partner's expectations and intentions. Global business representatives will want to ensure that they make the best impression on potential clients. This desire means that in addition to understanding preconceived notions about American business practices, the international representative should have at least a basic familiarity with the customs and practices of the country in which the company is considering conducting business. Gift giving, proper forms of address, appropriate dress, entertainment, holidays, business hours, and sense of time are a few cultural differences of which to be aware. Mastering international business etiquette and understanding foreign customs is imperative for success in global business.

Introduction

Culture is the set of shared attitudes, values, goals, and practices that characterize a society, or in the business sense, an organization.[1] Culture provides answers to questions pertaining to who, what, why, and when for a specific group of people. Business culture provides answers to questions pertaining to who, what, why, when, and how of any particular organization or type of business. The concept of business culture becomes increasingly complex when applied to a multinational corporation (MNC). Since the MNC culture evolved from the employees of more than one nation, the variables that comprise that specific culture are potentially limitless. Within the confines of the culture in any particular nation, one can commonly find that numerous different subcultures exist. The global manager must understand the complexities of the relationships between the different subcultures within any particular culture or nation and organizational operations in several different nations.

The purpose of this chapter is to discuss the relational complexities that potentially exist between a culture and a foreign organization seeking to do business in that culture. Major topics of this chapter include the following:

- Cultural paradigms,

- The dimensions of culture,

- An examination of the major aspects of cultures (major world religion, ethics across cultures, values and attitudes across cultures, business manners and customs across cultures, social structures and organizations, and education), and

- The major theories of cultural dimensions.

Managerial Cultural Paradigms—Ethnocentric, Polycentric, Geocentric

When the topic of culture is discussed within the context of international business management, one should consider the influence of three major cultural paradigms: ethnocentric, polycentric, and geocentric. Ethnocentrism is the belief that one's own culture is superior to all others and the standard by which all other cultures should be measured. Ethnocentric cultures hold a general contempt for members of other cultures. Ethnocentrism may manifest itself in attitudes of superiority or sometimes hostility. Violence, discrimination, proselytizing, and verbal aggressiveness are other means whereby ethnocentrism expresses itself.[2] Ethnocentric corporations are home-country oriented, with key management positions located at the domestic headquarters. Ethnocentric managers believe that home-country nationals are more intelligent, reliable, and trustworthy than foreign nationals. Home-country nationals are recruited and trained for all international positions. Many international companies exhibit an ethnocentric philosophy. The standard international company finds great difficulty communicating in different languages and accepting cultural differences. International strategic alternatives are limited to entry modes, such as exporting, licensing, and turnkey operations— because "it works at home it must work overseas."[3]

Polycentrism, as the opposite of ethnocentrism, promotes openness towards other cultures, opinions, and ways of life. Thus, intercultural actions and correlations are interpreted not only with the background of own cultural experiences, but when the independence of other cultures is recognized. Polycentric cultures relativize values and see them in the whole context.[4] Polycentric organizations are host-country-oriented corporations. The polycentric firm establishes multinational operations on condition that host-country managers "do it their way."

Headquarters is staffed by home-country nationals, while local nationals occupy the key positions in their respective local subsidiaries. Host-country nationals have high or absolute sovereignty over the subsidiary's operations. There is no direction from headquarters and the only controls are financially oriented. No foreign national can seriously aspire to a senior position at headquarters. Strategically, the MNC competes on a market-by-market basis because it believes that "local people know what is best for them.[5]

The geocentric organization's primary objective is to develop an integrated system with a worldwide approach; therefore, subsidiaries operate in a highly interdependent manner. The entire organization focuses on both worldwide and local objectives. Every part of the organization makes a unique contribution using its unique competencies. Geocentrism requires collaboration between headquarters and subsidiaries to establish universal standards with permissible local variations. Diverse regions are integrated through a global systems approach to decision making: good ideas come from and flow to any country, resources are allocated on a global basis, geographical lines are erased and functional, and product lines are globalized. Within legal and political limits, the best people are sought to solve problems. Competence is what counts, not national origin. The reward system motivates managers to surrender national biases and work for worldwide objectives.[6]

The astute, global-business professional is aware of the impact of the managerial-cultural paradigm in use for each overseas situation. Regardless of the managerial-cultural paradigm in use, the business professional recognizes that an understanding of the major dimensions of culture are essential for success in doing business overseas.

Dimensions of Culture

The dimensions of culture may be categorized as Communication, Religion, Ethics, Values and Attitudes, Manners, Customs, Social Structures and Organizations, and Education. The savvy global manager seeks to understand each of these dimensions as they impact decision making, negotiations, and ongoing operations critical to long-term success. The astute global manager knows how to effectively integrate the new culture with the existing culture.

Communication

Global business professionals encounter various cultures throughout the world. Individuals and organizations within each culture communicate in manners unique to their culture. The necessity for the global business professional to understand the dimensions of culture has become increasingly important:

> In international business, people of different cultures have difficulty communicating effectively without some caring and appreciation of each other's points of view, values, and goals. If individuals do not attempt to develop this awareness, stereotyping of people, information, and behavior takes place. This eventually can lead to systematic discrimination.[7]

Communication between two cultures can be awkward if professionals do not conduct proper research. In the global business arena, a misinterpretation can be very costly. As a result of using wrong or inappropriate words, business leaders from other countries may become offended and refuse to close important business deals. For instance, Japanese firms tend to involve the senior business officials in the negotiation of major business agreements. Prior to a meeting with a Japanese firm, U.S. negotiators must identify the senior Japanese executives to avoid embarrassment. Business leaders should provide important documents only to the senior Japanese executives at the start of the meeting. If global leaders do not follow this protocol, Japanese executives will perceive this as an insult and a show of disrespect.

Successful MNCs acknowledge cultural differences and adapt parts of the business to recognize the unique differences and variables in communication. Major communication variables include different meanings of words across languages, verbal communication, non-verbal communication, and context (high and low).

Different Meanings of Words across Languages

The various languages spoken throughout the world may use similar terminology, but different meanings may exist for the same word or phrase.

Differences in accent and usage can lead to misunderstandings. Cross-cultural or cross-language barriers exacerbate the misunderstandings that arise when trying to communicate a message. Different cultures and languages may not always present or interpret messages in the same context. The effective global business manager recognizes these differences and makes every effort to understand the culture, not assuming that those in the foreign culture will understand him or her. Global businesses outside of the U.S. typically operate in multilingual environments or those in which more than one language is spoken.

Verbal

Verbal communication involves the actual speaking of words. In the United States, English is the dominant verbal language. In France, French is the dominant language. All countries have a spoken language. Effective global managers must become very familiar with the language that is spoken in the countries in which they intend to do business. Global business professionals, in speaking the language of a host country, must understand the appropriate times to use certain words and phrases.

Language affects communication in two ways: (1) the ability to encode our thoughts and purposes clearly, and (2) the ability to formulate those thoughts and purposes.[8] Effective, cross-cultural communicators must know how to properly pronounce words, how to properly spell words, and how to use these words in proper grammatical form. Those doing business in a foreign nation may have to learn the language in order to make a respectable impression among the inhabitants of that country. This knowledge would, in turn, result in more respect towards the business person and their business firm.[9]

Four distinct areas relate to verbal communication: jargon and slang, acronyms, humor, and vocabulary and grammar.[10] People use jargon in business sessions or in everyday conversation. The expression "that's par for the course" is a jargon statement that describes a particular situation where the results meet the expectations. Acronyms are letters of the alphabet that represent a series of words. "FYI" is an abbreviation that means "for your information." When conducting international business, acronyms should not be used; these letters will be confusing and misunderstood. Humor should also be avoided: what is humorous in one country may be offensive or misunderstood in another. All written communications should follow proper grammar rules, and sentences should be complete and properly punctuated. Abbreviations should not be used when dealing with vocabulary and grammar.[11]

Nonverbal

When conveying messages, non-verbal communication is just as important as verbal communication. Nonverbal communication includes various forms of facial expressions and body language. While in foreign locations, the global business professional must "do his homework" concerning the use of acceptable and unacceptable body language. Those interested in doing business in other cultures must realize that well-accepted body language in their home country may be perceived as offensive in the country of business.

Thus, the business professional should study the body language requirements of the culture before arrival in that culture. The use of inappropriate or wrong body language could be quite costly to a corporation. Business travelers and corporations may be unable to counteract the negative perceptions of inappropriate body language. Consequently, host country officials may decide to discontinue business relations with a MNC due to misinterpreted body language. One small incident can be very detrimental to all future business negotiations.

High Context vs. Low Context

Context is another major cross-cultural communication variable to consider. A high-context culture is "a culture that relies heavily on nonverbal and subtle situational cues in communication." A low-context culture is "a culture that relies heavily on words to convey meaning in communication."[12] High context refers to societies or groups where people have close connections over a long period of time. As a result of years of interaction with each other, many aspects of cultural behavior are not made explicit, because most members know what to do and what to think.

Figure 2.1

Characteristics of High-Context Communication

- Less verbally explicit communication

- Less written/formal information

- More internalized understanding of what is communicated

- Long term relationships

- Strong boundaries—"insiders" vs. "outsiders"

- Knowledge is situational and relational.

Communication in high-context cultures implies considerably more trust by both parties. Despite how an outsider may perceive this type of communication, casual and insignificant conversation is important because it reflects the desire to build a relationship and create trust. Oral agreements imply strong commitments in high-context cultures.

Low-context refers to societies where people tend to have many connections, but of shorter duration. In these societies, cultural behavior and beliefs may need to be spelled out explicitly so that those coming into the cultural environment know how to behave.

Characteristics of Low-Context Communication

- Rule oriented: people play by external rules
- More knowledge is codified, public, external, and accessible
- More interpersonal connections of shorter duration
- Knowledge is more often transferable

Figure 2.2

In low-context cultures, enforceable contracts will tend to be in writing, precisely worded, and highly legalistic. Low-context cultures value directness. Managers are expected to be explicit and precise in conveying intended meaning.[13]

As can be seen by the comparison of high-context cultures and low-context cultures, many subtle nuances exist. Since the communication styles are very different, the wrong message can easily be sent, or the communication can be misinterpreted. Does this mean that high-context cultures are more effective in terms of communication than low-context cultures? The answer is no. Regardless of the cultural-communication context, the differences must be understood, and proper actions must be displayed at the appropriate time.

Religion

The term "religion" may mean many things to different people. When discussed across cultures, the topic of religion is open for misunderstanding. This misunderstanding may originate from either a preconceived notion or a lack of knowledge concerning the topic. Thus, global business professionals must understand and be well versed in this important cultural aspect. In general, religion has been defined as an action or conduct indicating a belief in, reverence for, and desire to please a divine ruling power; the exercise or practice of rites or observances implying a particular system of faith and worship. The following brief summaries of the major world religions may be helpful in understanding this cultural variable in the global business environment.

Christianity

Jesus Christ of Nazareth is the central figure in Christianity. Jesus was conceived by Immaculate Conception and born around 3 AD to the Jewish virgin, Mary. He was fully man in that he was born to Mary, and yet he was the only begotten Son of God, living a perfect and sinless life. Jesus performed numerous miracles, taught with absolute authority about his Father in heaven, and proclaimed that He was the Christ, the Son of God. For this, he was crucified at the age of thirty three. Christ's suffering and death upon the cross paid for the sins of all mankind; and through Him, God grants salvation to anyone who believes in Christ's sacrifice. Following Christ's death, He rose from the grave and returned to the earth, appearing to over five hundred of his followers and telling them of the Kingdom of God, to which He was going. He also promised his disciples that He would return one day to bring all believers with him to that Kingdom, to enjoy eternal life in the presence of God.

The only authoritative Christian holy text is the Bible, which includes the Old Testament (also considered sacred to Judaism and Islam) and the New Testament. The Old Testament chronicles the history of God's plan for man through Abraham's descendents, who had been promised a Savior by God and were waiting for Him. The New Testament is unique to Christianity in that it focuses on the figure of Jesus and His teachings. Christians believe that Jesus is the foretold Savior of the Old Testament; therefore, Christians are not looking for a savior but are waiting for the return of Jesus so that He can take them to his Kingdom, or Heaven. The Apostle's Creed contains the core beliefs of Christianity. This document distinguishes Christianity from other religions and proclaims Christian doctrine in a concise manner. It reads as follows:

> I believe in God the Father Almighty, maker of heaven and earth. And in Jesus Christ, His only Son, our Lord; who was conceived by the Holy Spirit, born of the Virgin Mary, suffered under Pontius Pilate, was crucified, died and was buried. He descended into hell; the third day He rose again from the dead; He ascended into heaven and is seated at the right hand of God the Father Almighty; from there He shall come to judge the living and the dead. I believe in the Holy Spirit, the holy Christian Church, the Communion of Saints, the Forgiveness of sins, the Resurrection of the body, and the Life everlasting. Amen.[14]

Judaism

Judaism is a monotheistic religion which believes that the world was created by a single, all-knowing divinity. God designed all things within that world to have meaning and purpose as part of a divine order. According to the teachings of

Judaism, God's will for human behavior was revealed to Moses and the Israelites at Mount Sinai. The Torah, or commandments, which decreed how humans should live, was a gift from God. The beliefs of Judaism can be seen in the words of Moses Maimonides, a Spanish Jew who, in the twelfth century, condensed the beliefs into a concise thirteen articles of faith. It reads as follows:

1. I believe with perfect faith that the Creator, blessed be His Name, is the Creator and Guide of everything that has been created; He alone has made, does make, and will make all things.

2. I believe with perfect faith that the Creator, blessed be His Name, is One, and that there is no unity in any manner like unto His, and that He alone is our God, who was, and is, and will be.

3. I believe with perfect faith that the Creator, blessed be His Name, is not a body, and that He is free from all the properties of matter, and that He has not any form whatever.

4. I believe with perfect faith that the Creator, blessed be His Name, is the first and the last.

5. I believe with perfect faith that to the Creator, blessed be His Name, and to Him alone, it is right to pray, and that it is not right to pray to any being besides him.

6. I believe with perfect faith that all the works of the prophets are true.

7. I believe with perfect faith that the prophecy of Moses, our teacher, peace be unto him, was true and that he was the chief of the prophets, both of those who preceded and of those who followed him.

8. I believe with perfect faith that the whole Torah, now in our possession, is the same that was given to Moses, our teacher, peace be unto him.

9. I believe with perfect faith that this Torah will not be changed and that there will never be any other Law from the Creator, blessed be His name.

10. I believe with perfect faith that the Creator, blessed be   His name, knows every deed of the children of men, and all their thoughts, as it is said. It is He that fashioned the hearts of them all, that gives heed to all their works.

11. I believe with perfect faith that the Creator, blessed be His Name, rewards those who keep His commandments and punishes those that transgress them.

12. I believe with perfect faith in the coming of the Messiah; and, though he tarry, I will wait daily for his coming.

13. I believe with perfect faith that there will be a revival of the dead at the time when it shall please the Creator, blessed be His name, and exalted be His Fame for ever and ever. For Thy salvation I hope, O Lord.[15]

Three branches of Judaism circulate that form the framework for the type of lifestyle and beliefs of Jewish individuals: (1) Orthodox or traditionalists who observe most of the traditional dietary and ceremonial laws of Judaism; (2) Conservatives, who do not hold to the importance of a Jewish political state but put more emphasis on the historic and religious aspects of Judaism, doctrinally falling somewhere between the Orthodox and Reform branches; and (3) the Reform or liberal wing of Judaism, which is culture and race oriented with little consensus on doctrinal or religious belief.

Islam

The teachings of Islam include aspects of both faith and duty. Muslims receive instruction only from those who consider themselves adequately learned in theology or law. Muslims base their doctrine on the teachings in the Qur'an (Koran), the scripture of Islam. Muhammad's disciples have said that sometime during the seventh century AD, the Angel Gabriel dictated the contents to him, infallible and without error. For Muslims, the Qur'an is the word of God, and the carrier of the revelation of Muhammad, the last and most perfect of God's messengers to mankind. Five articles of faith comprise the main doctrines of Islam. All Muslims are expected to believe the following:

1. There is one true Allah, who alone is the creator of the universe.

2. Angels exist and interact with human lives. They are made of light, and each has different purposes or messages to bring to earth. Each man or woman has two angels who record his actions; one records good deeds, the other bad deeds.

3. The four inspired books include the Torah of Moses, the Psalms (Zabin) of David, the Gospel of Jesus Christ (Injil) and the Qur'an. All but the Qur'an have been corrupted by Jews and Christians.

4. God has spoken through numerous prophets throughout time. The six greatest are Adam, Noah, Abraham, Moses, Jesus, and Muhammad. Muhammad is the last and greatest of Allah's messengers.

5. Last Days: The last day will be a time of resurrection and judgment. Those who follow Allah and Muhammad will go to Islamic heaven, or Paradise. Those who do not will go to hell.[16]

In addition to believing the Five Articles of faith, Muslims observe the Five Pillars of Faith: duties each Muslim must perform.

1. One must state, "there is no God but Allah, and Muhammad is the Prophet of Allah" publicly to become a Muslim.

2. Prayer must be done five times a day (upon rising, at noon, mid afternoon, after sunset, and before going to sleep) towards the direction of Mecca. The call to prayer is sounded by the muezzin (Muslim crier) from a tower (minaret) within the mosque.

3. Muslims are legally required to give one-fortieth of their income to the needy. Since those to whom alms are given are helping the giver achieve salvation, no sense of shame results from receiving charity.

4. During the holy month of Ramadan, faithful Muslims fast from sunrise to sunset each day. This develops self control, devotion to God, and identity with the needy.

5. Each Muslim is expected to make the pilgrimage to Mecca at least once in his or her lifetime, if he has the means to do it and is physically capable of the trip. This pilgrimage is an essential part of gaining salvation, so the old or infirm may send someone in their place. It involves a set of rituals and ceremonies.[17]

A sixth religious duty associated with the Five Pillars is Jihad, or Holy War. This duty requires that if the situation warrants, men must go to war to defend or spread Islam. If killed, they are guaranteed eternal life in Paradise.

Hinduism

Hinduism has no specific founder or theology. It developed as the combination of religious practices of Aryan tribes, who migrated from central Asia around 1500 BC to India, and the early inhabitants of India, the Harappans. Over time, both groups developed similar religious belief systems: Aryan polytheism and Harappan sanctity of fertility. The predominantly Aryan society eventually developed the caste system, which ranked society according to occupational class. The caste system is structured as follows:

1. Brahmins or the priests

2. Kshatriyas or the king-warrior class

3. Vaishyas or the merchants, farmers, Sutras laborers, craftspeople

4. Harijahns or the "untouchables". These individuals are believed to be descended from the Harappan aboriginal people. They are extremely poor and discriminated against.

The higher a person's caste, the more that person is blessed with the benefits and luxuries life has to offer. Although the caste system was outlawed in 1948, the

Hindu people of India still embrace the system and recognized it as the proper way to stratify society.

Hinduism is based on the concept that human and animal spirits reincarnate or come back to earth to live many times in different forms. The belief that souls move up and down an infinite hierarchy, depending on the behaviors they practiced in their life, is visible in many of the Hindu societal policies. As the caste system survives, charity towards others is unheard of, because Hindus believe that each individual deserves to be in the social class in which they were born. A person is born into the highest class because he or she behaved well in a past life. A person is born into poverty and shame because of misbehaviors in a past life.

A Hindu can be polytheistic (more than one god), monotheistic (one god), pantheistic (god and the universe are one), agnostic (unsure if god exists), or atheistic (no god) and still claim to be Hindu. This open theology makes discussing basic beliefs difficult because many ideas and definitions of Hinduism exist. However, these universal ideas must be mentioned.

Central to Hinduism are the concepts of reincarnation, the caste system, merging with Brahman (or the ultimate reality), finding morality, and reaching Nirvana (the peaceful escape from the cycle of reincarnation). The Hindu paths to salvation include the way of works (rituals), the way of knowledge (realization of reality and self reflection), and the way of devotion (devotion to the god that you choose to follow). If the practitioner follows the paths of these ways, salvation can be achieved.[18]

Buddhism

Buddhism is a religion that is based on the teachings of Siddhartha Gautama, the son of a wealthy landowner born in northern India (now part of Nepal) around 560 B.C. In order to achieve spiritual peace, Gautama renounced his worldly advantages and became known as Buddha, or "the enlightened one." He preached his religious views his entire life throughout South Asia. The five precepts of Buddhism include the following:

1. Kill no living thing.

2. Do not steal.

3. Do not commit adultery.

4. Tell no lies.

5. Do not drink intoxicants or take drugs.

Other precepts apply only to monks and nuns:

1. Eat moderately and only at the appointed time.

2. Avoid that which excites the senses.

3. Do not wear adornments.

4. Do not sleep in luxurious beds.

5. Accept no silver or gold.[19]

Confucianism

Confucius (K'ung Fu Tzu), born in 551 BC, wandered through many states of China, giving advice to its rulers and accumulating a small band of students. His writings deal primarily with individual morality and ethics and the proper exercise of political power by the rulers. In China and other areas in Asia, the social ethics and moral teachings of Confucius are blended with the Taoist communion with nature and the Buddhist concepts of the afterlife to form a set of complementary, peacefully coexistent, and ecumenical religions. Taoism originates with Tao (pronounced "*Dow*"), meaning "path or the way." The term is basically indefinable and has to be experienced:

> [Tao] refers to a power which envelops, surrounds and flows through all things, living and nonliving. The Tao regulates natural processes and nourishes balance in the Universe. It embodies the harmony of opposites (i.e., there would be no love without hate, no light without dark, no male without female.)[20]

The adherents of Confucianism consider it to be a philosophy of life, not a religion. According to Confucius, the nature of man is fundamentally good and inclined towards goodness. Perfection of goodness can be found in sages and saints. Every man should attempt to reach the ideal by leading a virtuous life, possessing a very noble character, and doing his duty unselfishly, with sincerity and truthfulness. He who possesses a good character and divine virtue is a princely type of man. The princely man sticks to virtue, but the inferior man clings to material comfort. The princely man is just, but the inferior man expects rewards and favors. The princely man is dignified, noble, magnanimous, and humble, but the inferior man is mean, proud, crooked, and arrogant. In the "Great Learning," Confucius revealed the step by step process by which one attains self development and by which it flows over into the common life to serve the state and bless mankind.[21] The order of development that Confucius set forth is as follows:

1. Investigation of phenomena,

2. Learning,

3. Sincerity,

4. Rectitude of purpose,

5. Self development,

6. Family discipline,

7. Local self government, and

8. Universal self government.[22]

Shinto

Shinto, an ancient Japanese religion that originated about 500 BC, was originally a mixture of nature worship, fertility cults, divination techniques, hero worship, and shamanism. Its name, derived from the Chinese words "shin tao," is translated "The Way of the Gods." Unlike most other religions, Shinto has no real founder, no written scriptures, no body of religious law, and a very loosely-organized priesthood. The Yamato dynasty consolidated its rule over most of Japan in the eighth century AD. Divine origins were ascribed to the imperial family, which then established Shinto as an official religion of Japan along with Buddhism. This situation remained until after the end of World War II, which resulted in the complete separation of Japanese religion from politics. The Emperor was forced by the U.S. army to renounce his divinity at that time.[23]

Of all the dimensions of culture, the religious dimensions typically provide the ethical foundations that define business relationships overseas. Those cultures that deny the existence of God through the practices of agnosticism or atheism still require standards of morality and conduct essential to the orderly functioning of society. The astute global business professional is well versed in the ethical foundations for both the home and host nations in which he or she is doing business.

Ethics

Ethics is the study of morality and standards of conduct. U.S. firms have developed and implemented standards of conduct for employees to serve as guidelines as to how they should comport themselves when representing the company. Some firms have employed knowledgeable consultants and subject-matter experts to teach corporate ethics, hoping to ensure that employees will conduct themselves in an ethical manner. What one culture considers moral may not be accepted as moral by another. A discussion of the concepts of ethics logically follows a discussion of religion because the two can be very related. On the other hand, one should consider the two issues separately, as ethical standards are not always a result of religious standards—although in many cases they are. One only needs to consider the founding of the U.S.A. The religious beliefs and faith of the Founding Fathers greatly influenced the writing of the Declaration of Independence and the U.S. Constitution. These documents continue to influence, in part, what many consider ethical conduct today. However, all cultures do not agree. Understanding the ethics of a particular culture is important when it comes to doing business in that culture.

Definitions

A general definition of ethics is as follows: the discipline dealing with what is good and bad and with moral duty and obligation. Business Ethics is the study of ethical dilemmas, values, and decision making in the world of business. Business ethics should not be considered a separate disciple from ethics. International business ethics examines the many practical issues that result from the international context of business. In the global context, the cultural relativity of ethical values receives more emphasis than when considering domestic business ethics. However, universal values do exist to form the basis for international business ethics, such as those relating to killing, lying, cheating, etc.

Figure 2.3

Global Business Professionals Must be Able to do the Following

1. Compare business ethical traditions across cultures.

2. Compare business ethical traditions from various religious perspectives.

3. Understand the ethical concerns of conducting international business transactions, including property rights and transparency.

4. Understand and respond appropriately to varying global standards, including various wage and labor practices.

5. Understand the ethics of outsourcing and other potentially controversial issues associated with globalization.

The ethical differences between cultures can be both vast and complex. One example of ethical differences can be seen in the exploitation of children in the workforce in Third World nations. Other cultures do not universally accept the ethics driving specific laws that govern the employment of children in the U.S. The global business professional may encounter this ethical dilemma while working overseas and have to craft strategies that are in line with the ethical standards of the business. The trafficking of narcotic drugs provides another example of ethical differences across cultures. U.S. law prohibits the trade of these harmful substances, yet it may be legal, even ethical, in other nations to engage in such trade. One should note that no legitimate business operating overseas would engage in drug trafficking to the U.S. Those firms involved in the legitimate global business community recognize that they have a social responsibility to their trading partners, based upon mutually agreed ethical principles.

Corporate Social Responsibility

Ethically speaking, one of the most important issues global business professionals may face is that of being socially responsible in the cultures in which they choose to do business. Nothing will sour the relationship between a foreign business and the community in which it operates more quickly than the perception that the company is operating in a way that is harmful to that community. Socially responsible organizations investigate ways in which to reinvest in those communities, contributing in terms of growth and economic development. Greed and corruption must be avoided at all costs, by both global businesses and their trading partners.

The Issue of Corruption

Corruption is a major concern for those engaged in global business. The issue of corruption has been addressed across the globe in numerous venues, such as international conferences, policy forums, government official speeches, international organizations, including the OECD and Transparency International—an international nongovernmental organization. Government leaders increasingly cite corruption as a reason for withholding foreign aid or debt relief. Many believe that a nation's inability to pay interest on its loans is due to its leaders siphoning off national earnings into their own bank accounts. Thus, extending aid or canceling the debt may encourage further corruption. While many international initiatives to combat corruption focus on developing nations, these nations are increasingly being scrutinized by potential investors as well. "Corruption is a source of concern for governments, entrepreneurs, private individuals, nongovernmental organizations, companies and indeed for society as a whole."[24]

A strong correlation exists between poverty and corruption. This correlation reinforces the growing evidence that corruption hampers efforts to lift people out of poverty and provide them with new economic opportunities. "Corruption clearly results in the misallocation of resources and tends to be more prevalent where systems of governance and political will to combat corruption are weak."[25] Corruption helps to fuel poverty, especially when high-level public officials steal from their nations or mismanage public resources intended to finance their people's aspirations for a better life. In many parts of the world, government officials have lined their own pockets instead of funding development such as new roads, schools, and hospitals.

Corruption eventually may lead to economic stagnation and increase economic and social disparities over time—when the high costs of providing public services and low capacities to collect taxes occur together. Investment opportunities and economic growth do not materialize easily in places where corruption is rampant. Investors are demanding a higher assurance of market integrity to mitigate potential risks from poor governance. Government leaders can address corruption more effectively when a strong political will exists to combat it—by enforcing countries' laws criminalizing bribery and prosecuting corrupt individuals at all levels of society.[26]

Figure 2.4

Transparency International (TI) is an international non-governmental organization dedicated to fighting corruption worldwide. TI succeeds through the following mission:

1. Curb corruption through international and national coalitions, encouraging governments to establish and implement effective laws, policies, and anticorruption programs.

2. Strengthen public support and understanding for anticorruption programs and enhance public transparency and accountability in international business transactions and in the administration of public procurement.

3. Encourage all parties involved in international business transactions to operate at the highest levels of integrity.[27]

TI provides guidelines for organizations wishing to develop anticorruption programs. These guidelines are derived from its "Survey of Best Practices for Corporate Anti-Corruption Programs."[28] Because the resource materials are from U.S. companies, the primary focus of the guidelines is compliance with the Foreign Corrupt Practices Act. However, the material can also be adapted for compliance with non-U.S., antibribery initiatives, including those of the OECD.

Foreign Corrupt Practices Act. As a result of Securities and Exchange Commission (SEC) investigations in the mid 1970s, over four-hundred U.S. companies admitted making questionable or illegal payments in excess of $300 million to foreign government officials, politicians, and political parties. The abuses ran the gamut from bribery of high foreign officials to secure some type of favorable action by a foreign government to so-called facilitating payments that allegedly ensured that government functionaries discharged certain ministerial or clerical duties. Congress enacted the Foreign Corrupt Practices Act (FCPA) to bring a halt to the bribery of foreign officials and to restore public confidence in the integrity of the U.S. business system.

The FCPA was intended to have and has had an enormous impact on the way American firms do business. Several firms that paid bribes to foreign officials have been the subject of criminal and civil enforcement actions. These actions resulted in large fines, suspensions, debarment from federal procurement contracting, and employee jail time. To avoid such consequences, many firms have implemented detailed compliance programs to prevent and detect any improper payments by employees and agents.

Following the passage of the FCPA, the Congress became concerned that U.S. companies were operating at a disadvantage compared to foreign companies. These foreign companies routinely paid bribes and, in some countries, were permitted to deduct the cost of such bribes as business expenses on their taxes. In 1988, the Congress directed the Executive Branch to commence negotiations in the OECD to obtain the agreement of the U.S. major trading partners to enact legislation similar to the FCPA. In 1997, the U.S. and thirty three other countries signed the OECD Convention on Combating Bribery of Foreign Public Officials in International Business Transactions. The antibribery provisions of the FCPA make it unlawful for a U.S. person, and certain foreign issuers of securities, to make a corrupt payment to a foreign official for the purpose of securing business with or directing business to any person. Since 1998, these provisions also apply to foreign firms and persons who attempt corrupt payments while in the United States.[29]

Values and Attitudes

The study of culture must include values and attitudes. Values are generally accepted beliefs about what is right and wrong. Values are an interpretation of culture by societal members. A society derives its culture from its history and environment. The developed values of a society influence the members of the society. The values are a basis for developing social norms and decision making. If a citizen behaves according to social norms, the society accepts and respects the individual. If the citizen behaves contrary to social norms, he or she stands out and may be subject to correction. An attitude is the manifestation of values, beliefs, feelings, and states of mind.[30]

To value something is to consider or rate it highly. In a cultural context, a value would then be anything that a particular culture holds in high esteem. Consequently, an attitude is "a mental position with regard to a fact or state or a feeling or emotion toward a fact or state."[31] An attitude is what one thinks or feels about someone or something. Values and attitudes are interrelated, as attitudes often shape values, and vice versa.

Variances in Attitudes across Cultures

The astute global business professional recognizes the variances in attitudes between the home culture and the host culture. Differences in attitudes toward time, work, change gender, social status, and social mobility impact all stages of the business relationship. Time differences effect meeting attendance, as well as ongoing employee attendance. Gender differences impact female employment.

Concept of Time

Different cultures approach the concept of time and corresponding time management practices very differently. For example, in some South American cultures, meeting might begin thirty minutes late.[32] French businesspeople are also relaxed about time but find it rude to visit unannounced.[33] Middle-Eastern nations that are predominantly Muslim do not hold a schedule tightly. Middle-Eastern businessmen prefer an open office space design. Interruptions will be frequent. Visitors who value time should invite Middle-Eastern businessmen to meet away from the business to minimize the interruptions.[34]

U.S. businesses tend to view time as a resource. Time is allocated and used to deliver maximum value to the organization. Australian, Japanese, Canadian, and British business people also see punctuality as respectable. Germans place great value on punctuality but never make decisions quickly. Many meetings may be required because negotiators typically must receive approval from an advisory board before action is taken. Italians expect visitors to be punctual, but the Italian businessperson may be acceptably late. Like the Germans, Italians make decisions slowly because of a slow bureaucracy and legal system.[35]

Some cultures view work as the purpose for life. Other cultures view work as means to support life. Global business professionals must make this important distinction, as a misunderstanding in this area can be debilitating. For example, workers in some European nations, such as France and Italy, are accustomed to taking one-month-long vacations every summer. Most Italian workers take the month of August for vacation. The same occurs in France during July. The global business professional should be prepared for this eventuality. Vacation takes priority over work in some cultures. This cultural tendency will impact production during the affected month, as well as others in the supply chain who rely on the Italian and French organizations to provide resources or support. The mass vacation does not preclude Italy or France from consideration for expansion by an international manager. The cultural approach to a summer vacation requires the manager to plan for shut down so that it does not impact other operations. Another example affects time during the day. In Mexico, lunch begins between 2:00 p.m. and 3:00 p.m. and may last three to four hours.[36] The impact of this attitude will be lost production time or management challenges when trying to adjust to the local culture.

Dealing with Change

Cultural attitudes differ in the approach to change. A culture that is open to change encourages creativity and individualism. Germany targets its children into education tracks that fit the learner, thus developing a society of technical experts instead of developers. Without the tension created in school that challenges students to be creative in how they learn, there will be little creativity in later productive years. Japan, with its group orientation, is producing experts at reverse engineering rather than design. Japanese industry has become very successful by mastering production efficiency through Total Quality Management and Quality Circles—both team-oriented efforts. Societies readily accept change in a culture that rewards creative thinking and embraces diversity. The United States and Canada are examples of cultures that embrace change. These cultures lead the world in technological innovation, transportation, and agricultural sciences.

The Role of Gender

Cultural attitudes differ in terms of the role of gender. Some cultures treat women as equals, while others view women as subservient. If a culture does not consider women eligible to work outside the home, an international manager knows that the workforce and diversity are limited. Women have affected German culture in powerful ways twice in the last century. Though Germany was a historically male-dominated society, women were pivotal in caring for injured soldiers during World War II and assisting in reconstruction after the war. The second instance occurred during the transition after the Berlin Wall came down. As the German economy grew, women were needed to satisfy the demand for labor.[37] Iranian women were pivotal in the revolution that overthrew the Shah in 1979; however, in the post-revolution society, many women's freedoms have been curtailed. Once again, they must wear a veil. However, Iranian women do work outside of the home, and they do have the right to vote.[38] Gender differences in Mexico have been narrowing since the 1970s. The number of women in the workforce has doubled in the last ten years. Educated women are pursuing careers. Unfortunately, wages are lower for women than men, and women are often subjected to sexual harassment.[39]

Social Status

Cultural attitudes differ by social status structures. The cultural attitude of social status impacts business. Training and promotional opportunities from within are limited whenever a culture forbids mobility across social classes. This suppression minimizes potential motivation techniques and creativity. Four social classes exist in Iran: Upper, Middle, Working, and Lower. The upper class includes large landowners, industrialists, financiers, and high-ranking clergy. Middle-class members are professionals, business and landowners, high-ranking government officials and military officers, teachers, and low-ranking clergy. The working class is made up of skilled labor. The lower class consists of unskilled labor and the unemployed.[40] France is another country with stratified social classes. Citizens are not expected to make large jumps from one class to another.

Business Manners and Customs across National Cultures

Etiquette, manners, and cross-cultural or intercultural communication have become critical elements required for the global business professional. As international, multinational, transnational, multidomestic, and global business continues to expand and bring people closer, the most important element of successful business outcomes may be the appreciation and respect for regional, country, and cultural differences. Understanding cultural diversity is a critical success factor for the global business professional.

Global professionals must have a knowledge and respect for the following issues:

- General information, including population, cultural heritage, language, and religion.
- Appearances, including do's and don'ts involving dress, clothing, body language, and gestures.
- Behavior, including do's and don'ts involving dining, gift giving, meetings, customs, protocol, negotiation, and general behavioral guidelines.
- Communication, including do's and don'ts involving greetings, introductions, and conversational guidelines.

Figure 2.5

Finally, gaining insight into the cultural dynamics of a country or region can be very helpful in understanding why people act the way they do. This insight also reveals the appropriate ways one should act while in that country.

Social Structures

The social structure of a culture refers to the manner in which the society is organized, including its institutions, social groups, statuses, and roles. An institution is an established and enduring pattern of social relationships. Traditional institutions include family, religion, politics, economics, and education. Nontraditional institutions have recently gained influence. These nontraditional institutions include science and technology, mass media, medicine, sport, and the military. Inadequacies in social institutions may engender many social problems within a culture. The educational institution's failure to prepare individuals for the job market and alterations to the structure of the economic institution significantly influence unemployment.

Institutions are made up of social groups. A social group is defined as two or more people who have a common identity, who interact, and who form a social relationship. Examples of social groups include the family and religious associations. Social groups may be categorized as primary or secondary. Primary groups tend to involve small numbers of individuals and are characterized by intimate and informal interaction. Families and friends are examples of primary groups. Secondary groups often involve small or large numbers of individuals, are task oriented, and are characterized by impersonal and formal interaction. Examples of secondary groups include employers and their employees and clerks and their customers.

Institutions consist of social groups; social groups consist of statuses. A status is a position a person occupies within a social group. The status one occupies largely defines one's social identity. Statuses may be either ascribed or achieved. An ascribed status is one that society assigns to an individual on the basis of factors over which the individual has no control: gender, race, ethnic background, and socioeconomic status, into which one is born. A society assigns an achieved status on the basis of some characteristic or behavior over which the individual has some control. Achieved status depends largely on the outcome of one's own efforts, behavior, and choices. However, one's ascribed statuses may affect the likelihood of achieving other statuses. In some cultures, one born into a poor socioeconomic status may find it more difficult to achieve the status of "college graduate" because of the high cost of a college education. Every individual has numerous statuses simultaneously. A person's master status is the status that the society considers the most significant to the individual's social identity. A society typically regards a person's occupational status as his or her master status.

Every status is associated with many roles—the set of rights, obligations, and expectations associated with a status. Roles guide behavior and allow one to predict the behavior of others. A single status involves more than one role. The status of a manager includes one role for interacting with superiors and another role for interacting with subordinates.[41]

Understanding the Dimensions of Culture

The study of culture and personality, which many experts consider a subset of anthropology and psychology during the first half of the twentieth century, concentrated on traditional and preliterate societies, with its conclusions coming from psychoanalysis.[42] From 1967 to 1973, Geert Hofstede applied the subset of cultural dimensions to the field of business management, segregating them into independent areas to be further divided in order to get a more precise understanding.[43] Not long after Hofstede began his work, another researcher, Fons Trompenaar, expanded on Hofstede's research and developed another framework for understanding the different dimensions of culture.

Through their employment in large multinational corporations, both Hofstede and Trompenaar conducted research that would lead each man to draw his own conclusions about the theories of cultural dimensions. Each postulated theories based on the research of a somewhat captive audience: the employees of the multinational companies. Years of research led both men to their respected cultural guidelines.

Geert Hofstede developed four initial theories and later added a fifth. Hofstede's understanding of different cultures led to the understanding that both national cultures and organizational cultures simultaneously occur within the same society. National cultures can be studied by examining the known facts, which will historically remain stable and very difficult, if not impossible, to change. On the other hand, organizational cultures can be quite dynamic, managed, and changed to varying degrees of difficulty, depending on how ingrained the organizational culture is.

Fons Trompenaar developed a seven-cultural-factors theory model that expanded on the thinking and research of Geert Hofstede, further exploring cultural diversity on a large multinational scale. His model concentrates on intercultural diversity and how well these different cultures assimilate in the workforce.

Hofstede's Dimensions of Culture

Geert Hofstede conducted perhaps the most comprehensive study of how culture influences values in the workplace. He analyzed a large data base of employee values scores, collected by IBM between 1967 and 1973, covering more than seventy countries. The results of that research led to the development of his model of Cultural Dimensions. The dimensions of culture include individualism, power distance, masculinity, and uncertainty avoidance.

1. Individualism focuses on the degree to which the society reinforces individual or collective achievement and interpersonal relationships. A High Individualism ranking indicates that individuality and individual rights are paramount within the society. Individuals in these societies may tend to form a larger number of loose relationships. A Low Individualism ranking typifies societies of a more collectivist nature, with close ties between individuals. These cultures reinforce extended families and collectives where everyone takes responsibility for fellow members of their group.

2. Power Distance focuses on the degree of equality or inequality between people in the country's society. A High Power Distance ranking indicates that inequalities of power and wealth have been allowed to grow within the society. These societies are more likely to follow a caste system that does not allow significant upward mobility of its citizens. A Low Power Distance ranking indicates the society de-emphasizes the differences between citizens' power and wealth. In these societies, equality and opportunity for everyone is stressed.

3. Masculinity focuses on the degree to which the society reinforces, or does not reinforce, the traditional masculine work role model of male achievement, control, and power. A High Masculinity ranking indicates that the country experiences a high degree of gender differentiation. In these cultures, males dominate a significant portion of the society and power structure, including females. A Low Masculinity ranking indicates the country has a low level of differentiation and discrimination between genders. In these cultures, females are treated equally to males in all aspects of the society.

4. Uncertainty Avoidance focuses on the level of tolerance for uncertainty and ambiguity within the society, e.g., unstructured situations. A High Uncertainty Avoidance ranking indicates that the country has a low tolerance for uncertainty and ambiguity. This high ranking creates a rule-oriented society that institutes laws, rules, regulations, and controls in order to reduce the amount of uncertainty. A Low Uncertainty Avoidance ranking indicates the country has less concern about ambiguity and uncertainty and has more tolerance for a variety of opinions. This low ranking reflects a society that is less rule-oriented, more readily accepts change, and takes more and greater risks.

Geert Hofstede added the following fifth dimension after conducting an additional international study using a survey instrument developed with Chinese employees and managers. Subsequently, the new dimension, Confucian Dynamism, was described as a culture's Long-Term Orientation, which focuses on the degree to which the society embraces, or does not embrace, long-term devotion to traditional, forward-thinking values. High Long-Term Orientation ranking indicates that the country prescribes to the values of long-term commitments and respect for tradition. This orientation is thought to support a strong work ethic where a society expects long-term rewards as a result of today's hard work. However, business may take longer to develop in this society, particularly for an "outsider."

A low Long-Term Orientation ranking indicates that the country does not reinforce the concept of long-term, traditional orientation. In this culture, change can occur more rapidly as long-term traditions and commitments do not become impediments to change. As with any generalized study, the results may or may not be applicable to specific individuals or events. Although Hofstede categorized his results by country, more than one cultural group often exists within that country. Therefore, the results of a multicultural country may deviate significantly from the study's typical results. An example is Canada, where the English-speaking majority and the French-speaking minority in Quebec have moderate cultural differences. Regardless, Hofstede's dimensions analysis can assist the business person or traveler in better understanding the intercultural differences within regions and between countries.[43]

Hofstede's approach to interpreting cultural dimensions is not without its share of criticism. That his research was conducted at IBM between 1968 and 1973 raises questions about whether the information can still be applicable today. Another criticism is the narrow scope of his research, because it involved only one company. Others have said that Hofstede's data is not concrete enough to warrant granting assumptions on societies and cultures. Hofstede responded to much of the criticism against his research, stating that even though surveys are not the only way to obtain information, they provide a solid tool for gathering data. He also pointed out that cultures do not change their ways of life rapidly, so information that is a few decades old should not be dismissed as inaccurate.[44]

Trompenaar's Model of Culture

Fons Trompenaar has worked as an author and as a consultant for companies such as General Motors, Merrill Lynch, Motorola, and Nike. From 1986-1993, Trompenaar conducted extensive research on different countries, from which he developed his "Seven Dimensions of Culture Model."[45] Trompenaar believed that every culture distinguishes itself from others by the specific solutions it chooses to certain problems and dilemmas. One can categorize these problems under three headings: (1) those which arise from our relationships with other people, (2) those which come from the passage of time, and (3) those which relate to the environment. Trompenaar identified seven fundamental dimensions of culture:

1.   Universalism vs. Particularism

People in universalistic cultures share the belief that general rules, codes, values and standards take precedence over particular needs and claims of friends and relations. In a universalistic society, the rules apply equally to the whole "universe" of members. Any exception weakens the rule. Particularistic cultures see the ideal culture in terms of human friendship, extraordinary achievement and situations, and in intimate relationships. The "spirit of the law" is deemed more important than the "letter of the law".

2.   Individualist vs. Communitarian

In a predominantly individualistic culture, people place the individual before the community. Individual happiness, fulfillment, and welfare set the pace. Society expects people to decide matters largely on their own and to take care primarily of themselves and their immediate family. The culture sees the quality of life for all members of society as directly dependent on opportunities for individual freedom and development. People judge the community according to how it serves the interests of individual members. In a predominantly communitarian culture, people place the community before the individual. The individual has the responsibility to act in ways which serve society. By doing so, individual needs will be met naturally.

3.   Specific vs. Diffuse

In specific cultures, the whole is the sum of its parts. Each person's life is divided into many components that can only be entered one at a time. Interactions between people are highly purposeful and well defined. The public sphere of specific individuals is much larger than their private sphere. People are easily accepted into the public sphere, but it is very difficult to get into the private sphere, since each area in which two people encounter each other is considered separate from the other—a specific case. Specific individuals concentrate on hard facts, standards, and contracts. On the other hand, people from diffusely oriented cultures start with the whole and see each element in perspective of the total. All elements are related to one another. These relationships are more important than each separate element. Thus the whole is more than just the sum of its elements. Diffuse individuals have a large private sphere and a small public one. Newcomers are not easily accepted into either. But once they have been accepted, they are admitted into all layers of the individual's life.

4. Affective vs. Neutral

In an affective culture, people do not object to a display of emotions. These cultures do not consider it necessary to hide feelings and keep them inside. Affective cultures may interpret the less explicit signals of a neutral culture as less important. They may ignore or not even notice these signals. In a neutral culture, people are taught to the error of showing one's feelings overtly. These people do have feelings, but they limit the degree to which feelings become manifest. Individuals from a neutral culture accept and are aware of feelings, but they maintain control over them.

5. Achievement vs. Ascription

Achieved status refers to what an individual does and has accomplished. In achievement-oriented cultures, individuals derive their status from what they have accomplished. A person with achieved status has to prove what he or she is worth over and over again; status is accorded on the basis of his or her actions. Ascribed status refers to what a person is and how others relate to his or her position in the community, in society, or in an organization. In an ascriptive society, individuals derive their status from birth, age, gender or wealth. A person with ascribed status does not have to achieve to retain his status; it is inherent.

6. Sequential vs. Synchronic

Every culture has developed its own response to time. The time orientation dimension has two aspects: the relative importance cultures give to the past, present, and future, and their approach to structuring time. Time can be structured in two ways. In sequentialism, time moves forward, second by second, minute by minute, hour by hour, in a straight line. People structuring time sequentially tend to do one thing at a time. They view time as a narrow line of distinct, consecutive segments. Sequential people view time as tangible and divisible. They strongly prefer planning and adhering to plans once they have been made. Sequential individuals take time commitments seriously. Staying on schedule is a must. In the synchronism approach, time moves around in cycles: of minutes, hours, days, and years. People structuring time synchronically usually do several things at a time. To them, time is a wide ribbon, allowing many things to take place simultaneously. Time is flexible and intangible. Time commitments are desirable rather than absolute. These people change plans easily. Synchronic people especially value the satisfactory completion of interactions with others. Promptness depends on the type of relationship.

7.	Internal vs. External

Every culture has developed an attitude towards the natural environment. The way people in a particular culture relate to their environment is linked to the way they seek to have control over their own lives and destiny. Internalistic people have a mechanistic view of nature. They see nature as a complex machine, and machines can be controlled if one has the right expertise. Internalistic people do not believe in luck or predestination. They are inner-directed—one's personal resolution is the starting point for every action. Externalistic people have a more organic view of nature. Mankind is one of nature's forces, so it should operate in harmony with the environment. Mankind should submit to nature and go along with its forces. Externalistic people do not believe that they can shape their own destiny. "Nature moves in mysterious ways," therefore one never knows what will happen to him or her. The actions of externalistic people are outer-directed—adapted to external circumstances.[46]

Brief Summary of Major Points

- One's paradigm is how one views the world. Three cultural paradigms in operation throughout global business dealings include ethnocentric, polycentric, and geocentric. These paradigms may be held by people, organizations, and cultures.

- The dimensions of culture may be categorized as Communication, Religion, Ethics, Values and Attitudes, Manners, Customs, Social Structures and Organizations, and Education. The savvy global manager seeks to understand each of these dimensions, as they significantly impact decision making, negotiations, and ongoing operations critical to long-term success. The astute global manager knows how to effectively integrate the new culture with the existing culture.

- Global business professionals encounter various cultures throughout the world. Individuals and organizations within each culture communicate in manners unique to their culture. The necessity for global business professionals to understand the dimensions of culture has become increasingly important.

- Successful MNC's acknowledge cultural differences and adapt parts of the business to recognize the unique differences and variables in communication. Major communications variables include different meanings of words across languages, verbal communication, non-verbal communication, and context (high and low).

- The term "religion" may mean many things to different people. When discussed across cultures, the topic of religion is open for misunderstanding. This misunderstanding may originate from either a preconceived notion or a lack of knowledge on the topic. Thus, global business professionals must understand and be well versed in this important cultural aspect.

- Ethics is the study of morality and standards of conduct. U.S. firms have developed and implemented standards of conduct for employees to serve as guidelines for how they should comport themselves when representing the company. What one culture considers moral conduct, another may consider immoral.

- The astute global business professional recognizes the variances in attitudes between the home culture and the host culture. Differences in attitudes toward time, work, change, gender, and social status and mobility impact all stages of the business relationship. Time differences affect meeting attendance and ongoing employee attendance. Gender differences impact how women can be employed.

- Etiquette, manners, and cross-cultural or intercultural communication have become critical elements required for the global business professional. As international, multinational, transnational, multi-domestic, and global business continues to expand and bring people closer, the most important element of successful business outcomes may be the appreciation and respect for regional, country, and cultural differences. Understanding cultural diversity is a critical success factor for the global business professional.

- The social structure of a culture refers to the manner in which the society is organized, including its institutions, social groups, statuses, and roles. An institution is an established and enduring pattern of social relationships. Traditional institutions include family, religion, politics, economics, and education. More recently, nontraditional institutions are increasingly in influence. These nontraditional institutions include science and technology, mass media, medicine, sport, and the military. Inadequacies in social institutions may engender many social problems within a culture.

- Through their employment in large multinational corporations, Geert Hofstede and Fons Trompenaar conducted research that would lead each man to draw his own conclusions about the theories of cultural dimensions. Each postulated theories based on their research of a somewhat captive audience: the employees of the multinational companies. Each formed conclusions based on years of research that led to their respected cultural guidelines.

Moving from Theory into Practice

The following summarizes a question and answer session with coauthor Joe Robinson. His answers are useful in contemplating how the global business professional can translate the theories and concepts covered in this chapter via practical answers to the questions from real life experiences.

<u>What is perhaps one of the worst things a global manager does, even unintentionally that hurts his business?</u>

On a daily basis, questions emanate from the global manager's overseas customers, representatives, and business contacts. Often questions come to the global manager in clusters—some of which deal with multiple unrelated topics. This is the source of the difficulty in responding. Frequently, a global manager must check with various departments and staff within a corporation to provide complete and accurate answers. The tendency is to wait to reply until all pertinent information is available before responding to the inquiry. The result of this approach is to potentially negate two aspects of the relationship. First and foremost, when a response is not acknowledged and handled in a timely manner, the inquirer feels ignored and slighted. To be ignored is in some cultures unacceptable. Second, by holding back on the reply until all questions can be answered, deprives both parties of taking action and moving forward on those answers that can be handled right away.

The solution is to reply to those questions that can be readily answered and to advise that answers to additional questions are forthcoming. In some cases, it may require time to answer all questions. In this case, immediately acknowledge that the questions require additional time and will be forthcoming as soon as available.

Remember, to be ignored is in some cultures paramount to being treated as a nonperson, and this can be construed as an insult. Always reply quickly to all inquires in a timely manner and advise that complete answers will be provided as accurate and pertinent information is obtained.

<u>Is misunderstanding the single most troublesome cause of business going awry?</u>

The answer is "no." It is miscommunication rather than misunderstanding. Actually, the two parties negotiating and having business dealings understand each other. One party has something of value for sale that the other party needs or wants and is willing to pay for it. The miscommunication is created by either or both parties omitting details necessary to accurately communicate with each other. The professional global business manager remembers that the two parties are dealing in different cultures, time zones, languages, currencies, and regulations.

An example of miscommunication is to assume that all individuals involved in the international process know who and how to communicate with overseas reps, partners, and customers. Internal training to inform especially clerical and support staff on how to communicate is a must-do for companies who engage in international business—in order to avoid miscommunication and the consequent problems it causes in unnecessary delays and sometimes costly mistakes.

Additionally, certain export documents often are needed for multiple purposes by multiple parties. For example, a Pro Forma Invoice is needed by the potential customer to establish the Purchase Order. The Pro Forma Invoice may also be used by the customer to open a Letter of Credit at his bank. It may be required to obtain a foreign exchange license from the foreign government. It may be needed to obtain an import license for the foreign customs officials. Export documents and related communication may not at first appear to be a culture issue. But when you consider that documents are so very important to those abroad for the multiple purposes for which they are used, and that most overseas personnel are communicating in English that is most likely not their native language, then it is easy to recognize that accurate, complete, and understandable documentation is indeed a communication and cultural issue.

The solution to this "miscommunication" is to consider how and who will need the information you wish to convey and to give pertinent information to enable all parties involved in the transaction the details necessary to carry out the desired business at hand.

Can you share a business example of a common miscommunication versus misunderstanding scenario?

The president of a one-hundred-year-old major Japanese trading company with whom I worked on a daily basis during a posting in Osaka stated to me that he could judge the reliability and integrity and dependability of a foreign company by the degree that their documents were prepared and presented. This is a culture issue as well as a commercial issue. Because we Americans do not treat this aspect as both a commercial and a cultural issue, we sometimes make our exporting and importing work more complicated and difficult that it really needs to be. The solution is to have trained and skilled personnel who know well how to prepare international documents and the many uses the documents are used for and to apply some empathy for the recipients of the documents. These skills will go a long way in saving time and money and make the export process smoother and create more harmony in daily transactions.

An example may be as simple as the terminology or nomenclature issue of a single word. A case in point is the frequent problem that may develop when an exporter offers a quote or Pro Forma Invoice regarding the term "delivery." For example, *"Delivery…thirty days after receipt of your order."*

The problem here is that the exporter and the buyer have different concepts of the term delivery. To the exporter, the term delivery means to have the product "ready to ship." To the buyer, the term "delivery" means he will receive the product—in other words—the product will be delivered to him at his factory or facility. I advise my clients to avoid the term "delivery" and to substitute the statement, *"Available for shipment from our factory thirty days after receipt and acknowledgement of your order."* This puts both parties on the same page and avoids any misunderstanding, resulting in good communication.

<u>Culturally speaking, what are some examples of "good" body language that work well across most business cultures?</u>

The open hand slightly extended with the palm up is generally considered a sincere gesture emanating from integrity.   Non threatening eye contact is also appropriate in most cultures. Another example is to not get too physically close when talking to others in a formal business setting. Leaning slightly forward is a good position to take when you want to influence or persuade someone to your way of thinking. These are especially meaningful when done together to enhance the meaning of the words spoken during business meetings with business leaders of other cultures.

<u>What is a common example of "wrong" body language?</u>

I once interpreted for an American exporter visiting Japan who was negotiating for a multimillion dollar order. He essentially had the order consummated, but during the negotiations, when he explained the quality of his product, he emphasized the point by a tightly balled fist that he tapped on the table numerous times. This "wrong" body language was received by the potential buyer as condescending and arrogant and that perhaps there was some overstatement in the honesty of the exporter. The result was a lost order that I am sure would have been awarded had the exporter known better how to communicate. Later that night during dinner, I mentioned to the exporter my observation of his "wrong" body language, and he admitted he was not even aware of what he had done but did recall the incident. He stated that he used the tight fist approach to emphasize the point he wanted to make but realized the fallacy in this technique that comes off as being condescending, insincere, and arrogant. This incident took place over fifteen years ago. Today, when I meet the exporter who is now a senior executive in his company, he thanks me for having brought this to his attention, and he now shares this with his younger global managers before he sends them on their overseas work travel.

Can you give some advice about the art of asking questions?

The purpose for asking questions is to obtain information. It is confusing to use questions to preempt the conversation for this purpose of seeking information. The better the questions, the better chance you have to receive the information you need to be successful in your global business. Avoid the "yes" and "no" type questions. An example of a bad question is, *"Will thirty days be an acceptable shipment date?"* A better question is, *"When do you need the product?"* In the first question, a "yes" reply in some cultures could mean "Yes, I hear you." The response may or may not mean "Yes, thirty days is acceptable."

Another technique in the art of asking questions is to avoid using preemptive questions. For example, it could be self defeating to ask a question such as, "You want us to ship the product on a pallet, don't you?" The term "don't you" is weak and preemptive, and in some cultures, where it is impolite to say "no," you will receive a false reply resulting in misunderstanding. A better question in this case is, "What method of packaging do you want us to use for your shipment?"

Remember, miscommunication creates misunderstanding that could later necessitate time consuming corrective measures—and it could be costly as well, so it is always best to use questions for the purpose of ascertaining information you need in order to conduct your global business, based upon a basis of being well informed by learning the technique of using good questions.

What are some words that are misinterpreted in the global business world where the meaning of the word; not their literal translation could be different?

In Mexico, the term "mañana" literally means tomorrow. A successful and wealthy Mexican businessman once explained to me that Americans do not understand the "meaning" of the word "mañana". When one Mexican executive asks another when the order will be placed, the term "mañana" does not mean the order will be placed tomorrow; the true meaning is *"not today."* The order may or may not be placed tomorrow. It may be placed next month. It may even never be placed. However, it will not be placed today.

In Japan, the word for "yes" is *"hai"* Frequently, if you ask a Japanese a yes/no type question, the reply (not the answer but the reply) *"hai"* could mean, "Yes, I hear you," not "Yes, I agree." In Japan it is impolite to say "no" to someone's face. This is one reason why it is so important to avoid yes/no type questions.

It is invariably better to use why/when/how/what type questions for optimum communications and to avoid miscommunications and misunderstandings.

What place do jokes and idioms have in international business parlance?

Simply put, don't do it. It is best to avoid jokes and idioms. Another example is to avoid sports metaphors. An American who says that his system is a "slam dunk" will not relate to someone in many foreign cultures, and the overseas customer may be just as confused about the meaning of this term as an American would be confused if a Japanese stated that his system is an "oseki," referring to the terminology of summo wrestling, a national sport in Japan.

What is more important when considering anticorruption laws: the letter of the law or the spirit of the law?

Both. The U.S. Foreign Corrupt Practices Act (FCPA) states that it is illegal (determined by law to mean not immoral, but illegal) for American businesses to engage in bribery or actions of unjustifiable influence with foreign government officials, politicians, and political parties. What some business men may not be aware of is that it is also illegal to commit the action of "self blind," which could happen when a salesman or over zealous executive tells his agent, representative, or joint venture partner, "Don't tell me what you are doing. I don't want to know." This is called self blinding. Under the interpretation of U.S. law, the U.S. business person needs and is expected to know the extent of his business overseas and how it relates to acceptable business practices and how it conforms to the letter of the law.

Can you give an example of a common difference in cultural business norms, say between Japanese and American businesses?

In the U.S., the individual is strong. We are a nation distinguished by attributes of individuals who make up the whole. In Japan, the group is strong, made up of a collective group of individuals. For example, when I answer the phone in my office in Virginia, I say, "This is Joe, may I help you?" In Japan, the Japanese businessman answers the phone saying, "Mitsubishi Tanaka speaking, may I help you?

Another example is the decision-making-time-frame difference between America and Japan. It is said that in the U.S. a decision is quickly made and then nothing happens until others know what and how to proceed. In Japan the method typically is to get a consensus and a joint informative understanding and then a decision is made and then something happens right away because those involved know what and how to proceed. This is admittedly an over simplification however it does illustrate a cultural difference that the global businessman needs to be aware of in order to be successful in the international arena.

One can relate to the Geert Hofstede model of understanding the dimension of cultures by observing multinational companies as they operate today. One example is a triventure of two Japanese firms and a U.S. firm with operations in the U.S. I have worked with this firm for the past seven years. Each of the three companies in this example is in the top one hundred world wide manufacturing conglomerates. In addition to having both Japanese and U.S. employees, there are numerous other nationalities employed at this facility. From an *"individual"* point of view, the Japanese side tends to be "improvement" driven. The American side tends to be "innovation" driven. From a *"power"* point of view, this triventure is made up of and run by highly–skilled, technical individuals and professionals. This is an example of a multinational corporation that de-emphasizes ranking and seeks harmony and cooperation among all staff rather than a high top few and low bottom "many" type of structure. The *"masculinity"* factor is evident in this firm as the technical and professional nature of their operations is dominated by the masculine values. This firm exhibits a low degree of *"uncertainty avoidance."* They thrive on seeking change and being leading edge providers on a global scale in what they do and offer their clients in major multimillion dollar projects on a worldwide basis. This firm is anchored in a strong work ethic *"dynamic"* that permeates throughout the company. They do work on major projects that take a lot of time and effort, and the final results and gains are not immediate, so the long-term rewards for their diligence is understood by the employees as they go about their daily tasks and work.

Key Concepts

- Dimensions of culture: communications, language, religion, ethics, transparency, values, attitudes, social structures and organizations

- Global business culture

- Managerial paradigms: ethnocentric, polycentric, geocentric

- Communication across cultures: verbal and non-verbal

- Communication across cultures: high context vs. low context

- Christianity

- Judaism

- Islam

- Hinduism

- Buddhism

- Confucianism

- Shinto

- Ethics in global business

- Corporate social responsibility in global business

- Values and attitudes across cultures

- Hofstede's dimensions of culture

- Trompenaar's dimensions of culture

Chapter 3 GLOBAL BUSINESS ENVIRONMENTS AND RISKS: POLITICAL, LEGAL, ECONOMIC SYSTEMS

Global Business in Practice

The World Bank Assists in Assessing Business Environments.

The World Bank provides financial and technical assistance to developing countries around the world. While more of a development and assistance organization than a bank, in the usual meaning of the term, it is comprised of two development institutions owned by 185 member countries—the International Bank for Reconstruction and Development (IBRD) and the International Development Association (IDA).

> Our mission is to help developing countries and their people reach the goals by working with our partners to alleviate poverty. To do that we concentrate on building the climate for investment, jobs and sustainable growth, so that economies will grow, and by investing in and empowering poor people to participate in development.[*]

The IRBD and the IDA contribute to the World Bank mission of global poverty reduction and the improvement of living standards. The IBRD focuses on middle income and creditworthy poor countries, while IDA focuses on the poorest countries in the world. Working in cooperation with each other, the institutions "provide low-interest loans, interest-free credit and grants to developing countries for education, health, infrastructure, communications and many other purposes."[†]

The World Bank also provides an annual report entitled "Doing Business." These reports investigate the regulations that enhance business activity and those that constrain it. "Doing Business presents quantitative indicators on business regulations and the protection of property rights that can be compared across 175 economies—from Afghanistan to Zimbabwe—and over time."[‡]

---

[*] The World Bank. Retrieved August 15, 2007 from http://web.worldbank.org/WBSITE/
EXTERNAL/EXTABOUTUS/worldbank.org/WBSITE/EXTERNAL/EXTABOUTUS/
0,,contentMDK:20040565~menuPK:1696892~pagePK:51123644~piPK:329829~theSite
PK:29708,00.html

[†] The World Bank. Retrieved August 20, 2007 from http://web.worldbank.org/WBSITE/
EXTERNAL/EXTABOUTUS/0,,pagePK:50004410~piPK:36602~theSitePK:29708,00.
html

[‡] Doing Business. Retrieved August 20, 2007 from http://www.doingbusiness.org/

The following aspects of the business environment within each nation are addressed:

- Starting a business
- Dealing with licenses
- Employing workers
- Registering property
- Getting credit
- Protecting investors
- Paying taxes
- Trading across borders
- Enforcing contracts
- Closing a business

The indicators can be used by the global business professional to analyze economic outcomes and compare the elements of risk across the 175 nations. The Doing Business report is an important resource for those investigating and analyzing business environments across nations and the risks associated with doing business across borders.

Introduction

The global community is experiencing unprecedented integration of business, governments, and nongovernmental organizations. Multinational corporations (MNCs) and nations increasingly rely on each other to improve cross-border trade necessary for survival in the global community. Policy issues can have a major impact upon businesses in the global market. Global business professionals must be knowledgeable of the history, tradition, and laws of nations in which they wish to conduct business. Sometimes these regional aspects create dilemmas for firms wishing to do business in the region. As discussed in chapter two, a practice or tradition in one country may actually be offensive to people in another country. Complying with local guidelines can be a financial burden on a company, but the loss of business or the cost of a lawsuit would undoubtedly cause the company far more.

The decision to conduct business overseas entails determining what is an acceptable level of risk. The competent global business professional evaluates the levels of risk by carefully considering the political, legal, and economic environments for each offshore location. The purpose of this chapter is to integrate the elements of these three global business environments with the realities of the types and causes of risk one might encounter internationally.

The Political Environment

Figure 3.1

Political Issues That Significantly Impact Global Business
• Government intervention in trade.
• Government promotion of trade.
• Government restriction of trade.

Why Governments Intervene in Global Trade—Importance to Nation, Businesses, Workers, and Consumers

International trading is very important to a nation because it generates business and government revenue and promotes varying levels of trust between trading partners. These levels of trust can have both positive and negative outcomes. Some nations are better suited for producing certain items that other countries may demand. Nations profit by trading with other nations better suited to producing products in demand. On the other hand, governmental disagreements may lead to embargoes and the cessation of international trade between the countries' businesses. Consumers are the main beneficiaries of trade, which also makes them the primary victim of embargoes. Consumers will have to pay higher prices for hard-to-find items if their government imposes an embargo on a country that is the main producer of the item.[1]

Governments may also intervene in order to protect their domestic market. A developing market, not ready to fully engage in international trading on its own, may require the protection of the government. On the other hand, domestic businesses may be ready to begin trading in the international market; however, they may not have the finances needed to undertake the endeavor. Some government agencies may choose to financially assist their domestic businesses in order to spur the whole nation's economic growth.

Governments are also aware of trade deficits that may develop between nations. A trade deficit occurs when a country is importing more than it is exporting. The government has the responsibility of ensuring that extreme deficits are monitored and corrected. If a trade deficit becomes excessive, then the government must correct the deficit before the entire nation's economy is at risk of faltering.

Whether motivated by the desire to improve standards of living for its citizens, the protection of domestic industries, or the management of trade deficits, a number of options are available for governments to promote cross-border trade. These include special government agencies, subsidies, export financing assistance, and foreign trade zones.

Government Actions that Promote Trade	Figure 3.2
• Special government agencies	
• Subsidies	
• Export Financing	
• Foreign Trade Zones	

Special Government Agencies

In 1994, as business and policy makers alike saw the potential growth of global business, the World Trade Organization (WTO) was created by several countries in order to monitor trade around the entire world. Since then, many other nations have formed regional trade agreements, such as the North American Free Trade Agreement (NAFTA) and the European Union (EU), to promote regional trade in their respective areas.

The U.S. Department of Commerce developed the International Trade Administration (ITA) in order to stimulate economic opportunities for U.S. businesses and their employees. Specifically, the ITA assists U.S. companies in navigating foreign markets by teaching them about marketing, financing, logistics, etc. Because the United States exports goods and services extensively, the ITA has created the U.S. Commercial Service to oversee and promote international trade.[2] The ITA has placed many offices in the U.S. and numerous other nations, in order to continue to encourage international trade.

Most U.S. states have developed special government agencies to partner with constituent companies to do business overseas. The Virginia Economic Development Partnership has created the Division of International Trade. This division has developed multiple programs and services to assist both manufacturing and service firms, located within the state, to increase their exports. Services include operating overseas state offices, conducting overseas trade missions, and providing resident, subject-matter, expert advice and counseling at all levels in the exporting process. The astute global-business professional should take full advantage of these services and programs, utilizing both federal and state special government agencies to expedite and supplement their global business presence.

Subsidies

Subsidies are special privileges offered by the government in order to attract businesses to a region or to provide them with the funding to operate successfully. A nation's government may provide tax breaks, lower the cost of required land, or offer other money-saving techniques to businesses that it wishes to attract or maintain in a region.[3] Providing subsidies may allow a region to acquire a company that will bring more jobs to the area, thus increasing productivity and strengthening the economy. These subsidies are designed to attract overseas firms and their foreign direct investment into the local government's economy. This type of subsidy should not be confused with those subsidies that the government frequently offers to domestic firms in an effort to protect local industries from the effects of free trade and world-wide competition. Foreign investment funding and other outside resources have greater potential to elevate local economic well being than money that merely circulates within a local economy.

Export Financing

Export financing differs from commercial lending, mortgage lending, or insurance. A company increases payment time when it sells and ships a product overseas. This type of transaction requires extra time and energy, to make sure that buyers are reliable and creditworthy. In addition, foreign buyers—just like domestic buyers—prefer to delay payment until they receive and resell the goods. Due diligence and careful financial management can mean the difference between profit and loss on each transaction. Diligence and management is especially important for small businesses engaged in exporting, as these organizations may need government assistance in obtaining finances for export activities. The Export-Import Bank (Ex-Im Bank) is the official export credit agency of the United States. The Ex-Im Bank is a valuable tool for small businesses because it does not require a minimum transaction limit. Using an organization to finance the cost of the exported goods will allow all parties involved to have more time to gather the finances needed to complete the transaction.[4]

Other institutions that operate underneath government agencies, private companies, or general organizations are available to finance exports.[5] Export credit institutions, export banks, and export finance institutions specialize not only in financing exports but also in circulating capital and providing insurance on the items being traded. Two forms of credit are associated with export financing. The first is the supplier's credit: a loan in which the exporter is covered, but the value of the cover will be less than the value of the contract. The second, buyer's credit, is more closely associated with long-term loans. Some international projects may take more than four years to complete; therefore, the financial institution needs the importer's credit to protect parties from potential problems that might arise during this extended time period.

While many governments have created institutions that oversee export finances, some allow the private sector to control its own financing. Because governments have different economic policies, some government-controlled credit institutions may not be successful or required. However, newly emerging governments could take advantage of financing agencies in order to assist their business community in the creation and maintenance of sustainable global trade. Financing can help protect businesses from potential losses by providing them with insurance against political and commercial risks, while also increasing their international business confidence.

Foreign Trade Zones

The United States' capitalistic economy allows citizens to engage in a free-trade system within the country and with other countries that operate under the free-trade model. Operating under a free-trade model provides many benefits, but as with any model, the costs can be significant. The Foreign-Trade Zones (FTZ) program alleviates some of the costs associated with free trade in the rapidly increasing global economic environment.

The Foreign Trade Zones program was created with the enactment of the U.S. Foreign-Trade Zones Act of 1934.[6] This program was created during a defining moment of American history when Americans were beginning to open doors to foreign policy, as well as to foreign business opportunities. U.S. policy makers hoped to encourage foreign commerce in order to spur the declining U.S. economy. The United States designated certain areas "Customs Ports of Entry," where commercial merchandise would "receive the same Customs treatment it would if it were outside the commerce of the United States. Merchandise of every description may be held in the Zone without being subject to Customs duties and other ad valorem taxes."[7] These zones are supervised by the U.S. customs service through audit-inspection checks.

During the 1950s and 1960s the global trade environment underwent tremendous change. Tariff barriers were continually reduced, and international trade began to flourish. However, as more countries began to open their doors to international trade, unexpected costs, hidden within the free trade system, became apparent. Each country was attempting to gain as much profit as possible, while spending less on imported goods. Countries spent much time deliberating on trade negotiations so that all countries involved could reap the benefits of international trade. In order to ensure the prosperity of all parties involved in global trade, the National Association of Foreign Trade Zones (NAFTZ) was created in 1972. In 1980, the U.S. Customs Service issued a new ruling that allowed U.S. based manufacturers to bring foreign-sourced parts into free-trade zones, without paying extra duties. This act, coupled with the continued increase in global trade, greatly spurred the U.S. economy and the U.S. Foreign-Trade Zones program. More than 230 Foreign-Trade Zone projects and nearly 400 sub-zones currently exist within the United States.

FTZs offer numerous benefits to manufacturers and distributors in the United States. Organizations investigate overseas options when deciding to locate or expand a new manufacturing or processing facility. Such location and expansion decisions must take into account all costs of manufacturing in a certain nation. As do most other nations, U.S. law may have unintended import tax penalties for firms located, or considering locating, in the United States. The FTZ program plays an important role in providing a level playing field when investment and production decisions are made. While the U.S. government might incur a reduction in Customs duty revenue through the FTZ program, these reductions are offset by the income taxes from created or existing jobs. In addition, local governments benefit from sales and property taxes.

Government Actions that Restrict Trade

- Tariffs
- Quotas
- Embargoes
- Local content Requirements
- Administrative Delays
- Currency Controls

Figure 3.3

Governments may attempt to restrict trade with other countries, especially in circumstances of large trade deficits or excessive currency outflows. Such actions may result in protectionism—when a nation deliberately reduces the number of imports it receives. As with any government action, advantages and disadvantages may accrue. Common forms of government actions that restrict trade include, but are not limited to, tariffs, quotas, and embargoes.

Tariffs, Quotas, and Embargoes

A tariff is a tax applied to selected categories of imports. Governments design tariffs to raise revenues and to generally provide a competitive advantage for domestic businesses. Tariffs are similar to excise taxes (taxes on cigarettes and alcohol, for example) in design and economic impact. Governments design tariffs, which they normally impose as a fixed percentage of the value of imports, to discriminate against selected imports by raising the price of imports relative to domestic prices for the same products. The tariff or duty is collected at a product's point of entry into a country. Since World War II, multilateral trade negotiations under the General Agreement on Tariffs and Trade (GATT) have resulted in large reductions in tariff and non-tariff barriers to international trade. A guiding principle for increasing international trade for goods and services has been the eventual elimination of all tariffs on imports.

Governments use quotas, also known as quantitative restrictions, to limit the quantity of imports allowed into a nation. Quotas typically "raise the price of imports, reduce the volume of imports, and encourage demand for domestically made substitutes."[8] Quotas and tariffs are similar in that their general purpose is to control the number of imports that enter a domestic market. While tariffs generate money for the government, because they are essentially an import tax, quotas can have some negative effects on a government. Quotas place power in the hands of customs officials. These officials determine which nations will be allowed to import goods into the domestic system, while denying other nations because no room exists for their products. This refusal can cause a nation to become disgruntled with the government of the nation in which they are trying to import their goods. Customs officials may even choose a favorite exporter, rather than importing goods on an equal level. Such corruption may be harmful to a country's economy, as well as its foreign relations.

Tariffs and quotas may increase smuggling activity. If the quota is extremely low or if a tariff is unreasonably high, smugglers may attempt to push goods through a country's borders without paying the proper taxes. Tariffs would be easier to control in this situation, because no quota dictates the amount of goods that can enter the nation. The incidence of smuggling may then be reduced by lowering the tariff while still collecting revenue from the taxes.[9]

Embargoes are economic and trade sanctions against targeted foreign countries, groups, organizations, and individuals. Embargoes can be motivated by political, economic, or moral reasons. The United States Department of the Treasury oversees and enforces all U.S. economic sanctions through the Office of Foreign Assets Control (OFAC). The following reveals some of the purposes behind embargoes:

- Punishing a country or group for unacceptable behavior;
- Influencing the behavior of the target;
- Signaling disapproval of a government's or group's behavior;
- Warning the target nation that harsher measures could follow;
- Limiting a target's freedom of action;
- Denying resources or technology;
- Increasing the cost of engaging in unacceptable behavior;
- Drawing international attention to unacceptable behavior;
- Challenging allies to take more forceful action themselves in support of common objectives;
- Signaling to a government or group that is engaging in practices which violate core values that a "business-as-usual" approach is not acceptable;
- Protecting the assets of allies from hostile actions;
- Assuring that the assets of targets will be available to meet future claims.

The various methods of imposing economic sanctions include the following:

- Limiting exports and re-exports to the targets (including exports to third countries predominantly for use in products for the targets);
- Limiting imports from the targets;
- Blocking assets of the targeted country, company or individual;
- Restricting investments in the targets;

- Prohibiting private financial transactions; and

- Restricting government trade financing and investment assistance regarding the target.

Local Content Requirements

Local content requirements are means by which governments can block open trade within a country's borders. These requirements, which can hinder foreign exports from reaching a nation or from being purchased in the domestic market, place restrictions on domestic businesses. The World Trade Organization is striving to eliminate local content requirements, so that the global market may profit from free trading. However, the WTO has not yet been completely successful in its efforts. In 2006, China and the United States disagreed over China's local content requirements concerning imported auto parts. China's requirements have increased taxes from 14 percent to 28 percent. China previously committed itself to eliminating all local content requirements; therefore, the U.S. believes China must decrease its taxes on imported auto parts. In addition, the U.S. government perceives that the government of China is promoting an action to restrict trade.[10]

Administrative Delays

Administrative delays impose a waiting period between the determination of a product's quality and the determination of when it can actually be sold in a market. This prohibits the producer of the product from improving the quality of the product during the waiting period. This delay causes the producer to miss an opportunity to gain profits. Furthermore, administrative delays do not provide any extra revenue to the nation that imposes the delay—they do not bring in any extra revenue aside from the standard tariff.[11] If a popular item becomes available in other nations while in administrative delay, then smugglers may attempt to introduce the item into the country's economy—hurting the country's revenue from the tariff. If the delay is excessive, the demand for the new item may decrease by the time the item makes the shelves of the importing country. Both countries would lose profits in this scenario Administrative delays have the potential to be harmful to all parties involved.

Currency Controls

Some governments practice strict control over their country's currency. The Chinese government will not allow its employees to remit funds that exceed $10,000 outside of China, unless it has been approved by the government. In addition, Chinese citizens may not purchase foreign currency for investments.[12] In

May of 2006, The People's Bank of China vowed to decrease its currency controls in order to stabilize international payments and control credit growth.[13]

The Legal Environment

The astute global business professional understands the impact of political issues and regulations on commerce. In addition to the political issues, a keen awareness of the legal aspects of doing business overseas is essential for success. Legal aspects of international business focus on the types of laws and legal issues used across nations and borders. The basic legal issues include standardization of laws, property rights, and copyrights.

Types of Law

Laws are essential to the efficient and effective operation of businesses establishments and corporations within a society. They provide standard rules, regulations, and protocols necessary for fairness and ethical treatments of customers, employees, and suppliers. Each sovereign nation has the right to establish laws that govern the conducting of business within its borders. Such laws typically fall into one of three categories: common, civil, and theocratic.

Common Law

The common law, originally developed in historical England, is the result of judicial decisions that were based in tradition, custom, and precedent. Common law may be unwritten or written in statutes or codes. The common law, as applied in civil cases (as distinct from criminal cases), was devised as a means of compensating someone for wrongful acts—known as torts—including both intentional torts and torts caused by negligence, in order to develop the body of law that recognizes and regulates contracts. In a common law system, an adversarial approach is used to investigate and adjudicate guilt or innocence. The adversarial system assumes that truth is most likely to result from the open competition between the prosecution and the defense. Primary responsibility for the presentation of evidence and legal arguments lies with the opposing parties, not with a judge. Each side, acting in its self-interest, is expected to present facts and interpretations of the law in a way most favorable to its interests. The approach presumes that the accused is innocent, and the burden of proving guilt rests with the prosecution. Through counterargument and cross-examination, each side is expected to test the truthfulness, relevancy, and sufficiency of the opponent's evidence and arguments.[14]

Civil Law

Civil law, with its origins in Roman law, is the predominant system of law in the world, which sets forth a comprehensive system of rules—usually codified—that are applied and interpreted by judges. Historically, the original difference between common law and civil law was that common law developed by custom, beginning before any written laws existed and continuing to be applied by courts after they were written, and civil law developed out of Roman law. The difference between civil law and common law is grounded in the methodological approach to codes and statutes. Civil law nations view legislation as the primary source of law. Courts base their judgments on the provisions of codes and statutes from which they derive their particular solutions to cases. Courts must reason extensively on the basis of general rules and principles of the code, often drawing analogies from statutory provisions. By contrast, in the common law system, cases are the primary source of law, while statutes are seen only as incursions into the common law, and thus, interpreted narrowly.

Theocratic Law

Theocratic law refers to laws which are derived from religion. Due to the numerous religions in the world, such as Christianity, Islam, Buddhism, and Hinduism, nations find difficulty coming to agreements over theocratic laws. Because of the increase in globalization within the marketplace, as well as communities, a common secular law is needed in order to ensure the prosperity of international trade.

Standardization of Laws

Each nation has its own distinct set of laws that govern its people. While some nations rely on civil law, others focus on either common or theocratic law. As globalization continues to grow, the efforts to form a set of standardized international laws continue to increase. Theocratic law presents an especially difficult challenge in global trade because of the wide variance of religious groups in the world whose theocracies can vary greatly. Another issue with international law is that ultimately, an economically independent country can refuse to follow international law without fear of economic sanctions. This refusal to observe international law could become dangerous and potentially lead to physical war between two nations. International laws will be difficult to enforce unless all participants can come to an agreement on the laws and appoint a governing body to settle disputes.

A widely used tool in law and development programs is the supply of well-designed laws from the outside. This method of law development has now been embraced by international organizations as a way to improve the legal framework for global markets. The International Monetary Fund (IMF) has endorsed attempts by various organizations to develop legal standards with special emphasis on corporate and financial institution laws. The common idea behind these attempts is that the supplied laws once incorporated into domestic legal systems will improve the existing legal framework, and thus further economic development.[15]

Property Rights

Protecting property is an important part of promoting the global trade. Trade, simply put, is the trading of property in order to receive monetary value. Property can be classified as both physical and intellectual. Ideas spur innovation, which spurs the development of new goods that will be available for trade. The World Trade Organization (WTO) allows for a minimum level of property rights to provide its members with a global standard of protection.

Figure 3.4

The WTO's System of Property Covers the Following Issues

- How basic principles of the trading system and other international, intellectual property agreements should be applied.

- How to give adequate protection to intellectual property rights.

- How countries should enforce those rights adequately in their own territories.

- How to settle disputes on intellectual property between members of the WTO.[16]

Intellectual property. The WTO defines intellectual property rights as "the rights given to persons over the creations of their minds. They usually give the creator an exclusive right over the use of his/her creation for a certain period of time."[17] Examples of intellectual rights include patents, trademarks, and copyrights.

Industrial Property. (patents and trademarks). Industrial property rights protect specific signs and trademarks that distinguish specific goods and services from other goods and services. The property on a trademark can last as long as the trademark is easily distinguishable. Patents protect individuals who are in the process of creating a new invention. Individuals can receive a patent protection for approximately twenty years.[18] This protection allows the individual enough time to develop the product into a working invention without threat of competition. After the patent expires, other persons or companies may attempt to reproduce a similar product.

Copyrights

Copyrights are a form of intellectual property rights designed to encourage and reward creative intellectual work by protecting the author's work. Copyrights protect the rights of authors in regards to literary and artistic works. These works include all books, songs, compositions, paintings, films, and computer programs. Authors are protected by copyright for at least seventy years after their death. The modern copyright system can be traced back to the Berne Convention (1886). The Berne Convention provides a minimum protection of property rights that arc independent of the nation in which the work originated. The agreement made at the Berne Convention protects the artistic domain of authors in regards to literary works, such as novels, songs, and compositions. The following is a list of rights authorized for protection by the Berne Convention:

- The right to translate,

- The right to make adaptations and arrangements of the work,

- The right to perform in public dramatic and musical works,

- The right to recite in public literary works,

- The right to communicate to the public the performance of such works,

- The right to broadcast (with the possibility of a contracting State to provide for a mere right to equitable remuneration instead of a right of authorization),

- The right to make reproductions in any manner or form (with the possibility of a contracting a nation to permit, in certain special cases, reproduction without authorization, provided that the reproduction does not conflict with the normal exploitation of the work and does not unreasonably prejudice the legitimate interests of the author, and with the possibility of a contracting State to provide, in the case of sound recordings of musical works, for a right to equitable remuneration),

- The right to use the work as a basis for an audiovisual work, and the right to reproduce, distribute, perform in public, or communicate to the public that audiovisual work,[19]

- The Convention also allows authors to possess moral rights in which they can object to anyone using their work in a manner that would dishonor the reputation of the author.[20]

Global Economic Systems

The global economy involves complex national and regional economic systems with many variables. These economic systems span developed, newly industrialized nations, and they include centrally planned, market, and mixed systems. Organizations such as the United Nations and the International Monetary Fund (IMF) use various measurement tools to determine the economic status of all nations. These tools include the Human Development Index (HDI), Gross National Product (GNP), Gross Domestic Product (GDP) and Purchasing Power Parity (PPP). However, an understanding of the economic systems of the world must be preceded by an understanding of the beliefs and values of various cultures.

Individualist vs. Collectivist Economic Values

As cultures converge across the globe, companies must be engaged in learning the converging patterns that underlie a vast array of societies. The U.S. economic value system has developed from the Puritanical belief that endorsed individualistic values and characteristics.[21] Other nations, such as Great Britain, Australia, and Canada also have similar value systems; however, cultures such as China, North Korea, and Cuba believe that an economic value system should be founded on cumulative efforts, controlled by greater entities or governments. A distinction between individualist and collectivist societies is crucial to the proper understanding of cross-cultural beliefs and values.[22]

Individualism refers to a self-orientation, an emphasis on self-sufficiency and control, the pursuit of individual goals, which may or may not be consistent with the in-group goals, a willingness to confront members of the in-group to which a person belongs, and a culture where people derive pride from their own accomplishments. In an individualistic environment, people are motivated by self-interest and achievement of personal goals. Individualists are hesitant to contribute to collective action, unless their own efforts are recognized, preferring instead to benefit from the efforts of others.[23]

The benefits of individualism include the following:

- Employee develops stronger self-concept and more self-confidence
- Consistent with achievement motivation
- Competition among individuals encourages greater numbers of novel concepts, ideas, and breakthrough innovations
- Stronger sense of personal responsibility for performance outcomes
- Linkage between personal effort and rewards creates greater sense of equity

The drawbacks of individualism include the following:

- Emphasis on personal gain at expense of others; selfishness, and materialism
- Individuals have less commitment/loyalty and are more "up for sale"
- Differences among individuals are emphasized
- Interpersonal conflicts are encouraged
- Greater levels of personal stress; pressure for individual performance
- Insecurity can result from overdependence on one's self
- Greater feelings of loneliness and alienation
- Stronger incentive for unethical behavior, expediency

Collectivism involves the subordination of personal interests to the goals of the larger work group, an emphasis on sharing, cooperation, and group harmony, a concern with group welfare, and hostility toward out-group members. Collectivists believe that they are an indispensable part of the group and will readily contribute without concern for being taken advantage of or whether or not others are doing their part. They feel personally responsible for the group product and are oriented towards sharing group rewards.[24]

The following list contains the benefits of collectivism:

- Greater synergy from combined efforts of people with differing skills
- Ability to incorporate a diverse perspective and achieve a comprehensive view
- Individuals treated as equals
- Relationships more personalized, synchronized, harmonious, while interpersonal conflicts are discouraged

- Greater concern for welfare of others; network of social support available

- More consensus regarding direction and priorities

- Credit for failures and successes equally shared

- Teamwork produces steady, incremental progress on projects[25]

The subsequent list includes the drawbacks of collectivism:

- Loss of personal and professional self to group/collective

- Greater emotional dependence of individuals on the group or organization

- Less personal responsibility for outcomes

- Individuals "free ride" on efforts of others; rewards not commensurate with effort

- Tendency toward "group think"

- Outcomes can represent compromises among diverse interests, reflecting need to get along more than need for performance

- Collectives can take more time to reach consensus: may miss opportunities[26]

Types of Economic Systems

The three primary types of global economic systems are centrally planned economy, market economy, and mixed economy. Depending on a nation's governmental control, combinations of economic systems usually emerge, making it difficult to accurately analyze their economic system. However, in most instances, one economic orientation tends to dominate.

Centrally Planned Economic System

A centrally planned economy most often refers to an economic system that is under comprehensive control and regulation by a government, in accordance with the plan of economic development. The centrally planned economy is in contrast to a market economy, in which market forces dictate supply, demand, production, pricing, etc. In a centrally planned economy, an overriding hierarchy (usually the government) attempts to control supply, demand, production, distribution, and pricing. Most centrally planned economic systems are associated with communism. Several governments, including Cuba and North Korea, still adhere to its practices.

Cuba became a member of the Council for Mutual Economic Assistance (CMEA), which was a part of the Soviet trading bloc in 1972, as it transformed from a capitalist economic system to a centrally planned economic system, led by President Fidel Castro. Prior to its revolution in 1959, Cuba, because of its great resources, strategic location, and trade relationship with the United States, was a major economic force in the Caribbean. During the period of 1945 through 1958, Cuba was able to double its gross national product, ranking third among Latin American countries. Economists estimate that Cuba's GSP or gross social product—Cuba's measure of economic production—decreased 30 percent from 1989 through 1992.[27] In addition to the dissolution of the CMEA in 1990, several items have contributed to the distress of the Cuban economy since the late 1980s:

- The failed system of ownership, where collective ownership has proven to be a disastrous economic policy.

- Artificially valuing the peso and continuing to issue money into circulation.

- Production of sugar beyond what is economically rational, thus causing low productivity in other areas.

- Misallocated investment resources into large projects with no economic basis.

- Technological retrogression in that rather than adopting economic reform, they have reverted back to ox carts and bicycles.[28]

To stimulate growth and trade, Cuba attempted to introduce economic reform in the early 1990s. These reforms included the establishment of a new "unofficial" exchange market to replace the black market, transformation of many state farms into co-operatives, and steps towards decentralization of economic management.[29] Although these initial reforms were thought to be the beginnings of a transition to a market economy, subsequent events have shown that the reforms were no more than Cuban officials' claims of an increased use of market mechanisms within a framework of continued state ownership and economic control.

Market Economic System

A market economy, also known as a free-market economy and a free-enterprise economy, is an economic system in which the production and distribution of goods and services takes place through the mechanism of free markets. The market is guided by a free price system rather than a planned economy, controlled by the state.[30] The free-market economy is controlled by the supply and demand of goods and services rather than a hierarchy control, such as government. Many nations, most notably the U.S., are considered free market economies; however, no nation operates with a true, free-market economy. All economies have some governmental control, and none are completely free to operate unrestricted. Nations that primarily functioned under the centrally planned economic system prior to the 1980s, such as China and Russia (formerly know as the Soviet Union), have embraced the market economy. While their overall economies have improved, they face many challenges in the transition from a centrally planned economy to a market economy.

Throughout the 1990s, Russia has worked to transition from a centrally planned economy to a market economy and has seen the explosion with new markets of previously neglected services and consumer goods. In 2004, services accounted for approximately 60 percent of GDP, compared to only 36 percent in 1990. GDP continues to grow annually at approximately 7.1 percent.[31] Although Russia has experienced increased markets and a higher GDP, the post-communist government inherited an economic catastrophe: a GDP decline in 1991 of 12 percent, a budget deficit at 26 percent of GDP, and inflation rates that advanced to triple digits. Several underlying factors caused this transitional collapse:

- Long-standing, political commitment to expanding heavy industry with little consideration for its impact on the new market system.

- The dissolution of the Council for Mutual Economic Assistance (CMEA) disrupted many supply chains.

- The government's inability to financially assist the agricultural market without raising food prices beyond the reach of its citizens.

- The Russian people were trained to operate under the disciplines of the planned, economic system and struggled with the disciplines needed to succeed under the market system.

- The old political elite resisted even the most moderate of economic reforms.[32]

Mixed Economic System

A mixed economy is an economic system that allows for the simultaneous operation of publicly and privately owned enterprises. Mixed economies combine the purest forms of the market system and the centrally planned system. Countries such as Cuba are typically defined by economists as centrally planned systems, which could be considered a mixed economic system, as characteristics from both planned and market systems contribute to its makeup. On the other hand, Hong

Kong, while being considered as close to resembling a free market system, should technically be classified as a mixed system because both planned and market system characteristics are apart of its functionality.

Classification of Nations

The United Nations, the World Bank, the International Monetary Fund (IMF), and the Central Intelligence Agency (CIA) have developed classifications for all nations. These organizations have broken the classification of nations into three distinct groups: developed, newly industrialized, and developing. Of the 193 nations currently in existence, developing countries make up one-third of this number.

Developed Nations

A developed nation is a nation that has great wealth and resources, as well as the knowledge to properly manage its resources to take care of the well being of its people. Developed nations have a high per capita income. Industrialized countries and First World countries are also used to refer to developed nations. A United Nations Human Development Index score of 0.8 or higher would indicate that a nation is developed. The following nations are classified as developed nations:[33]

- Andora
- Australia
- Austria
- Belgium
- Bermuda
- Canada
- Denmark
- Faroe Islands
- Finland
- France
- Germany
- Greece
- Holy See
- Hong Kong
- Iceland
- Ireland
- Israel
- Italy
- Japan
- Liechtenstein
- Luxembourg
- Monaco
- Netherlands
- New Zealand
- Norway
- Portugal
- San Marino
- Singapore
- South Korea
- Spain
- Sweden
- Switzerland
- Taiwan
- United Kingdom
- United States

Newly Industrialized

According to the Organization for Economic Cooperation and Development (OECD), many formerly third world countries are entering into the arena of newly industrialized nations.[34] Mainly because of the technology boom of the last twenty-five years, many Asian countries, such as Hong Kong, Singapore, South Korea, and Taiwan have seen considerable economic growth. Many consider newly industrialized nations as those transitioning from the status of developing nations (sometimes referred to as "third world") to that of a developed nation. A regional variation of newly industrialized nations include Caribbean nations—such as Barbados, Guyana, Jamaica, Trinidad, and Tobago—where per capita incomes, access to healthcare, education, and technology are significantly greater than in regions such as Africa, Asia and Latin America.[35] Because tourists from around the globe can access these island nations, they are progressively becoming classified as industrialized or developed nations.

As technology improves and the movement of people between nations becomes blurred, more nations will transition from developing to the developed or newly industrialized category of nations.

Developing

The United Nations and other global monitoring agencies classify nations with the lowest economic status as developing nations. Developing nations typically have a Human Development Index of less than 0.5 according to the Human Development Reports office.[36] Economists also consider developing nations third world nations, where poverty and disease run rampant, education is nearly nonexistent, and life expectancy is very low. Approximately two-thirds of the world's population lives in developing countries, as population growth is high versus the population growth of developed nations.

For decades, governmental and nongovernmental agencies have attempted to help poverty-stricken nations move towards true development through various programs of financing, agricultural training, and basic-needs focus. Due to the high cost to sustain the programs, the agencies have not deemed the programs universally successful. Many experts believe the answer to truly developing third world nations is through the small business venue.[37] Small businesses have traditionally played a vital role in the success of developed nations, such as the United States, Japan, Israel, and the United Kingdom. With time, small business could be the answer to developing impoverished nations. However, several challenges exist in promoting small business in third world nations. The first challenge centers on the significant difference in economic data that is available in the developed countries, as opposed to developing countries. Although this information is becoming increasingly available for developing nations, it is still far short of the quantity of data available for a developing nation. The second challenge centers on the lack of consideration of current models of entrepreneurship development. The factors of success for entrepreneurial ventures in developing countries differ significantly from those faced in developed countries.[38] Small business development has always been a catalyst for improved employment and transforming agrarian economies. While obstacles such as lack of technology, obtaining financing, unskilled and uneducated workforce, lack of infrastructure, and price volatility are present in developing nations, small business development is crucial to developing economies.[39]

Basic Issues in Economic Development

One way to properly analyze data in order to help develop solutions for economies that are newly industrialized (or in the developing stage) is the use of reliable economic data. Such data is often organized into meaningful categories, or indices. These indices provide indicators that can be used to forecast development trends. Such indicators include Gross National Product (GNP), Gross Domestic Product (GDP), Purchasing Power Parity (PPP) and the Human Development Index (HDI).

National Production—GNP vs. GDP

Gross Domestic Product (GDP) is the total market value of all the goods and services produced within the borders of a nation during a specified period. GDP is the more common measure of income and production for countries around the world. Gross National Product (GNP) is the total market value of all the goods and services produced by a nation during a specified period. GNP includes the income produced in other countries to GDP. GNP per person is often used as a measure of the welfare of the citizens of a country. Countries with higher GNP often score high on other measures of welfare, such as life expectancy. However, there are serious limitations to the usefulness of GNP as a measure of welfare. GNP does not take into account several key factors: (1) unpaid economic activity such as domestic work; (2) inputs used to produce the output; (3) movements in exchange rates; and (4) factors that may be important to quality of life, such as the quality of the environment (as distinct from the input value) and security from crime. Because of these limitations, other measures— Purchasing Power Parity and the Human Development Index—should be used in any economic development analysis.

Purchasing Power Parity (PPP)

Purchasing Power Parity is based on the idea that changes in exchange rates should balance the price of a basket of traded goods in a foreign country. Once the foreign prices are converted to domestic currency at the exchange rate, the traded goods in the foreign country should roughly equal the price of the same basket in the domestic country.[40] The Big Mac Index is often used as an example for PPP in that the product is the same wherever you are in the world and involves several commodities—agriculture, labor, advertising, real estate cost, and transportation. Suppose one purchases a Big Mac in the U.S. for $3 (USD) and a Big Mac in Great Britain for £2 (GBP). The exchange-rate Purchasing Power Parity is $3 (USD) to £2 (GBP). While PPP seems to make sense on the surface, this simplistic approach creates several problems:

- Even the most homogeneous goods have different degrees of quality.

- Even products sold with the most rigorously controlled distribution will be different (e.g., the Big Mac).

- Even if two identical items were sold in two different places with one at a lower price, it would not make sense to buy the cheaper item and ship to the more expensive area (consider cost of shipping and distribution channels at arrival).[41]

Human Development Index

Understanding the Human Development Index (HDI) is essential to comprehend how various organizations, including the United Nations, the World Trade Organization, and the World Bank classify nations. The HDI includes a number of human development indicators that provide a global assessment of country achievements in different areas of human development. Table 3.1 shows the breakdown of nations and their HDI score. Nations with a score of 0.8 or higher are typically considered developed nations. Nations with a score of 0.5 or lower indicate developing nations, while nations who score in the range of 0.5 and 0.8 characterize newly industrialized nations. Below is the 2006 HDI index ranking for the top ten countries: [42]

Table 3.1

HDI rank[a]	Human development index (HDI) value 2004	Life expectancy at birth (years) 2004	Adult literacy rate (% ages 15 and above) 2004[b]	Combined gross enrolment ratio for primary, secondary and tertiary schools (%) 2004[c]	GDP per capita (PPP US$) 2004	Life expectancy index	Education index
High Human Development							
1 Norway	0.965	79.6	..e	100[f]	38,454	0.91	0.99
2 Iceland	0.960	80.9	..e	96[g]	33,051	0.93	0.98
3 Australia	0.957	80.5	..e	113[f]	30,331	0.92	0.99
4 Ireland	0.956	77.9	..e	99	38,827	0.88	0.99
5 Sweden	0.951	80.3	..e	96	29,541	0.92	0.98
6 Canada	0.950	80.2	..e	93[g,h]	31,263	0.92	0.97
7 Japan	0.949	82.2	..e	85	29,251	0.95	0.94
8 United States	0.948	77.5	..e	93	39,676	0.88	0.97
9 Switzerland	0.947	80.7	..e	86	33,040	0.93	0.95
10 Netherlands	0.947	78.5	..e	98	31,798	0.89	0.99

a. The HDI rank is determined using HDI values to the 6th decimal point.

b. Data refer to national literacy estimates from censuses or surveys conducted between 2000 and 2005, unless otherwise specified. Due to differences in methodology and timeliness of underlying data, comparisons across countries and over time should be made with caution. For more details, see www.uis.unesco.org.

c. In 2006 the United Nations Educational, Scientific and Cultural Organization (UNESCO) Institute for Statistics changed its convention for citing the reference year of education data to the calendar year in which the academic or financial year ends—

d. from 2003/04, for example, to 2004. Data for some countries may refer to national or UNESCO Institute for Statistics estimates. A positive figure indicates that the HDI rank is higher than the GDP per capita (PPP US$) rank, a negative the opposite.

e. For purposes of calculating the HDI, a value of 99.0% was applied.

f. For purposes of calculating the HDI, a value of 100% was applied.

g. Preliminary national or UNESCO Institute for Statistics estimate, subject to further revision.

h. Data refer to a year other than that specified.

Global Business Risk

Knowledge of the political and economic environments of international business can empower the global business professional in their pursuit of global markets. From a practical perspective, this knowledge is valuable in terms of assessing and confronting the numerous risks associated with doing business overseas. Operating a domestic-only business can have many risks. However, engaging in global business—due to the increased complexity—has more and greater levels of risk that must be identified and managed for success.

Global business risk is any worldwide factor—outside the laws of supply and demand—that could impact the success or failure of any venture moving into the international arena.[43] The three types of risk for global international business are ownership risk, operation risk, and transfer risk.

Ownership Risk

Ownership risk ranges from property title uncertainty, property line encroachment, squatting, and even government expropriations, such as capital levies and unexpected export or excise taxes.[44] Ownership risk may be categorized as follows: (1) the risk of a claim from a previously dispossessed owner, and (2) the risk that the current owner will be dispossessed.

Operation Risk

Operation risk appears to be one of the main risks that companies can actually do something about. Operation risk is defined by the Bank for International Settlement (BIS) as "the risk of loss resulting from inadequate or failed internal process, people and systems or from external events."[45] Operation risk can include differences in language, cultures, accounting methods, and data entry between different branches of a company, located across the globe.

Transfer Risk

Transfer risk occurs when debtors in a country are unable to ensure timely payments of foreign currency debt service because of either transfer or exchange restrictions or a general lack of foreign currency.[46] Transfer risk can range from governmental regulations that restrict the flow of dollars to governments taking over funds or industries to civil disturbances that make it impossible for borrowers or lenders to make wire transfers or send mail.

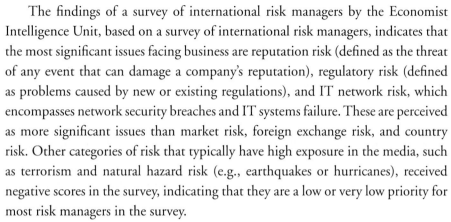

Sources of Risk

The findings of a survey of international risk managers by the Economist Intelligence Unit, based on a survey of international risk managers, indicates that the most significant issues facing business are reputation risk (defined as the threat of any event that can damage a company's reputation), regulatory risk (defined as problems caused by new or existing regulations), and IT network risk, which encompasses network security breaches and IT systems failure. These are perceived as more significant issues than market risk, foreign exchange risk, and country risk. Other categories of risk that typically have high exposure in the media, such as terrorism and natural hazard risk (e.g., earthquakes or hurricanes), received negative scores in the survey, indicating that they are a low or very low priority for most risk managers in the survey.

"The focus for risk managers is shifting from financial risk to less understood areas, with reputation and regulatory issues topping their list of priorities," says Daniel Franklin, editorial director of the Economist Intelligence Unit. "By regularly tracking changes in the risk environment, the Risk Barometer will help risk professionals understand how their peers are responding to these new trends and challenges."[47]

Global-business risk has many sources: corruption and bribery, unstable political systems, excess involvement of military or religious leaders in government, internal conflict among ethnic and religious groups, and unstable relations with other nations. Astute business professionals should always monitor any threat to the success of their business.

Corruption and Bribery

"Corruption is the misuse of public power for private profit or political gain—represents a hazard to free trade and investment, a threat to democracy and development, and, in collusion with international crime, a danger to national security."[48] The Organization for Economic Cooperation and Development (OECD), the World Trade Organization, the World Bank, and the International Monetary Fund have all indicated that corruption is the greatest single barrier to economic development worldwide.[49] Two things have contributed to global business corruption over the past twenty years: the end of the Cold War and the explosion of democracy and markets.[50] As more economies move from planned economies to market economies, each society must confront the specter of corruption. A bribe is "an inducement that influences a public official to perform his/her duties in a manner contrary to the course that would otherwise be adopted."[51] International bribery is disguised in various forms and hinders global, economic development, disrupting the flow of distribution channels, destroying any incentives to compete solely on quality and price, distorting market efficiency and predictability, and eventually denying people the right to a fair standard of living.[52]

Unstable Political System

Because of political unrest in the countries of Eastern Europe, the Middle East, Latin America, Africa, and Southeast Asia, many companies looking to enter or expand in the international arena are not willing to commit resources to these and other similarly afflicted areas of the world. Companies cannot afford even the smallest of investments to risk a potential overnight change in a political regime that would force new laws and regulations upon the management of a new international venture. Before entering the market of any foreign country, businesses must properly investigate and analyze the political climate to assure themselves of no threats from political instability.

Excess Involvement of Military or Religious Leaders in Governments

Because historians have only recorded three-hundred war-free years, a good look at the military status of a country would be an important consideration before establishing a business in a foreign country. Even though civilian regimes have become powerful and effective in many Latin American countries, a number of these countries, such as Columbia, Ecuador, and Venezuela, are still heavily influenced by military leaders.[53] Amid the influence of military leaders in Latin America, countries such as Argentina, Chile, Brazil, and Uruguay are thriving economically from less military control.[54] Whether the influence is in the U.S., the Middle East, or India, religious leaders play a very powerful part in the economic success of any country. The Saudi Arabian government has recently faced challenges in attempting to open its economy—a result of Islamic leadership on the Saudi Arabian government and economy for generations.[55] As its population continues to grow and economic growth remains flat, Saudi Arabia is more willing to invite new markets into its economy. As foreign influence arrives with the new markets, the traditional rule of Islamic leaders in the school systems, government agencies, and judicial systems may need to be adjusted to accommodate economic growth.[56] Any company considering moving into a foreign economic market must consider the powerful influence of the military and religious leadership.

Internal Conflict among Ethnic and Religious Groups

Religious beliefs among ethnic groups have always been a source of internal conflict in countries around the world. This conflict frequently arises when one ethnic group wants to ethnically cleanse its country from another ethnic group. After the end of the Cold War in the early 1990s, Bosnia experienced civil war because the Bosniaks (Muslims), the Serbs (Eastern Orthodox Christians), and the Croats (Roman Catholics) had differing opinions as to the establishment of Bosnia as a state.[57] The Serbs and Croats wanted to partition Bosnia and establish ethnically pure states; however, the Bosniaks were seeking a unified multiethnic Bosnia.[58] The war ended in 1995 with the Dayton Agreement, establishing Bosnia as a multiethnic state; nevertheless, the tragic consequences of this ethnic religious conflict still exist today.[59]

Unstable Relations with Other Nations

Relations among nations appear to be an extension of ethnic religious group conflicts that have crossed borders and involve two or more nations. Usually, when two nations are in conflict, a heightened sense of alarm extends around the globe, negatively impacting the global economy. When terrorists destroyed the World Trade Center in New York in 2001, the stock market, as well as the U.S. economy, suffered The ripple effect was felt on economies around the world. Although no one can predict unstable relations among nations, astute business managers must be aware of and prepared for the risk.

Causes of Risk

Many sources of risk are associated with conducting domestic business. This is amplified with international business because of added pressures caused by sovereign governments, geography, and culture. The successful global business professional identifies the potential risks, assesses the potential profits, and puts the appropriate risk mitigation tools into place. A number of causes of risk are associated with international transactions, including violence and conflict, terrorism and kidnapping, confiscation, expropriation, and nationalism. Understanding the causes of global business risk helps managers properly address risk before it becomes detrimental to the success of the organization.

Violence and Conflict

Violence and conflict in overseas markets can occur at a moment's notice, disrupting business operations for anyone involved in global trade. Companies can experience violence and conflict, resulting from foreign governments and third parties, potentially leading to forced shutdowns, relocations, and other unforeseen expenses. The origin of the conflict and violence could be legislative, executive, judicial, popular revolt, or various combinations of these factors. In formulating a definition of country risk, the difference between risk and uncertainty is paramount. Uncertainty is an unknown chance that an event will occur.

Terrorism and Kidnapping

Terrorist acts in modern times have impacted the global business environment by temporarily disrupting economic gain and the pursuit of capitalism. At the same time, these acts have backfired on those against free-market economies, as an entire industry has emerged that is devoted to antiterrorism. In addition, "thanks to good economic crisis management (monetary and fiscal policy adjustments) including international co-operation, the short-term adverse economic impact of the September 11 attacks was far less serious than initially feared."[60] The U.S. economy bounced back as the strength of capitalism proved to be more resilient than the terrorists who were willing to destroy innocent people.

Kidnapping is another action that increases global business risk, and protection from this action has emerged as a reality of doing business in a global economy.[61] The problem can be compounded when managers do not know how to handle the risk of employee kidnapping. Expatriates and those working overseas should be aware of the following protective measures:

1. Avoid any country that has potential for this kind of behavior.

2. Plan for it to occur if you must do business in a hostile country, and be sure to have an extraction plan in place.

3. Communicate and develop relationships inside and outside the company and continue to communicate after an incident occurs.[62]

Terrorism, kidnapping, and extortion are all common occurrences around the world. The best way to handle them is to be prepared.

Confiscation, Expropriation, and Nationalism

A mutual mistrust exists between international companies and the government of hostile foreign countries in which they enter.[63] From the perspective of the company, this mistrust is based on government actions, such as the rise of confiscation, expropriation, and nationalization. These have become a great concern for the business community.[64] Confiscation is the seizure of private property for the public treasury. Expropriation is to deprive of possession: a government could take away a private business from its owner. Nationalism converts ownership from private to governmental control.

Brief Summary of Major Points

Globalization will continue to be an important topic in both the government and the private sector. International trade has reduced many global trade barriers between countries, while allowing the countries involved to profit from each other's resources. Due to the increasing importance of international trade, many international organizations have been created to manage international affairs. Companies considering growth in the international arena must do extensive research before committing to that growth. Because of the different value systems around the globe, a company should examine whether or not the values of a country or a region match those of the company. Companies must consider risks when looking to progress into the international market. Managers must do extensive research into political, religious, and economical systems to establish, in advance, a plan to combat such risks.

- The governments of most countries actively monitor and regulate international trade in order to sustain economic stability. Governments may use subsidies and other tax breaks in order to attract trade, but times will arise when governments must decrease the amount of imports it receives in order to protect the domestic market. Governments may also place embargoes on foreign nations to economically punish them for a conflict or difference in ideology. International trade is also important for governments, because it generates positive revenues through taxes and tariffs.

- The World Trade Organization (WTO), World Intellectual Property Organization (WIPO), International Trade Centre (ITC), International Intellectual Property Alliance (IIPA), Consumers International (CI), Licensing Executives Society International (LESI), Entertainment Software Association (ESA), United Nations (UN), and International Organization for Standardization (ISO) are working together in an effort to create a level of standardization to promote free trade among all nations. However, they must actively engage the challenge of the different types of laws that govern the diversity of nations. These international organizations are also diligently working on securing the property rights of all nations.

- Nations may be categorized into one of the three types of economic systems: centrally planned economy, market economy, and mixed economy. While most countries fall into the mixed economic system, countries such as Cuba and North Korea fall into the centrally planned systems. Most consider Hong Kong to be primarily a market system.

Nations may also be classified into three economic development types: developed, newly industrialized, and developing. The United Nations, the World Bank, and the International Monetary Fund use such measures as the Gross National Product, Gross Domestic Product, Purchasing Power Parity, and the Human Development Index to report and assess development.

- Risk, a natural element of global trade, may be classified as ownership risk, operation risk, and transfer risk. Sources of global business risk would include corruption and bribery, unstable political systems, excess involvement of military or religious leaders in government, internal conflict among ethnic and religious groups, and unstable relations with other nations. Causes of global business risk include violence and conflict, terrorism and kidnapping, confiscation, expropriation, and local content requirements.

Moving from Theory into Practice

The following summarizes a question and answer session with co-author Joe Robinson. His answers are useful in contemplating how the global business professional can translate the theories and concepts covered in this chapter via practical answers to the questions from real life experiences.

<u>What main political issue does the successful global business professional look for when evaluating whether or not to put time, money, and manpower into developing a new market?</u>

A stable government is a must. If a country has raw materials, wealth, and a number of attractive attributes to attract foreign commerce to enter its markets, it still could be a major risk and could be a bad decision to try to penetrate the market—if the government is politically unstable or is in constant turmoil. A current example is Venezuela. International banks shy away from transactions in Venezuela, so I tell my clients to beware of any foreign market where they cannot find banks readily willing and able to assist with risk financial management. In the case of Venezuela, there is political unrest nationwide and the possibility that the government will instigate policies and procedures that may make doing business there financially and commercially risky. The nationalization of industries is a potential issue. Graft and bribery are also issues. My question to exporters is, "Why do you want to focus on business in a country with higher than normal risks, when there are so many other countries that are less risky and your chances to succeed are much greater and easier?" It is best to find those countries and to do business where the political and economic climate is most conducive to good global, commercial standards and practices.

<u>How does a government's long-term approach to global business ethics affect its economic well being and the prospect for successful growth in global commerce?</u>

Good government and political ethics is essential for long-term economic well being and prosperity. You have probably noticed that I like to use Japan as real-life examples. That is because Japan has been traditionally one of our largest trading partners in the USA. Japan is a good example of a country where government and politics basically operate with integrity. The insistence by the Japanese government that international business be conducted in a fair and equitable manner, backed by good ethics practices, is one of numerous beneficial traits, resulting in the economic growth experienced by Japan during the 60s and 70s. An example of an opposite effect is the case of the Philippines during the same period that

Japan expanded. In the late 60s and early 70s, the Philippines was a country that appeared to be leading South East Asia in economic prosperity. However, due to the graft, greed, and unethical practices that began to proliferate in the mid-70s, perpetuated by the Marcos government, the Philippines today is not in the same economic class of prosperity as Thailand and Malaysia. Companies today will shy away from those countries that do not practice good ethics. It is my advice to companies looking for new overseas ventures to first seek those countries where governments and politics operate with acceptable global standards of ethics.

Other than a stable and ethical political structure, what is a current major concern of global corporations regarding the legal system of the countries in which they do business?

Concern for intellectual property protection is a major concern. I get phone calls and emails weekly regarding this issue. Global companies need protection for their branding, copyrights, patents, and trade marks. Fortunately, the WTO, on a global scale, and the ITA, on behalf of US companies, is diligently working on this issue. My advice is to seek good legal counsel with regards to intellectual property rights protection. This is especially important where brand name recognition and patent protection is essential to business growth. In seeking good legal council, it is good business practice to find and work with competent attorneys with experience in international Intellectual Property issues.

Can I take my U.S. domestic representative agreement that I have been using for years here in the States and simply use it as a template for my international representative agreement?

This is not a good idea and is actually inviting problems that will surely surface in the future. Remember that there are inherent differences in doing business overseas. Time, language, laws, and business codes need to be taken into account when establishing working contracts or agreements with overseas reps or partners.

An example is the termination clause that Americans put into their domestic contracts that states that the agreement may be terminated with written, registered mail notice sixty days in advance to either party. This is not acceptable in Latin American and many European countries. Their laws for termination are much more involved and stringent, such that termination needs "permission" and negotiation before an amicable parting–of-ways is concluded.

Can you give an example of an "administrative delay" that might negatively impact my exports to a foreign country?

One example is the process to register a product to be compliant for a standard in the country to which you are exporting. Electrical standards, food label standards, medical regulations approval, and environmental certification all fall into this category. If you feel you are unduly discriminated against by an "administrative delay," I advise you to get in touch with your regional U. S. Department of Commerce, Bureau of Export Assistance, Trade Specialist (202)482-2000 and seek their help. If the situation warrants serious consideration you can ask the ITA (International Trade Administration) Foreign Commercial Service, (202) 205-2000 for assistance.

Other examples are inconsistent customs procedures, lack of transparency and burdensome paperwork that serve as trade barriers, created by "administrative delay," creating a drain on the exporter and resulting in increased costs, so that the exporter is placed in a less competitive position to conduct business in the country that exercises "administrative delays." Additional examples include inconsistent licensing requirements, incoherent inspection standards—both of which add costly process and time constraints on exporters—especially to small firms who do not have the staff or the talent to deal with these encumbrances.

What is a quick and simple method to initially evaluate a new market before spending a lot of time, effort, and money when considering the political and economic environment?

Find out if your competitors are already in the market and ascertain how they are doing. This can be done by checking trade organizations, government export/import figures, and similar statistics. You can also find out the competitive situation from a potential representative or distributor, and at the same time, determine how knowledgeable and market savvy your potential representative or partner is about his commercial environment and your targeted customer base. This is an initial approach, and if the new market appears attractive, it is always a good strategy to then visit the country to verify your initial findings.

How risky is it to do business in countries where intellectual property rights are not well governed by their legal system and their business environment is not respectful of intellectual property rights?

It is very risky to do business under these circumstances. In addition to lack of protection for your patents, trademarks, logo and branding recognition, the country that is weak or nonrespective of other's intellectual property most likely has other problems that will complicate and make your entry and dealings within the market very risky. These impediments may include all three risks: political, legal, and economic.

If bribery is a common way of conducting business in a particular country, does my company have to engage in these practices in order to do business there?

The answer is "no." Keep in mind that if an American company engages in or practices bribery or influences foreign government officials, it is illegal by U.S. law, and the individual or individuals engaged in this practice could face criminal charges, the company could be fined or lose its export privileges, and the actions most likely will be published, creating an unwanted and damaging public for the company engaged in bribery. The best action is to simply not engage in bribing foreign government officials. This includes customs officials, government agents, and foreign military officials.

What is good protocol for gift giving? Is gift giving considered bribery?

Gift giving is a common and acceptable practice, provided it is done in good taste, within moderation, and performed openly. This is not considered bribery and is a good idea for relation building. Giving, for example, small gifts with the company brand or logo is done routinely—and is acceptable. I find that hand crafted gifts are well received when I travel abroad. By their very nature, each hand crafted item is unique and has a history of the locality from which it comes. An example of this are the Jefferson pewter cups that are crafted in Williamsburg, which are easy to carry, and lightweight. In some cases, I have inscribed on the gift the name of the person receiving it and the date of the gift giving occasion.

When I travel to Saudi Arabia, what do I give the billionaire sheik who has everything? I gave him a jar of sourwood honey that comes only from the sourwood tree available for harvest only two weeks of the year. No one would consider this bribery, it is done in good taste (pun intended) and it is well received.

Large picture books are also a good gift. An example is the book I have given, entitled, "Wildflowers of the Blue Ridge," which is well received in Europe, China, Japan, and the Middle East. Be careful that you review the pictures before you decide to use it as a gift. For example, when I first thought of a large photo book, I looked at "Scenes from Virginia." The pictures were lovely from the mountains, to plantations, to rivers, to old style homes, to Virginia Beach. Whoops, the Virginia Beach scenes had bikini clad ladies and girls and this is definitely not a good gift for Saudi Arabia. So I chose the wild flower book instead.

<u>You talk about company and commercial risks but what advice can you give about personal and individual risks involved in global travel and doing business in foreign countries?</u>

First, be sure your company insurance policies cover you in foreign countries when you travel on company business. For example, some life insurance and major medical policies will not cover you in marshal-law countries, unless you advise your insurance company beforehand of the country you will visit and your intended length of stay. And you pay a daily additional premium for risk protection. This was the case when I checked my personal situation while working for a former company when I made a one-week business trip to Korea. The daily additional premium was very small but a necessary fee for adequate protection. I had a wife and two small children at home at the time and wanted to be sure that both my life insurance and major accident coverage were in place just in case an unexpected catastrophe might arise.

Two web sites to check out for individual travel risk management are,

- US Department of State: www.travel.state.gov
- Centers for Disease Control: www.cdc.gov/travel

Key Concepts

- Why governments intervene in global trade 78
- Special government agencies for international trade 79
- Import/export subsidies 80
- Export financing 80
- Foreign trade zones 81
- Tariffs, quotas, embargoes 83-84
- Local content requirements 85
- Administrative delays 85
- Methods of imposing economic sanctions 84
- Common, civil, and theocratic law 86-87
- Standardization of international law 87
- Intellectual property rights across nations 88
- Industrial property rights across nations 88
- Individual vs. collectivist economic values across nations 90-91
- Central, market, and mixed economic systems 92-94
- Developed, newly industrialized, and developing nations 95-96
- GNP vs. GDP 97
- Purchasing power parity 98
- Human development index 98
- Ownership, operation, and transfer risk 100
- Sources of risk in global business 101
- Cause and effect risk factors in global business 103

4 INTERNATIONAL TRADE, GLOBAL TRADING SYSTEMS, AND FOREIGN DIRECT INVESTMENT

Global Business in Practice
Embracing the Challenge of International Trade

Ben S. Bernanke, Chairman and a member of the Board of Governors of the Federal Reserve System, summarized the importance of embracing international trade, as well as dealing with its challenges. The following remarks were excerpted from his speech, "Embracing the Challenge of Free Trade: Competing and Prospering in a Global Economy," at the Montana Economic Development Summit 2007, Butte, Montana.

International trade in goods, services, and assets, like other forms of market-based exchange, allows us to transform what we have into what we need or want under increasingly beneficial terms. Trade allows us to enjoy both a more productive economy and higher living standards.

Of course, current trading arrangements are far from perfect. Some features of the world trading regime, such as excessive restrictions on trade in services and the uneven protection of intellectual property rights, are both unfair and economically counterproductive. Working through the World Trade Organization or in other venues, we should continue to advocate the elimination of trade distortions and barriers in our trading partners even as we increase the openness of our own economy. We should also work to ensure that both we and our trading partners live up to existing agreements under the World Trade Organization. When trading partners do not meet their obligations, we should vigorously press our case. Ultimately, a freer and more open trading system is in everyone's best interest.

Although expansion of trade makes the U.S. economy stronger, as I have noted today, the broad benefits of trade and the associated economic change may come at a cost to some individuals, firms, and communities. We need to continue to find ways to minimize the pain of dislocation without standing in the way of economic growth and change. Indeed, *the willingness to embrace difficult challenges is a defining characteristic of the American people. With our strong institutions, deep capital markets, flexible labor markets, technological leadership, and penchant for entrepreneurship and innovation, no country is better placed than the United States to benefit from increased participation in the global economy. If we resist protectionism and isolationism while working to increase the skills and adaptability of our labor force, the forces of globalization and trade will continue to make our economy stronger and our citizens more prosperous.**

* The Federal Reserve Board. Retrieved on August 20, 2007 from http://www.federalreserve. gov/boarddocs/Speeches/2007/20070501/default.htm

Introduction

International Trade and Investment is the trading of goods, services, or funding that crosses international borders. Funding may be in the form of Foreign Direct Investment (FDI), the amount invested in property, equipment, or services capability in a foreign country. The expansion of international trade and investment in the last half century has helped to create a global economy, affording increased opportunity to investors and manufacturers, both foreign and domestic.[1]

A primary indicator of a nation's status, in terms of international trade, is its balance of payments. The national balance of payments is a gauge to track the coming and going of international trade dollars. The ideal is that a nation's net income from trade in goods and services would be positive. A nation's capital account defines the net change in foreign ownership of domestic assets and foreign assets and records the purchase and sale of domestic and foreign assets. Governments attempt to attract foreign direct investment and promote those industries that will use national endowments most intensely, increasing a nation's competitiveness and the competitiveness of the region for FDI. Therefore, the global business professional has a keen awareness of the benefits of international trade and knowledge of international trade patterns.

Benefits of International Trade

International trade serves as the foundation for the new global economy. Developed nations are reaching out to find more places to sell their goods, more places to house their factories, and new people to work in those factories. These nations are also searching for the best products and services that the world has to offer and attempting to bring them to their marketplace. The developing world is desperately trying to find a way to share what they have to offer with the rest of the world in a way that is economically beneficial for them. Those developing nations that actively seek trade open the possibility for numerous global marketplaces, which can eventually lead to the enhancement in the quality of life for their citizens. Developing nations participating in globalization and international trade have experienced tremendous growth when compared to nations that have chosen to marginalize the possible benefits of global trade. The Ministry of Foreign Affairs of Denmark has proclaimed that "international trade is a crucial precondition for growth. Many of the poorest countries in the world have not sufficiently managed to take advantage of the trade liberalization that has taken place since the end of World War II."[2]

The natural resources of developing nations dictate that one crop or one product will monopolize exportation potential. International trade is the key to unlocking the potential of the developing world and lifting millions out of poverty. Agriculture is one of the primary exports of many developing nations; however, slow globalization in this industry has limited the ability of many countries to export. Globalization has reduced the tariffs on manufactured goods by 90 percent over the last fifty years; nevertheless, agricultural tariffs are largely unchanged over that period of time. Agriculture makes up a sizeable portion of the economies in developing nations. A reduction in the tariffs charged would have a significant impact in terms of improving the economic status of the developing nation. Additionally, the importing of technology would enable farmers to produce more crops, thus enabling these developing nations to have more to offer in the global market.

George W. Bush, the forty-third president of the United States, has expounded on the benefits of international trade: "Free trade is the only proven path out of poverty for developing nations. And when nations are shut off from the world, their people pay a steep price."[3] While the benefits of globalization to the developing world have great potential, industrialized nations also stand to see a large manifestation of economic gain by globalizing the market place. Additionally, industrialized nations benefit by importing the best goods a region has to offer, thus fostering specialization and improving the overall offering of goods in the global marketplace. Along with improving the quality of goods, international trade promotes competition, which lowers the cost of goods sold. As a general rule of thumb, companies do not want competition for their product offerings. Any organization seeking a profit seeks to capitalize on the highest percentage of market share possible. However, what is good for the company is not always good for the consumer or for the economy as a whole. While the U.S. has embraced market competition—even federally regulating it—many other nations, including western European nations, are slow to welcome the idea.[4] One of the major strengths of the U.S. economic model is the "competition is good" ideology. The American model has decreased unemployment, stabilized prices, and created an environment that fosters change in how the economy functions. The rapid growth of global trade, brought on by the advancements in U.S. technology during the twentieth century, is a major reason why the U.S. is currently the world's dominant economy. When compared to the economy of France, where the students and employees seek "secure lifetime employment," the American economy looks exceptionally strong.[5]

Table 4.1

WORLD OUTPUT GROWTH, 1990 - 2005[a]
(Percentage change over previous year)

Region/country[b]	1990 – 2000[c]	1999	2000	2001	2002	2003	2004[d]	2005[e]
World	**2.7**	**2.9**	**4.0**	**1.3**	**1.8**	**2.5**	**3.8**	**3.0**
Developed countries	**2.4**	**2.7**	**3.5**	**1.0**	**1.3**	**1.7**	**3.0**	**2.3**
of which:								
Japan	1.4	0.1	2.8	0.4	-0.3	1.4	2.6	1.8
United States	3.4	4.1	3.8	0.3	2.4	3.0	4.4	3.5
European Union	2.1	2.9	3.6	1.7	1.1	0.9	2.1	1.5
of which:								
European Union-15	2.1	2.9	3.5	1.6	1.0	0.8	2.0	1.4
Euro area	2.0	2.8	3.5	1.6	0.9	0.5	1.8	1.2
France	1.7	3.2	2.8	2.1	1.2	0.5	2.1	1.5
Germany	1.6	2.0	2.9	0.9	0.2	-0.1	1.0	0.8
Italy	1.6	1.7	3.0	1.8	0.4	0.3	1.0	-0.4
United Kingdon	2.7	2.8	3.8	2.1	1.7	2.2	3.1	2.0
South-East Europe and CIS	**-4.3**	**3.4**	**8.1**	**5.6**	**4.9**	**6.9**	**7.5**	**6.0**
Developing Countries	**4.8**	**3.5**	**5.4**	**2.4**	**3.5**	**4.7**	**6.4**	**5.4**
Developing Countries, excluding China	**4.0**	**3.0**	**5.0**	**1.5**	**2.7**	**3.9**	**5.7**	**4.6**

Source: UNCTAD secretariat calculations, based on UNCTA *Handbook of Statistics* 2004;
United Nations, Department of Economic and Social Affairs (UN/DESA),
Development Policy and Planning Office, Project Link estimates; national sources; IMF,
World Economic Outlook, April 2005; JP Morgan, *Global Data Watch*, various issues;
Economic Intelligence Unti (EIU), *Country Forecast*, various issues; and OECD,
Economic Outlook No. 77.

a   Calculations are based on GDP in constatn market prices based on 1995 dollars.
b   Region and country groups correspond to those defined in the UNCTAD Handbookd of Statistics 2004.
c   Average.
d   Preliminary estimates.
e   Forecast.

International Trade Patterns

Similar to the rise and fall of the stock market and the status of the economy in general, international trade experiences gains and losses over time. The U.S. economy, with its philosophy of embracing competition and free trade, has been the driving force for the overall economic results of the rest of the world. This is evidenced by a concurrent evaluation of the data reported in Table 4.1 and in Table 4.2. Table 4.1 data depicts the growth of world output from 1990 to 2005. Table 4.2 data depicts world export and import volumes from the same period. The mild recession in the United States in 2001 resulted in the lowest World Output numbers of the last six years and resulted in half the average from 1990 to 2000. Despite modest growth from other nations, including the strongest year ever recorded for South East Europe, the overall outputs were grim. Conversely, in 2000 and 2004, the strongest years for the United States, the world output numbers were at their greatest.

Table 4.2

EXPORT AND IMPORT VOLUMES OF GOODS, BY REGION AND ECONOMIC GROUPING, 1996 -2004

(Percentage change over previous year)

	Export volume					Import volume				
	1990 – 2006[a]	*2001*	*2002*	*2003*	*2004*	*1990 – 2006*[a]	*2001*	*2002*	*2003*	*2004*
World	7	-1	5	6	13	7	-1	4	7	13
Developed economies	7	-1	2	3	11	8	-1	3	5	11
of which:										
Japan	6	-8	8	9	13	4	1	1	6	6
United States	7	-6	-4	3	9	11	-3	4	5	11
Europe	7	2	4	3	12	8	1	2	5	11
Developing economies	8	-2	9	12	16	7	-3	7	10	19
of which:										
Africa	2	1	2	11	7	1	5	4	7	26
Latin America	10	1	2	3	10	9	-3	-4	0	13
West Asia	5	0	8	1	3	10	-4	7	-5	35
East and South Asia	10	-3	12	17	22	6	-3	11	15	18
of which:										
China	12	9	25	35	33	11	12	23	36	26
India	8	7	17	10	18	5	4	13	9	17
South-East Europe / CIS	1	7	5	9	13	-0	17	10	21	17

Source: UNCTAD secretariat calculations, base on UN COMTRADE; United Nations Statistics Division, United Nations Common Database (UNCDB); United States Bureau of Labor Statistics, Import/Export Price database; Japan Customs Trade Statistics database; UNCTAD, *Commodity Price Bulletin*, various issues; and other national sources.
a   Average.

Historical Development of International Trade and Investment Theory

International trade and investment theory can be used to forecast levels and consequences of export and import activities within specific economic, geographic, and political circumstances. This, in turn, allows for the prediction and prescription concerning the content, direction, and size of international trade flows. The history of modern economic theory can be traced to the sixteenth century, emerging at approximately the same time as the modern nation-state. Early economic theory, though later debunked by Adam Smith and others, likely facilitated the drive for growth and expansion of nation-states worldwide for the next three-hundred years. The historical development of international trade and investment theory serves as a framework for understanding global trade patterns and the underlying reasons for the growth of trade between nations. The following sections of this chapter will trace the major international trade theories, from mercantilism to new trade theory.

Pre-Industrial Revolution—Mercantilism

Mercantilism was the prevailing thought, in terms of international trade theory, during the Pre-Industrial Revolution period. Although mercantilism does not meet the above criteria established for a trade theory, many consider it can be considered an economic policy whereby governments accumulate wealth in the form of gold bullion. The gold is then used in efforts to control the domestic economy, invest in other wealth-building enterprises, and expand into other global markets. Mercantilism was a typical idea during the era of nation building, which preceded the Industrial Revolution. Mercantilism allowed the development of the notion that the principal source of wealth was global trade, thus shifting European political power from feudal lords and the church to national sovereigns.

The trade-policy implication of this concept was the generation of a national trade surplus, paid for by accumulation of gold reserves. Before fully developed financial systems, international credit was scarce. Therefore, a current-account surplus was not matched by net capital outflow (net loans or investment overseas); rather, it was matched by a net inflow of gold to pay for the excess of goods exported from the country. Some of this gold found its way to overseas investment by the ruling monarch. Mercantilism, as a national economic policy, collapsed because nations cannot export without another nation's willingness to import.[6] The United States Declaration of Independence in 1776 listed the "cutting off our trade with all parts of the world" as one of the reasons for declaring a separation from Britain.[7] These actions of Great Britain's King George were no doubt a reflection of the then waning economies of mercantilism. It is no coincidence that the founders of the United States of America were clearly influenced by the new economic theories of the eighteenth century, specifically Adam Smith's Absolute Advantage.

Absolute Advantage Theory

A nation is said to have an absolute advantage when it is able to produce more output than any other nation. In order to achieve an economic advantage, a nation should specialize, produce, and export only those products where the nation holds an absolute advantage. Adam Smith first proposed the theory of advantage in his *An Inquiry into the Nature and Causes of the Wealth of Nations* (1776) by pointing out that an individual would not make anything that would cost him less to buy. A farmer would not spend a whole day sewing a pair of pants when he could buy a pair of pants from the tailor with only a half day's worth of corn (his farm output). Absolute Advantage Theory says that the farmer should specialize where he has an advantage—in this case corn—and the corn output will "buy" more of other goods, where the farmer does not have a production advantage:

> What is prudence in the conduct of every private family can scarce be folly in that of a great kingdom. If a foreign country can supply us with a commodity cheaper than we ourselves can make it, better buy it of them with some part of the produce of our own industry employed in a way in which we have some advantage. . . . According to the supposition, that commodity could be purchased from foreign countries cheaper than it can be made at home. It could, therefore, have been purchased with a part only of the commodities, or, what is the same thing, with a part only of the price of the commodities.[8]

Any domestic resource that a nation can buy at a lower price than it would cost to produce domestically should be purchased and not produced. Smith proposed that nations should specialize to increase overall output and productivity, and his theory altered economic thought sufficient to promote the concept that governments should allow free trade and efficient allocation of resources. This, in turn, would raise the general welfare and standard of living of trading nations.

Comparative Advantage Theory

Adam Smith's Theory of Absolute Advantage served to demonstrate the benefit of nations specializing in producing outputs where it had an absolute advantage over all other nations. However, the theory was too simplistic. Nations can benefit from trade even when one trading partner does not have an absolute advantage on any of the products being traded. Thus, there was a need for a somewhat more sophisticated international trade theory. David Ricardo developed this when he proposed the Theory of Comparative Advantage in his 1817 work *On the Principles of Political Economy and Taxation*.[9]

In an effort to demonstrate Ricardo's theory, one should consider the possibility of trade that exists between a lawyer and an automotive mechanic. Both the lawyer and the mechanic are capable of performing automotive repairs or writing a will. In fact, the lawyer once worked as a mechanic and was exceptionally efficient in that trade. From Table 4.3 below, suppose each task requires a different length of time to complete, and that the lawyer, because of his proficiency in the trade, has an absolute advantage over the auto mechanic in terms of hours (or units of time) required to complete each task.

Table 4.3

	Time Required	
	Repair Car	**Write a Will**
Lawyer	2	3
Mechanic	3	15

To know whether the lawyer should repair his own car, or in order for the mechanic to know if he should write his own will, each must consider the opportunity cost and the cost of the object. Opportunity cost is the value of what had to be given up, or foregone, to consume or achieve the object. Table 4.4 presents the opportunity cost for the lawyer and the mechanic.

Table 4.4

	Opportunity Cost To:	
	Fix Car	**Write a Will**
(@ $100 / Hr) Lawyer	$200	$300
(@ $30 / Hr) Mechanic	$90	$450

The lawyer has absolute advantage in fixing the car and writing a will in terms of hours (or units of time) and has opportunity costs of $200 and $300 respectively for these tasks. The mechanic has an opportunity cost of $90 and $450 respectively. If the lawyer chooses to repair his own car, he would not be able to earn money as a lawyer while repairing the car, and thus he would forego $200 (2 hours at $100) in lawyer revenue. This example represents the lawyer's opportunity cost to perform the repair. If the mechanic chooses to write his own will, he will forego $450 dollars in mechanic revenue (15 hours at $30 per hour) while writing the will.

The lawyer and mechanic easily make the best decision once they know their opportunity cost. Though the mechanic does not have an absolute advantage in either repairing the car or writing a will, he does have a relative advantage when fixing the car—in that his disadvantage is the least with this task. Both lawyer and mechanic would be better off working in their specialty and buying the services that they do not specialize in. To conclude, the mechanic saves $150 ($450 opportunity cost MINUS $300 lawyer fee) by paying the lawyer to write the will, and the lawyer saves $110 ($200 opportunity cost MINUS $90 mechanic fee) by paying the mechanic to fix the car.

The following is a direct application of Ricardo's Comparative Advantage theory to international trade. Ricardo provided the example of England and Portugal to clarify his theory. Specifically, both nations were compared in terms of the production of two commodities (cloth and wine), with labor being the only input of production. Ricardo assumed productivity of labor—defined as the quantity of output produced per worker—to be varied between industries and both nations. While Adam Smith's theory assumed that England would be more productive in producing one good and Portugal in producing the other, Ricardo's theory assumed that Portugal would be more productive in both goods.

Consider the following Tables to help explain David Ricardo's Theory of Comparative Advantage. Table 4.5 shows that Portugal can produce both wheat and wine more cheaply than England—it has an absolute advantage in both commodities. Ricardo noted that it could still be mutually beneficial for both countries to specialize and trade. A unit of wine in England costs the same amount to produce as 2 units of wheat. Production of an extra unit of wine means foregoing production of 2 units of wheat. In other words, the opportunity cost of a unit of wine is 2 units of wheat. In Portugal, a unit of wine costs 1.5 units of wheat to produce; therefore, the opportunity cost of a unit of wine is 1.5 units of wheat. Some might wonder why it would be mutually advantageous for both countries to trade, even though Portugal has an absolute advantage in both commodities. The answer lies in the difference between the relative or comparative costs for each nation would be improved if trading occurs.

Table 4.5

Cost per Unit in Man-Hours		
	Wheat	**Wine**
England	15	30
Portugal	10	15

Because Portugal is relatively better at producing wine than wheat, it has a comparative advantage in the production of wine. England is relatively better at producing wheat than wine, thus it has a comparative advantage in the production of wheat.

Table 4.6 provides the example of how trade may be advantageous, according to Ricardo's theory. This table makes the following assumptions:
- England has 270 man hours available for production. Before trade takes place, it produces and consumes 8 units of wheat and 5 units of wine.
- Portugal, having fewer labor resources, has 180 man hours of labor available for production. Before trade takes place, it produces and consumes 9 units of wheat and 6 units of wine. Total production between the two economies is 17 units of wheat and 11 units of wine.

If both countries specialize—Portugal producing only wine and England producing only wheat—total production is 18 units of wheat and 12 units of wine. Specialization has enabled the global economy to increase production by 1 unit of wheat and 1 unit of wine. In other words, the result of each nation specializing where they have a comparative advantage is a total gain in output from the same labor inputs. The standard of living in each nation would be improved if trading occurs.

Table 4.6

	Production Levels			
	Before Trading		After Trading	
	Wheat	**Wine**	**Wheat**	**Wine**
England	8	5	18	0
Portugal	9	6	0	12
Total	**17**	**11**	**18**	**12**

One should note that Ricardo's theory is very simple, based on the following assumptions:

- Transport costs are not considered.
- Costs are constant with no economies of scale.
- Only two nations are producing two goods.
- Traded goods are homogeneous – identical.
- No tariffs or other trade barriers are considered.
- Perfect knowledge exists – merchants and customers know where the least-cost goods are located.

Factor Proportions Theory

The presupposition of Absolute Advantage and Comparative Advantage is that differences in productivity determine patterns of international trade. This too was a simplistic view of trade; thus, the need for another, more sophisticated theory of trade arose. The sophistication lies in the idea that factor endowments, not differences in productivity, determine the patterns of trade. One of the first theories to address this issue was the Factor Proportions Model, developed by two Swedish economists, Eli Heckscher and his student, Bertil Ohlin in the 1920s. The monograph "Interregional and International Trade" was published in 1933.[10]

Where the earlier theory of Comparative Advantage considers differences in productivity, the Factor Proportions Model considers also the dimensions of capital—equipment and machines—and the proportion—mix of technology and capital—along with the intensity that the factors of production are used. Technology in this context is the application of specialized knowledge to work. Factors of production include the following:

- Land—natural resources used in the production process, including timber, minerals and water resources.

- Labor—physical and mental work (intelligence) brought to bear in the production of goods and services.

- Capital—machinery and equipment, including facilities, used to manufacture and deliver products.

The Factor Proportions Theory recognizes nations as having different amounts of capital and labor, called endowments, and the ratio of those labor to capital endowments. Nations endowed with abundant labor can produce agricultural products using labor-intensive methods, just as nations with abundant capital–using, capital-intensive methods can also abundantly produce agricultural products. Examples might include Canada, using capital-intensive agricultural methods, and India, using labor-intensive methods in the production of wheat. The Factor Proportions Theory, as a model of production, attempts to explain that nations will produce and export goods that use the highest proportion of those factors of production that are most abundant to a nation.[11] For example, Japan, as a nation with abundant capital, skilled labor, and little land, will be a heavy importer of raw materials and an exporter of capital-intensive products, which only a highly capable labor force could produce.

Comparative Advantage and Factor Proportions are the foundational concepts of the traditional or neoclassical theory of international trade. In simple terms, neoclassical theory seeks to determine how one should proceed in trade if the goal was to maximize world production (the goods and services available to citizens of each country). This theory assumes that the (1) factors of production are immobile, (2) goods are mobile, and (3) technology is stable and ubiquitous. World production and the goods and services available to each country are thus maximized by using resources for the production of goods that face the lowest opportunity cost within each nation, trading locally unneeded products for other goods produced with the lowest opportunity cost for resources in other nations. The neoclassical theories provided the important theoretical frameworks for understanding international trade up until the 1950s, which ushered in the so-called "Space Age." New developments in technology and transportation required the formation of new theories to understand and predict emerging global trade patterns. The emerging theories assisted marketers to move beyond the previously predominant emphasis on production in their efforts to create and sustain competitive advantage across global markets.

International Product Life Cycle Theory

Raymond Vernon developed and published the International Product Life Cycle Theory in 1966. Vernon's three-stage theory proposes that new products are first (stage one) invented and produced to satisfy a domestic, (local) high-income customer in a highly developed nation. Products are also manufactured with higher-cost, local labor. In stage two, a maturing product begins to saturate the domestic market, while exports are growing to meet demand in foreign markets of high-income customers. Production capacity is added in these foreign markets with both domestic and foreign production satisfying a local, high-income customer. In stage three, the product demand world wide has been steady enough that the producer, now facing low demand uncertainty and a need to maintain or increase profit, is able to make investment in specialized equipment, to take advantage of economies of scale, building what is now a standard product. An investment in specialized equipment allows the producer to now use cheaper low-skill labor, which is abundantly available in less developed nations. Production moves to a less developed nation, and the cycle is complete, as highly developed nations become importers of this product.[12]

New Trade Theory

New Trade Theory, introduced in 1979 by Paul Krugman, shifted economic thinking by proposing that certain industries should not be modeled using the perfect-competition assumption, frequently used in economic theory. Today, the World Trade Organization acknowledges this assumption, noting that where producers exist with high fixed costs, perfect competition will not be the result.[13] Krugman recognized that increasing returns to scale in certain industries would lead to a few firms engaging in competition, growing larger, and obtaining not constant, but increasing returns to scale. Nations that vigorously pursue the quick development of economies of scale in a given export may gain comparative advantage in that export. Such nations can produce the product more efficiently, relative to other products, than can their trading partners, but not necessarily due to factor endowments. Rather, it is due to the development of industry support, such as skilled labor, specialized infrastructure, networks of suppliers, and localized technology. In this case, governments play a major role in support of technology by crafting industry-specific measures, such as tax credits for research and development of new technologies and trade policies that support essential technology sectors.

The New Trade Theory Model demonstrated that in certain industries, government protections of an industry prove advantageous. The implications of New Trade Theory may suggest protecting the same "infant industries" of classical economics.

Michael Porter's, *The Competitive Advantage of Nations* (1990) proposed that the role of government is as an indirect determinant, equal with chance. Porter's Diamond has four determinants that indicate the level of competitiveness of a national industry—in addition to the two indirect determinants of Government and Chance. The relationship between the four determinants or Diamond (see Figure 4.1[14]) model a nation's competitive environment for an industry The determinants are (1) factor conditions, (2) demand conditions, (3) firm strategy, structure, and rivalry, and (4) related and supporting industry.[15]

Factor conditions are not to be confused with factors of production, such as land, labor, and raw materials. Factor conditions refer to specialized or value-added factors that are developed because they do not naturally occur. Examples might include industry–specific, highly skilled people or processes of production that are the result of continuing industry investment. Demand conditions that increase the competitiveness of an industry are the result of demanding domestic customers that push, pull, and prod for innovation to occur. Satisfying demanding customers requires high-quality, innovative products. Firms in such a domestic industry are better prepared to meet the demands of customers in the global market. Factor Conditions and Demand Conditions are the horizontal components on Porter's Diamond model.

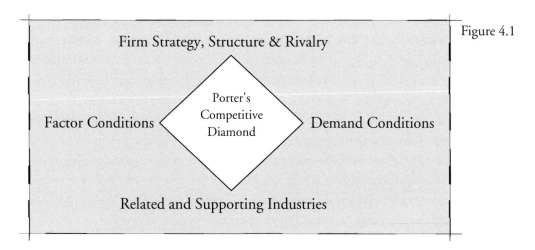

Figure 4.1

The interaction between the vertical components of rivalry and related and supporting industry drives a nation's national competitive advantage. The rivalry and related industry relationship stimulates a firm to achieve the capability necessary to take advantage of special factor conditions, which are available in order to meet the expectations of demanding customers. As this occurs within an industry and on a national level, industry "clusters" in a geographic concentration increase the interactions represented in the Porter's Diamond and expand and transform the diamond into an interrelated system. Porter's Diamond provides a systematic explanation and guide for developing national competitiveness.

Global trading systems evolved in a parallel manner to the theoretical frameworks. The astute global business professional understands this parallel development and seeks to apply the theoretical to the practical. The next few sections of this chapter will discuss these global trading systems and how they interact in terms of Foreign Direct Investment and Balance of Payments.

Modern Global Trading Systems

A global trading system should be without discrimination, freer, predictable, more competitive, and more beneficial for less developed countries. Trading systems, by definition, consist of multilateral agreements between several, and sometimes many, nations. Trade agreements are negotiated, legal documents pertaining to all manner of trade between nations. As a result, these documents are very complex. Trade agreements are the foundation for a common understanding of the rules governing trade. These agreements guide the trading conduct of nations that may not have similar legal foundations or business customs.[16]

A guiding principle of the ideal global trading system is equality between trading partners, when partners do not prefer domestic products, services, people, or the products of their trading partners over others. When trade operates under standard rules, it is more predictable, free, and competitive—positively impacting the economies of all participants. When the rules encourage lesser-developed nations to produce and trade, they also facilitate participation in the global economy, increasing their economic prosperity—which would not have been likely without a trading system. Synthesizing the dictionary definitions of the term "system" provides a working definition for the modern global trading system: an interdependent group acting as a unified whole, following shared principles, performing activities to achieve a common goal.[17] The common goal is to increase the global economy and raise the standard of living for all people.

General Agreement on Tariffs and Trade (GATT)

The historical development of GATT can be traced through the international trade theories, from mercantilism to new trade theory. Mercantilism posits a country could only gain at the expense of its rival, i.e., a country grew rich by the amount of gold that it amassed through the sale of domestic goods to foreigners and constraining the amount of foreign goods sold on the home market. Protection of the domestic market was the prime objective. Mercantilism gave way to the neoclassical theories of Adam Smith and David Ricardo. They argued that international trade could be a win-win proposition. This outcome was possible if each country specialized in producing and selling the goods that it could produce the most efficiently, relative to another country. The flow of goods also had to be free and unregulated among and between countries. While the era of free trade had begun, protection of domestic markets was still important to national economies. The dawn of the twentieth century ushered in modern wars—most notably the two World Wars. International trade was severely disrupted as nations sought to secure and protect domestic industries from the economic ravages of war. At the conclusion of World War II, the Allies recognized that nations might be able to prevent war if they were allowed to trade freely. Such free trade would require nations to adapt standards of free trade, which provide the legal foundations for global trade and the need for a general agreement among participating nations.

The General Agreement on Tariffs and Trade (GATT) was signed on January 1, 1948. Originally created by the Bretton Woods Conference as part of a larger plan for economic recovery after World War II, its primary purpose was to reduce barriers to international trade. Representatives from twenty-three nations accepted what would later be considered the precursor to the World Trade Organization (WTO). This first attempt at setting international trade rules covered forty-five thousand tariffs and 20 percent of the world trade.[18] The goal of this conference was to create a body called the International Trade Organization, which the United Nations was to organize. Not wanting to jeopardize the work that had already been accomplished in the new agreement, the signatory nations accepted the GATT draft provisionally. Even though this agreement was accepted as provisional, it existed as an international trade agreement until 1995. The Uruguay Round and the Marrakesh Declaration followed, leading to the creation of the World Trade Organization.[19]

World Trade Organization (WTO)

Though the World Trade Organization (WTO) has officially existed since 1995, the foundation for the rules in this trading system originates in the GATT. Like the GATT, the WTO deals with the rules of trade between nations at a global or near-global level. Where the primary focus of GATT was trade in goods, the WTO agreements include intellectual property and trade in services. The WTO provides a forum for negotiation between members, concerning the lowering or elimination of trade barriers, and freedom of trade. The WTO is not exclusively about lowering or reducing trade barriers, but "in some circumstances its rules support maintaining trade barriers—for example, to protect consumers or prevent the spread of disease."[20] The WTO encourages trading under the guiding principle of trading fairly by treating other nations equally, under the concept of most-favored-nations (MFN) status. This discourages excessive import duties that act as trade barriers, though exceptions can be made to favor developing nations. WTO rules emphasize and promote expanding and increasing trade between nations.

The WTO encourages nations to practice the Golden Rule on a national level, pointing out that foreigners and foreign industries should be treated just like the locals and domestic industries. The WTO refers to this as extending the "national treatment," and the application of any WTO rule assumes that developing nations will change and comply increasingly with time.[21] Rules in the WTO system serve to provide stability by guiding the conduct of agents operating in the system and by helping members in the system know what to expect as they follow the rules. Trading partners should not expect hidden trade policies, quotas, and other trade barriers, knowing that quotas and import duties are allowed in limited and controlled situations—and usually when a less-developed nation is involved.[22]

Foreign Direct Investment

As organizations become more involved in the global community, they may opt to purchase land or other resources in other nations. This activity, known as foreign direct investment (FDI), is commonly used to purchase real estate and existing properties. The idea is to buy physical assets or a significant amount of ownership of a firm in another nation to gain a measure of managerial control. While no standard percentage of ownership exists, most nations consider the threshold to be within the range of 10 to 25 percent. The U.S. Department of Commerce's FDI ownership threshold is 10 percent. In the event that the financial objective is not to gain a measure of managerial control, the investment is considered "portfolio investment." FDI typically takes two forms. The first, Greenfield Investment, involves the development of an entirely new operation in a foreign nation. The second entails acquiring or merging with an existing operation in a foreign nation. These forms of FDI allow the firm to achieve strategic goals, including (1) establishing a presence in a new geographic market, (2) creating and maintaining global competitiveness, (3) filling gaps in global product lines, and (4) reducing production and logistical costs.

Why Companies Engage in FDI

As companies become affluent, they begin looking globally for economic development potential. Additionally, they seek out foreign investment for a better value for their money, in terms of labor or material costs. The trend of foreign companies making foreign direct investments in the U.S. is increasing. An example would be Canada, who, attracted by U.S. technology firms, has sought to align itself with the creativity being generated in high-tech places, such as Silicon Valley. While FDI is a great enabler of international trade and competition fuels the U.S. economy, U.S. companies hesitate to join the increasing trend of FDI. The dramatic increase of foreign investment dollars in the United States has mixed results. Foreign dollars are good for U.S. companies looking to sell assets, because the price of these assets will likely rise. However, U.S. companies looking to expand their businesses may see an increase in prices because of the increased competition brought on by FDI.[23]

Foreign Direct Investment can also take place by injecting marketing dollars into the economy of a given country. Companies that are looking to gain brand awareness have turned to international sporting events as a means of self-promotion. Hyundai, the Korean auto-manufacturer, made a foreign direct investment in Athens, Greece, during the 2004 summer Olympic Games. Hyundai promoted its brand heavily by providing cars, buses, and signage at facilities.[24] Their focus, however, was not media coverage or the tourists attending the events, but the Grecian market itself. Hyundai is currently the second best-selling brand in Greece, and the sponsorship was designed to solidify their grip on the Grecian auto market. By investing their marketing capital in Athens during the Olympics, Hyundai not only promoted their brand to millions but also strengthened their position on the market.

Balance of Payments

Keeping track of the activity surrounding international trade and investment is done by maintaining a record of all international transactions, otherwise known as the balance of payments (BOP). The balance of payments is the sum of all monies that flow in and out of a given country; including imports, exports, goods, services, and financial investments. Usually calculated on a yearly basis, the balance of payments acts as a gauge to track the coming and going of international trade dollars. In a perfect world, the balance of payments accounting columns would cancel each other out. In theory, each dollar given in trade for goods or services goes to some source in the country providing the goods. In terms of recording the balance of payments, if a country has received money, it should be recorded as a credit. If Japan, for example, purchases wheat from the U.S., a credit is given to the U.S. balance of payments. Reciprocally, if the U.S. purchases Japanese cars, a debit is shown in the U.S. BOP.

Components

Similar to any accounting spreadsheet, the balance of payments is determined by measuring different factors to determine a result. The balance of payments for a country is the sum of the current account and the capital account. The current account is sometimes known as the financial account.

Current Account

The current account, sometimes called the financial account, is the sum of one country's net income from trade in goods and services. This includes what is known as net factor income, or interest payments from foreign debt, and also net unilateral transfers from abroad. Positive net income from abroad corresponds to a credit in the current account. Negative income from abroad corresponds to a debit in the current account. A current account surplus is usually associated with positive net exports, because a country's exports are usually the largest source of income they will receive from abroad.

Capital Account

The capital account is the net change in foreign ownership of domestic assets. These assets can include liquid, real estate, stock, or intellectual property. If foreign ownership increases faster than domestic ownership, then the country is said to have a capital account surplus. Conversely, if domestic ownership of foreign assets increases faster than foreign ownership of domestic assets, then the country has a capital account deficit.

The capital account entity records the purchase and sale of domestic and foreign assets. The assets are separated into categories, such as Foreign Direct Investment, Portfolio Investment, which includes stock and bond transactions, and Other Investment, which includes bank deposit and cash assets.

The Issue of Surpluses and Deficits

An inequity between the current account and the capital account will create a trade surplus or deficit, depending upon whether the inequity is positive or negative. For example, a trade surplus will be generated if a nation's exports outweigh its imports. In contrast, a trade deficit will be generated if the imports outweigh the exports. Surpluses and deficits will affect the current account holdings, which affect the overall balance of trade. Assume for a moment that the current account was much like a personal checking account. In order to purchase goods or services, funds must be available in the checking account before the transaction will be successful. If, however, funds are not available, the transaction can still occur, if the consumer is willing to borrow the capital needed. Essentially, a trade deficit is created in the same way. If a nation wished to import goods or services (in excess of what it is exporting), it does so by borrowing the capital necessary, which creates a trade deficit in the current account. If the nation that financed the transaction invests the money in the trading nation's economy, then the deficit will again disappear.[25] Assuming that the financing nation did not reinvest the money in the borrowing nation's economy, the financing nation now has a surplus in the current account. In mathematical terms,

$$\text{Exports} - \text{Imports} = \text{Savings} - \text{Investments}$$

The equation represents the relationship between trade deficits and surpluses. For example, if a country wanted to reduce its trade deficit, it would need to reduce the disparity between its savings and investments. Several factors can affect the international BOP and either create or reduce surpluses and deficits. A few of these factors are detailed below:

- Prices of domestic goods—typically the prices are affected by the raw materials required to produce the final products. A low supply in any one raw material required in the production of a particular commodity will cause an inevitable need to increase the cost of the final product.
- Trade agreements (or lack of trade agreements)—if a nation has an international trade agreement to purchase a particular commodity from another nation, this agreement will affect the ability for a third party nation to successfully compete in that market; furthermore, if a nation has established a trade barrier against a particular nation, the capacities for exports have been curtailed.
- Taxes and Tariffs—if a nation chooses to impose heavy taxes or import tariffs on goods from another nation, the furnishing nation will likely reduce exports into that nation.[26]

While these are just a few examples of factors that affect surpluses and deficits, one can see that nearly everything that affects the import or export of goods can generate lasting economic effects for a nation. The final sections of this chapter will discuss how governments and businesses deal with these issues relating to global trade.

Government and Global Management Issues in FDI

The relationship between government and multinational corporations can be mutually beneficial, promoting economic development and prosperity in the host country and business advantages for the multinational corporation. Successful FDI raises employment and the standard of living for nationals in the host county. From a business perspective, a successful FDI can secure access to customers in the host nation and increase sales or access to lower cost resources that will lower production costs of goods, which will be exported from the host nation. Successful FDI can be a win-win situation for governments and business.

Government Interventions

While governments do attempt to attract foreign direct investment with tax breaks, power subsidies, and reduced cost or no cost facilities, evidence shows that these incentives can be ineffective, bringing doubt about what most influences the location decision—incentives or adequate political stability and infrastructure.[27] After reviewing various FDI incentives, the WTO expressed the concern that it would be hard to make a case in support of investment incentives and that most of the world would be better off with limited use of them.[28] Though the result of intervention with incentives may be mixed, the government has a role concerning FDI. Government interventions, in the positive sense, can increase global competitiveness for their businesses, keep the balance of payments under control, and help acquire new technologies and managerial skills from foreign firms entering their markets. In a negative sense, government interventions may promote protectionism.

Increase Global Competitiveness

Government interventions may be used to increase global competitiveness. Nations have unique factors of production and unique proportions in the mix of technology and capital. The intensity of these national factors of production can be used to enhance cross-border trade. In other words, governments seek to specialize in specific industries that will use national endowments most abundantly and intensely. Because a nation offers unique and valuable factors of production to certain industries, the nation will be competitive in attracting those industries and increasing competitiveness of the region for future FDI. When national outputs are known by positive attributes in world markets—Japan for high quality cars, the U.S. for innovative software—the value of those outputs increases. The momentum of a positive national image and a strong industry image within the nation can "spillover" to other domestic industries, increasing their competitiveness in world markets and future FDI.[29]

Keep Balance of Payments under Control

Governments may intervene to keep the balance of payments under control. Prior to the mercantilism era, the balance of payments was not a major concern to nations. Commodities and currencies were allowed to flow without restriction. The primary concern for governments was tracking who controlled the gold. Since gold was the standard backing all currency, governments watched to ensure that potential threats did not control a large supply of the nation's gold, because a well-financed enemy posed a higher threat than one without proper financial backing. Hence, the term "war chest" was coined. If the "war chest" of a potential threat grew too large, then the government would be concerned. This idea gave way to mercantilism, one of the earliest economic theories, which sought to maintain a balance of payments of gold and silver in order to keep it out of the hands of the enemy.

Currently, the task of managing the balance of payments is primarily concerned with maintaining the surpluses and deficits owed to any nation for any commodity or currency that can be tracked. If a nation's surpluses far exceed its deficits, then the balance of payments is out of control, or more simply stated, out of balance. The same is true if the balance is reversed. Countries keep detailed accounts of the balance of payments and usually publish the findings at the end of each year. Nations should control the balance of payments so that deficits do not climb too high. This rise in deficits would indicate that a nation is merely paying (currency outflow) to other countries and not receiving investments in return (currency inflow).

Acquire New Technologies and Managerial Skills from Foreign Firms Entering their Markets.

Many countries today can benefit from the acquisition of new technologies and managerial skills from foreign firms. The acquisition of new technologies can be seen as a by-product of the international product life cycle. Although the international product life cycle theory does not describe acquiring new technology in this way, it remains a viable means for acquiring new technology. Most firms entering a foreign market try to send seasoned managers to the new market. These expatriates use their excellent management skills and know-how to train the managers and workers in the host countries.[30]

Technological change and economic development seem to go hand in hand in today's society. In an effort to stay competitive in the world market, nations have been pouring money into researching and developing new and advanced technologies. Nations can effectively tap into this resource for information by utilizing the management skills of foreigners operating in their country. In addition, nations can extract the new, existing technologies from foreign firms and capitalize on an already existing technology, saving millions of dollars in research and testing. This investment also allows domestic companies to remain globally competitive in the technological arena.

Protectionism—Restrictions in Ownership

Protectionism is the economic policy of restraining trade between nations. Methods to impose such restraints include high tariffs on imported goods, prohibitive quotas, restrictive government regulations on foreign imports and foreign ownership of domestic assets, and anti-dumping laws, which are meant to protect domestic industry from foreign take over or competition. Protectionism contrasts free trade, where such protective barriers are not used.

Nations use protectionism as a means of controlling foreign direct investment. For example China employs strict protectionism as a means of controlling foreign involvement in its economy. Censorship and restriction of certain business types are the norm in China. Recently the Chinese authorities have changed the rules on foreign investment in real estate. According to the *China Daily*, the new restrictions require that in order to own property in China, a foreign business must have offices in China or have officers who have lived or worked in China for at least one year. This example of protectionism is meant to slow the influx of western culture into China.[31]

In a historic sense, protectionism is the economic policy of applying tariffs on imported goods for government funding to reduce or eliminate the need for taxation on domestic industries. One can view this traditional protectionism as a type of sales tax on foreign goods in order to relieve the need for taxation on domestic products. Some critics of protectionism say that this economic shelter of domestic industry ultimately hurts the economy by discouraging competition and allowing the weaker products to remain on the market. Opponents of protectionism say that by increasing the cost of imported goods through tariffs, the government instituting the barrier penalizes the sending country as well as the citizens it is trying to protect. Like many other issues, economic ideas are often tied to political ideologies.

Business Managers

Issues for business managers may include degrees of ownership control, the need for "make or buy" decisions, consideration of labor and production costs, and seeking economic development incentives. Managers in large corporations may encounter international opportunities that require making a FDI decision. The United Nations Conference on Trade and Development defines FDI as investments outside the investor's home economy where the investor holds a 10 percent stake. The investment can be higher or lower, depending not necessarily on whether the investor has absolute control, but some level of influence over the foreign enterprise. The distinguishing characteristic between a portfolio of investments and a foreign direct investment is whether or not the investor's purpose in making the investment is to influence or control the target enterprise.[32] Business managers consider foreign direct investment in the effort to secure entry into nations with large markets for their goods and services. A business manager may also consider foreign investment to secure resources important to the production of domestic products, or in the case of services, access to knowledge and human resources.

Ownership Control

When considering FDI, the most important consideration facing a corporation is the type of ownership and control the investing corporation will have over the foreign entity. While in the case of alliances and joint ventures, the degree of ownership and control may be lower—significant potential benefits exist that may not be possible otherwise. These benefits include access to markets where the government restricts foreign ownership in certain industries, the lower risk associated with having a local partner to navigate the political environment, or by not being considered an "outsider" by the market or government.

Ownership in foreign entities can be a complete or a controlling stake in the form of either a wholly owned subsidiary or through mergers and acquisitions of existing corporations. Some nations use ownership control as a way of protecting their most valuable industries. Mexico, for example, relies heavily on the tourism industry. The hundreds of miles of pristine beaches are some of its greatest natural resources. The Mexican government restricts any foreigner from owning land within

100 kilometers of the border or 50 kilometers of the coast. These areas are known as Restricted or Prohibited Zones, which are designed to protect Mexican's rights to these valuable resources. The loophole that allows for the giant hotels that line popular destinations like Cancun or Acapulco to be owned by foreigners is a fiduciary trust, known as a *Fidelicomiso.* This is similar to a U.S. beneficiary trust. The owners can be foreigners, but they must own the property through a corporation that is formed in Mexico. This protects Mexico's tax interest in the property.[33]

Make or Buy Decisions

If the goal is complete ownership in a foreign entity, the next business decision is to "make or buy." In the case of buy, the investing corporation will seek an existing corporation in the target industry or market as a candidate for merger or acquisition. Frequently, the goal of having a wholly owned subsidiary leads management to make a Greenfield investment decision. Greenfield investments are investment in new assets. The Greenfield method is named literally from "green field," or what a grassy nonbuilt up area would look like, where a potential building could be built.[34] In some cases, a purchasable operation may not exist, so the only option is a Greenfield investment decision.

Labor and Production Costs

Labor and production costs are typically lower in less developed nations. These cost savings attract international corporations desiring to increase profits while maintaining competitive prices in the global market. This is frequently the case for corporations with products in stage three of the international product life cycle. At stage three, corporations are able to leverage economies of scale through investment in specialized equipment, which will facilitate production processes able to make use of cheaper, low-skill labor resources abundantly available in less developed nations.

Economic Development Incentives

The business manager must consider any and all economic development incentives in the FDI decision. When nations compete for FDI, the incentives can be significant. The WTO classifies investment incentives into three broad categories: equity capital, reinvested earnings, and other capital.

Equity capital is the value of the MNC's investment in shares of an enterprise in a foreign country. This category includes both mergers and acquisitions and "Greenfield" investments (the creation of new facilities). Mergers and acquisitions are an important source of FDI for developed countries, although the relative importance varies considerably. Reinvested earnings are the MNC's share of affiliate earnings not distributed as dividends or remitted to the MNC. Such retained profits by affiliates are assumed to be reinvested in the affiliate. This can represent up to 60 percent of outward FDI in countries such as the United States and the United Kingdom. Other capital refers to short or long-term borrowing and lending of funds between the MNC and the affiliate.[35]

There is an increasing global trend among nations to participate in the global economy, as governments see FDI as an important component to increasing economic prosperity and raising the standard of living for their citizens. This potential for prosperity is a nation's primary reason for offering significant incentives to attract FDI.

In addition to attracting FDI on the national level, the United States' FDI incentives are often offered on the state level to lure businesses and jobs to the local economy. Examples would be Hyundai's plan to build a plant in the United States and the response by Alabama, the state where one of the proposed sites would be located. In order to win the FDI from the Korean car manufacturer, the Alabama governor had to make a sales pitch of FDI incentives. If the offer was too low, then the business would go to another state; if it was too high, the FDI incentives would offset the benefit to the state. After much negotiation and much cost-benefit analysis, the Alabama executive agreed to "grant Hyundai a $252.8m incentive package including $76.7m in tax breaks, $61.8m in training grants and $34m in land purchase assistance."[36] The incentives were enough to win the business.

The global environment has increased competition. Today, every state, county, and city in the country has an economic development agency with funds available for incentive packages that will help their particular agency compete for business. The increased competition is particularly evident in the automobile sector. In 1978, for example, "the state of Pennsylvania gave Volkswagen incentives equivalent to $3550 per job created to set up a factory in the state. Two years later, in 1980, Tennessee paid Nissan $11,000 per employee. And in 1993, Alabama paid Mercedes Benz $150,000 per job created."[37]

Brief Summary of Major Points

In the competitive global environment, international trade and investments are tools that are used by nations to expand their horizons beyond their borders. Free trade is seen by many as the primary hope for lifting developing nations out of poverty and setting them on a footing that is equal to the rest of the developed world. Unfortunately, government corruption is rampant throughout these nations. Many times, aid sent to stimulate development of industries, primarily agricultural, goes to waste or is intercepted by local government officials. However, given time and proper training, local communities will be the key to bringing about change in their government and opening them up to the benefits of globalization. Like free trade, foreign investment is helping developed nations to increase their market competitiveness. Technological advancements in telecommunications has enabled FDI dollars to pour into places like India and the Philippines, providing much needed jobs for English speaking residents. Companies such as Dell have moved their call centers to India, finding that it is more cost effective to pay for the international phone call then pay high American wages. While it may sound like this type of FDI is taking jobs from American workers, Dell disagrees, saying that "for every $100 of call center work sent offshore by U.S. firms, $143 was invested back into the U.S. economy in the form of repatriated profits, increased sales, and cost savings."[38]

The debate about protectionism versus open trade between borders will continue to play out in the meetings of economic policy decision makers of the World Trade Organization and the G8. As the leaders prepare to guide their countries into the future, they will undoubtedly entwine their economies into one global force. The globalization that has taken place in recent history is undeniable and unstoppable. With technology leading the way, changes in the way the world does business are occurring and will continue to occur. To embrace these changes is to fully accept globalization and align oneself with the future. In summary,

- International trade and investment involves the trading of goods, services, or funding that crosses international borders.
- The expansion of international trade in the last half century has created a global economy as companies are driven by profit motive to increase sales and reduce costs. "International trade is a crucial precondition for growth" and economic prosperity in the world's developing countries. Access to natural resources in developing countries by foreign companies can potentially lift millions out of poverty. Free trade is the only proven path out of poverty for developing nations —when nations are shut off from the world, their people pay a steep price.

- The economic concept of mercantilism held that nations should export more than they import, and exports should be limited primarily to raw materials that are converted and exported as finished goods by domestic industry.

- Adam Smith is credited with establishing the economic theory of absolute advantage, first proposed in his 1776 work *An Inquiry into the Nature and Causes of the Wealth of Nations.* A nation has absolute advantage when it produces more of an output than any other nation; a nation should specialize in that product to achieve economic advantage, noting that a nation should buy goods and services that other nations can make at lower cost.

- David Ricardo developed the theory of comparative advantage in his 1817 work, *On the Principles of Political Economy and Taxation.* His writing demonstrated that absolute advantage is too simplistic, and that nations benefit from trade, even when one trading partner does not have an absolute advantage. Nations benefit by trading where they have a relative advantage, or, stated another way, where they have the least disadvantage.

- Bertil Ohlin published the factor proportions theory in 1933, also called the H-O (Hecksher-Ohlin) Model. This theory adds the dimensions of capital to economic theory—equipment and machines—the proportion of specialized knowledge and capital, and that nations have different endowments, capital and labor, and endowment ratios—showing that nations may produce the same outputs but use different endowment intensities.

- Raymond Vernon published the International Product Life Cycle Theory in 1966, showing that products are first invented and produced to satisfy a local customer, using higher-cost local labor, in a highly developed nation. Second, foreign markets are satisfied through exporting. Third, production capacity is added in these foreign markets. And fourth, a company will make investments in specialized equipment somewhere in the world-taking advantage of low-cost labor, usually in less-developed nations.

- Paul Krugman shifted economic thinking in 1979 with the idea of new trade theory. He recognized that increasing returns to scale led governments to further consider protections of industry, in the hope of eventually having within their borders one of the world's few producers within that industry.

- Michael Porter contributed to new trade theory in his 1990 work titled, *The Competitive Advantage of Nations.* He suggested four direct determinants to indicate the competitiveness of a national industry, along with two indirect determinants of Government and Chance. The model is known as Porter's Diamond and shows that industries will take advantage of special factor conditions and eventually form "clusters" in a geographic concentration, providing a systematic explanation and guide for developing national competitiveness.

- The World Trade Organization (WTO) provides a framework of rules for international trade—covering goods, services, and intellectual property—and provides a forum for negotiation between trading partners.

- Foreign Direct Investment (FDI) defines the amount invested in property, equipment, or services capability in a foreign country. Imperfect market theory explains situations where production is immobile and must remain fixed, not able to move and produce, where customers are plentiful because the mix of resources is unique. Eclectic theory, proposed by John Dunning, tied together the elements of location, ownership, and internationalization with the economic rationale for doing business in foreign markets. Market Power theory is the ability of a seller to set market price for any particular item. Any corporation seeking to make FDI must be sure it will be competitive and able to sell at a price that the company expects. Markets with superior products will find difficulty in recovering FDI.

- National balance of payments is a gauge to track the coming and going of international trade dollars. The ideal is that a nation's net income from trade in goods and services would be positive. A nation's capital account defines the net change in foreign ownership of domestic assets and foreign assets and records the purchase and sale of domestic and foreign assets. The assets are categorized as FDI, Portfolio Investment, and Other Investment. Governments do attempt to attract foreign direct investment and to specialize in specific industries, promoting industry that will use national endowments, most intensely, increasing a nation's competitiveness and the competitiveness of the region for FDI. As the region and nations outputs are known worldwide by positive attributes, the value of all outputs is increased. This increased value is also called "spillover."

- Business managers make FDI decisions to secure entry into nations with large markets for their goods and services. Ownership in foreign entities can be a complete or a controlling stake in the form of either a wholly owned subsidiary or through mergers and acquisitions with existing corporations. Where complete ownership is desired and there is no entity available to acquire, the manager must make a Greenfield investment decision—an investment in new assets. Lower labor and production costs in the less-developed nations are attractive to managers hoping to remain price competitive in the global markets. Managers will frequently leverage economies of scale through investment in specialized equipment near low-cost labor to achieve lower production and labor costs.

Moving from Theory into Practice

The following summarizes a question and answer session with coauthor Joe Robinson. His answers are useful in contemplating how the global business professional can translate the theories and concepts covered in this chapter via practical answers to the questions from real life experiences.

With more complications, difficulties and added paperwork involved in international commerce, why do people go global?

The short answer is, "That's where the money is." I once heard from a presenter at a US Department of Commerce seminar a few years ago that the world economy is twenty times larger that the US economy. I do not know where he got this figure or whether it is accurate; however, all agree that the world economy does offer opportunities for companies to expand their sales and increase profits.

Some companies seek overseas customers because of the added opportunities. Some companies seek overseas customers because they have to do so in order to survive. In this case, their domestic customers moved their factories and facilities to foreign countries, and in order to survive, it became necessary to follow their customers. This was the case in the early days of NAFTA when many US firms had to visit Mexico to continue doing business with their traditional customers, who moved entire factories into Mexico. Later this migratory trend went to China. Currently this migration is shifting to South East Asia and India and some countries in Latin America. This trend is a dynamic and will constantly evolve.

The best reason to engage in global business is to thrive rather than to survive. It is better to be proactive than to be reactive. Those who engage in global commerce in the pursuit of advancing their resources, sales, and profits will be the companies who will sustain their competitive edge and grow their business in a healthy and rewarding environment.

How can international commerce help developing countries?

There is as ripple effect when commerce takes place in a competitive and wholesome manner. When a company does well, its employees in turn spend money, and this contributes to the local economic well being of the countries financial environment. Money that is brought into an economy from outside has a greater propensity to spend that currency that merely circulates round and round solely within an economy. This effect is seen with the newly emerging markets.

Examples of successful emerging economies that have eagerly adopted foreign trade and good global business practices for their benefit include Thailand and

Malaysia. I know this because I currently provide export counseling to over a dozen small and medium firms that have joint ventures, technical sales liaison offices, or joint ventures in Thailand and Malaysia

Other countries that have not adopted or accepted global commerce and met international standards and practices that are not so well off include North Korea, Cuba and the Philippines. These countries are not up to standards in economic well being. The record speaks for itself in substantiating this phenomenon that international commerce is good for emerging countries.

Can you give a practical application of Michael Porter's *Competitive Diamond?*

Malaysia is a prime example of this theory that conditions, demand, strategy, and support can indeed provide a competitive edge for an industry, and consequently, for the nation. The case in point is the rubber tree industry in Malaysia. Traditionally the rubber tree plantations exported the rubber emulsion to developed countries to be produced into finished goods. Of particular value is the demand for medical protective gloves for doctors, nurses, and health care givers. The government of Malaysia collectively decided to support an entire industry from plantation management, to harvesting, to glove manufacture, to industrial research, to world-class, best, continuous improvement practices and procedures so that today most of the entire world's medical gloves are manufactured in and exported globally from Malaysia. To the benefit of Malaysia, the demand for these gloves greatly increased due to the need to prevent contamination and infection—from HIV, SARS, Avian Flu, and similar diseases. Fortunately for the medical industry, the gloves produced and exported from Malaysia are the strongest and provide the safest protection of any medical gloves manufactured anywhere.

The inflow of money from this competitive advantage situation is creating an economic well being and spreading to other industries and business activities in Malaysia, such that foreign companies are investing in Malaysia, and this in turn continues to produce an accumulative effect, and the cycle continues to move upward, as evidenced by the actual economic growth in Malaysia.

What is a good case example of foreign direct investment?

A good example of a foreign direct investment is one that results in higher sales and profits in the host country and also serves as an active secondary source of product for the investing company on a global basis. A real example is the case of a U.S. manufacturer of industrial valves that invested in a small factory in England to cover the U.K. and Europe, and they also invested in a factory in Japan for that market, as well as other parts of Asia. The beauty of this arrangement is that from time to time, due to difference in foreign exchange rates, it became more competitive for one of the "foreign" factories to sell the product than the product from the U.S. factory. Selling valves to the Middle East was and still is a big market for industrial valves. Say that at a given time the Japanese yen rate was more attractive in comparison to the U.S. dollar. In this case, the U.S. principal company would ask the Japanese factory to quote the project, and vice versa. The Japanese factory is actually a joint venture, and the U.K. factory is a wholly owned subsidiary in this case. The U.S.-Japanese JV is now in its thirty-seventh year of successful operation, and a good case study of all the things that are done right between two foreign partners.

How are a nation's balance of payments calculated and are they accurate and what does this mean for the global business professional?

Balance of Payments figures are inherently not completely accurate. Countries are not able to fully record exports with the same accuracy as imports. The result is there is some discrepancy between import and export figures between countries. However, over a period of time, the trends of the figures tend to be accurate, so the figures and charts do provide value to measure how one country is measuring up with other countries regarding importing-exporting balance of payments.

There is one exception to this and that is the case between the UDS and Canada. It is accepted that import figures are accurate, so the U.S. and Canada "exchange" import figures so that the result is the other knows their respective exports accurately between the U.S. and Canada.

Protectionism is considered a restraining policy imposed by a country. Can you give an example at the corporate level and how it negatively affected the company?

A few years ago, when I was the country manager for an American cosmetic firm in Japan, we needed to register our product name for brand recognition purposes. The particular product was our leading seller and recognized on a world wide basis. The product has been selling successfully since the 1920s. The Japanese Registration Office kept asking for more and more details—additional and sometimes unrelated information and comparison between the English and Japanese language. I went to my Japanese advisor to seek his wise counsel. He told me this was their way of delaying our entering the Japanese market until several Japanese cosmetic firms could "imitate" the product and then we would be "allowed" to enter the Japanese market. Fortunately the wise gentleman introduced me to the Japanese tradition of a private company approaching the government seeking *"administrative guidance,"* and this mater was quickly resolved to everyone's satisfaction Today, the product is indeed sold in Japan, in select retail outlets, rather than in mass retail stores, and there are several Japanese competitors, so that the ultimate impact is long term protectionism for the Japanese cosmetic firms.

<u>What country could you use as an example that government corruption prevents economic uplift of the country and actually reverts or keeps the nation in poverty by creating waste and limiting the competitive nature of the nation used as an example?</u>

I would think that the Philippines could be used as an example of corruption that prevented the economic uplift of a country. From 1960 through the 1970s, the Philippines appeared to be growing economically at a pace to become the leading, and perhaps most prosperous nation in South East Asia. Unfortunately, graft and political corruption became a way of life as a result of the Marcos government actions, such that corruption became rampart. The Philippines that could have become the economically shining star among the nations of Southeast Asia today is outpaced by both Thailand and Malaysia.

<u>Is lower labor costs the only reason for a company to make an FDI (foreign direct investment) in another country.</u>

The answer is "no." There are other ingredients than simply the cheap labor costs to be included in the formula needed for a company to make a successful and prosperous foreign direct investment. An example is an American company that bought a small factory in Mexico City to manufacture small machines for the purpose of supplying PEMEC, the petroleum conglomerate in Mexico. The initial "justification" for the investment was to be more competitive in price. After two years of operation, PEMEX started placing orders again on the U.S. factory instead of the Mexico City factory. The quality of the product from the Mexico City facility was not acceptable, so PEMEX decided to pay higher prices (this was before the NAFTA benefits) for the product and the higher freight and the import duty. When the production engineer visited the Mexico factory for a technical audit, he discovered that four out of ten shafts were rejected and not meeting standards, and this actually resulted in an overall increased cost that offset any savings in labor. Believe it or not, the ratio of rejects per labor costs was cheaper cost of goods from the U.S. factory than the Mexican factory at that time.

How can I get help from my state and local government to assist me in my export expansion program?

Most states have economic development offices with international divisions. In addition, there are local and regional economic developers that can assist your global efforts. These are decidedly directed towards exports rather than imports.

A great example of this is the State of Virginia. Their International Trade Division of the Virginia Economic Development Partnership offers resources, programs, and services that assist firms in their export endeavors, from the very smallest to multi national corporations. The VEDP received national recognition as the leading public-private partnership several years ago and continues to be the leading, and perhaps most innovative, state program in the nation as far as assisting their companies in the global market place. For details and an understanding of what they offer, visit www.ExportVirginia.org.

We are a very small company but have a good successful product in the U.S. How can I get help from government sources to help us get started in exporting?

Contact your local economic developer such as the SBA (Small Business Administration) or SBDC (Small Business Development Center) to be sure your basis business plan is financially sound. Then get the full commitment and support of your top management. Then contact your state international trade division and the US Department of Commerce for determining steps to take to be successful in your beginning exports. Be sure that your POA (Plan of Action) is based on proven techniques and best practices. Do not try to take on too many countries at once. Focus on only one country in the beginning, and then broaden your horizon as you become successful—one-by-one. Canada is as good a place to start. Then perhaps you could add Mexico. Local trade clubs are an excellent source of information and "how to" techniques in the larger metropolitan areas that you should get in touch with to aid your export endeavors. You may well be surprised at the amount and quality of assistance you can obtain by making the right contacts with your local, state, and federal government organizations.

Key Concepts

- The benefits of international trade   116
- International trade patterns   118
- Mercantilism   120
- Absolute advantage theory   120
- Comparative advantage theory   121
- Factor proportions theory   124
- International product life cycle theory   126
- New trade theory   126
- General Agreement on Tariffs and Trade (GATT)   129
- World Trade Organization (WTO)   129
- Foreign direct investments   130
    - Balance of payments   131
    - Current account   132
    - Capital account   134
- Government and global management issues in FDI   134
    - Government interventions   134
    - Business management issues   137
    - Economic development incentives   138

Global Business in Practice
World Federation of Exchanges

The World Federation of Exchanges is the trade organization for regulated securities and derivative markets, settlement institutions and related clearing houses, and their diverse services to capital markets. Membership of the World Federation of Exchanges identifies an exchange as having assumed the commitment to prescribed business standards, recognized as such by members, owners, and users of exchanges, as well as by regulators and supervisory bodies. According to its website:

As was true of other multilateral financial organizations, the need for international co-operation amongst stock exchanges was first felt in the 1930s. The International Chamber of Commerce, based in Paris, took the initiative to create an International Bureau of Stock Exchanges which existed until World War II.

After the war, it was not until 1957 that the first major steps towards international co-operation between stock exchanges took place, and in May of that year representatives of several European bourses met in Paris. Four years of informal co-operation followed, after which the participants chose to institutionalise this work in the form of a federation, and this was done in London in 1961. Since that time, the FIBV (Federation Internationale des Bourses de Valeurs) has grown constantly. Over time, the businesses run by members came to include derivative markets, clearing houses, settlement agencies and other financial services. For this reason, the General Assembly voted in 2001 to change the name to the World Federation of Exchanges.

Today membership encompasses 55 exchanges from all over the world. Members together account for over 97 % of world stock market capitalisation, and most of its exchange-traded futures, options, listed investment funds, and bonds. The combined market capitalization of the markets these exchanges operate is around $35,000 billion. There are a further 24 affiliates, and 32 bourses which are correspondents.

The Federation regularly holds committee meetings, general assemblies, and conferences. In recent years, it has organised committee meetings and specialised workshops for its members to transfer know-how and to share expertise.

As the global exchange industry trade organisation, the Federation has examined virtually every aspect of the securities business, be it technical, commercial, legal or economic. Over the past four decades studies have been published on such issues as self-regulation, enforcement, trading halts, securities business conduct, and other issues. [*]

The Ten Largest Stock Exchanges by Market Capitalization are:

1. NYSE Euronext
2. Tokyo Stock Exchange
3. NASDAQ
4. London Stock Exchange
5. Hong Kong Stock Exchange
6. Toronto Stock Exchange
7. Frankfurt Stock Exchange (Deutsche Börse)
8. Shanghai Stock Exchange
9. Madrid Stock Exchange
10. Australian Securities Exchange [†]

[*] World Federation of Exchanges (2007). Retrieved August 25, 2007 from http://www.world-exchanges. org/WFE/home. asp?action=organization
[†] World Federation of Exchanges (June 2007). Retrieved on August 25, 2007 from http://www.world-exchanges.org/publications/ EQU1107.pdf

Introduction

Global financial markets promote the exchange of goods and services across national borders. The price of goods and services exchanged is based on the supply and demand in the global markets. In addition to numerous industrial products exchanged within the global financial market, various types of commodities and resources are bought and sold, including food, shares of stock, national currencies, gold, and even labor services. Buyers and sellers negotiate the quality and quantity of a particular product, what buyers are willing and able to pay for the product, and the commissions paid for conducting the transactions.[1]

Global Financial Markets include both physical and virtual market places that make the cross-border exchange of goods and services between buyers and sellers possible. This exchange is accomplished by using a monetary unit of account to pay for various transactions. In most cases, these transactions are executed via the foreign exchange market—a global market in which people trade one currency for another. Major financial markets are located in cities throughout the world. The most prominent are located in New York City, Tokyo, and London.

The Importance of Global Financial Markets

The economies of the world have become highly interdependent because of improvements in communication and transportation technologies and the lowering of barriers to trade. This increase in the marketing of goods and services has contributed to standard of living improvements across national economies, most notably in developing nations. Specific goods produced in one nation are offered for sale in the world market and compete against products produced in other nations. This competition allows buyers and sellers to juxtapose quality and prices in their respective currency to other national currencies.[2] The end result of the global competition is higher quality products and lower prices for consumers. Mechanisms, such as the foreign exchange market, facilitate global financial market activities. Global financial markets involve both borrowers and lenders, which are important to both.

Importance to Borrowers

Global financial markets are important to borrowers for two reasons: (1) to expand the supply of money, and (2) reduce the cost of money. The supply and cost of money has a powerful effect on economic activities. Borrowers use the lending options of financial institutions to make major purchases of goods, property, and business ventures. The increased capital that borrowers acquire from financial institutions supplements disposable income, which encourages increased spending. Businesses react to increased spending by ordering more raw materials to increase the production of goods. This stimulation of business activity increases the demand for labor and raises the demand for capital goods.[3]

The quantity of money in a nation can affect the price of goods and services and employment. In the United States, the Federal Reserve Bank is responsible for regulating the growth of the economy, which is accomplished by the increase or decrease of money supply.[4] Other nations and economic unions have similar institutions: the Bank of England, the Bank of Japan, and the European Central Bank.

The overspending of money by borrowers (both consumer and industrial) helps perpetuate the expansion of the money supply. The public begins to experience the effects of inflation with an expanding money supply. Inflation essentially decreases a consumer's purchasing power, making goods and services more expensive, leading to wage-price spirals because too much money is circulating. Consumers attempt to offset inflation by exchanging the lower-value currency for something that is perceived to hold a value better, such as property, gold, or foreign currencies.

Importance to Lenders

Global financial markets are important to lenders for two major reasons: (1) expanding lending opportunities and (2) reducing risk. Financial institutions (commercial banks, credit unions, life insurance companies, and investment companies) are, simply put, in the business of making money. These institutions make money by accepting customers' deposits and using these funds for purchasing investments, such as government securities, or offering loans to businesses and individuals for business start-ups and real estate purchases. Earnings from the interest and fees charged to business and individuals on loans, in addition to purchased government securities, enable a financial institution to pay interest on depositors' accounts for the use of their funds. Conversely, this permits a financial institution to expand their activities and services to make more money.[5]

Expand lending opportunities. Lenders expand lending opportunities by offering borrowers different lending options. Typical options include the following:

- Variable Interest Rate Loans—the borrower and lender share the interest rate risks. Initially the lender offers a lower interest rate with the premise of rising along with the prime interest rate over the term of the loan.
- Secured Loan—interest rates on loans secured by some type of collateral property or savings account shares.

- Short-Term Loan—traditionally, short-term loans bear lower interest rates by comparison to long-term loans.
- Up-Front Cash.[6]

Reducing risk. Minimizing economic risk is a major consideration and task across global financial markets. In ideal functioning markets, speculation and insurance assist in the reduction of unavoidable risks associated with uncertainties, such as unemployment, catastrophic losses, and diminished business revenue. Speculators buy and sell commodities with the intention of making profits on price differentials across global markets. They are in the business of moving goods across regions where the price is low to markets where the price is high. Investors often will buy insurance to reduce the potentially disastrous declines in utility from natural disasters, death, and the like. Insurance helps spread large risks, to the extent that they become acceptable to a greater number of investors.[7]

 Foreign Exchange Market

Overview

The Foreign Exchange Market is a physical and virtual institutionalized structure through which the currency of one country is exchanged for the currency of another country. It is a market place where the exchange rate is determined and where transactions take place. The progress of trading relations between nations has enabled international trade to evolve into a multifaceted operation the conversion of one currency to another. International trade has evolved into the development of a market through which any currency can be traded or exchanged. After the Gold Standard was discontinued in 1971, the Foreign Exchange (FX) Market followed the rule of supply and demand, and currencies started to flow freely between sellers and buyers in currency markets.

The FX Market has gradually evolved into the largest, fastest, and most flexible currency trading market in the world. Operations continue around the clock every day with minimal breaks for weekends. The average daily amount of transactions on the FX Market exceeds $2.4 trillion.[8] The largest trading centers of the FX are located in Tokyo, London, and New York. Integration of modern technology and globalization of financial markets provides real-time information and real-time trading, which enables traders, investors, banks, multinational corporations, and governments to participate in FX daily trading operations from all over the world. Traders actively use modern technology to their advantage and to the advantage of their clients. Actual currencies do not change hands on FX

Markets; rather, all transactions are completed electronically and by phone. The FX Market is best described as an over-the-counter (OTC) market place, meaning negotiations include the amount, date, and price of the transaction.

Since the world thrives to trade and does not have a uniformed international currency, the exchange rate from one currency to another is determined by supply and demand on a given day on the FX Market. The main principle of trading on FX Markets is to select a pair of currencies and measure profit or loss by the fluctuation of one currency's market activity compared to the other. The most popular currencies traded in Foreign Exchange Markets, with a minimum transaction amount of $1 million, include the US Dollar (88.7 percent), the Euro (37.2 percent), the Japanese Yen (20.3 percent), and the British Pound Sterling (16.9 percent).[9] Although the majority of participants in the FX Market are banks, central banks, multinational corporations, and governments, the market is still open to individual investors through investment companies and multiple hedge funds.[10]

Functions

The FX Market serves many functions. These functions enable investors, banks and governments to facilitate and conduct international trade. The functions allow (1) hedging of currency for protection from unexpected fluctuations in exchange rates, (2) exchanging of currency and international investments, and (3) stabilization of weak currencies by purchasing more stable or "strong" currencies. Additionally, FX investment opportunities permit transactions to acquire profit by speculating the movements of exchange rates between different currencies. The major functions include conversion, hedging, arbitrage, and speculation.

Conversion. Many currencies can easily be exchanged for other currencies, which are referred to as convertible currencies. If a currency is converted, regardless of the circumstance to another currency, this currency is unrestricted. However, many nations restrict convertibility of their currencies due to their national and international policies and interests. A nation with a large and stable economy is able to trade freely and possess hard or reserve currency, in addition to nonrestricted currency. By comparison, smaller nations with weaker currencies, which have limitations and restrictions on their currencies, possess weak currencies. Large banks that are trading on FX usually use reserve currencies as a part of their transactions, or they refer to reserve currencies when quoting the exchange rates. Conversion rates are spot rates (or the day's rate offered by a dealer or a bank) and are quoted in pairs against another. FX vendors often quote the values of currencies against the value of the U.S. Dollar.

Hedging. Hedging is described as measures taken by a company or corporation to protect itself from the loss that may occur because of fluctuations in the exchange rate of currency. International corporations that operate globally conduct the majority of hedging in global markets. An example would be a major U.S. automotive firm that manufactures vehicles in Europe. The firm desires to protect its yearly gross earnings in Euros by entering into a hedging transaction. This transaction is accomplished by forecasting auto sales and approximating the gross amount of Eurocurrency that will be accumulated on a quarterly basis. The U.S. firm can enter into a hedging contract, where four times a year it will exchange earned Euros to U.S. Dollars, using a set exchange rate. Since hedging allows locking of future exchange rate fluctuations of Euros during the fiscal year, the U.S. firm's profits are unaffected. While hedging may protect against loss, it may eliminate a potential for unexpected gain.

Arbitrage. Arbitrage generally means buying a commodity when its price is low and then reselling it after prices rise in order to make a profit. Currency arbitrage, on the other hand, means buying a currency in one market at a low price and reselling moments later in another market at a higher price. However, because of the liquidity of the FX market and the number of transactions that occur each second, making a profit from arbitrage has become almost impossible.

Speculation. Speculation on the Foreign Exchange Market is a gamble. Traders who speculate are taking risks (staying open) because they buy and sell currencies based on the predicted rise and fall in price of a given currency. For instance, if investors expect a rise in the price of the U.S. Dollar (USD), traders go long (meaning purchase the rising currency). However, if predictions indicate a fall of the USD, speculators go short by selling the falling currency. As in arbitrage, only few opportunities exist to make a large profit, though the potential still exists.

Currency Quotations and Terminology

The USD remains the world's leading currency. The majority of transactions on the FX include operations with U.S. Dollars, where one party sells or buys dollars using other world currencies. Therefore, prices are quoted as "Currency A is worth X units of Currency B" or "Currency 1 in units of Currency 2."

Reuters is the largest informational platform that international traders use to communicate FX exchange rates. The Reuters codes for currencies are three-letter abbreviation codes. For instance, the value of one dollar in units of Japanese Yen would appear as "USD-JPY." This value may also be expressed as a fraction and will appear as JPY/USD, which causes confusion for some inexperienced traders. Professionals immediately recognize that the "U.S. Dollar is being quoted in Japanese Yen." Quotations may be delivered as being direct or indirect. Rates may be stated as spot, forward, or cross. Fluctuations may be calculated using percent change calculations. Finally, contracts may be written as swaps, options, and futures contracts.

Direct vs. indirect quotation. Direct and Indirect quotation is also known as American quote and European Quote. Direct (American) quotation is the exchange rate of a foreign currency in domestic currency units. Only the USD and British Sterling are quoted by one unit price; all other currencies are quoted in one hundred units. Indirect quotation (European) is exactly the opposite and expresses the value of domestic currency in foreign currency and is not as common as direct quotations. Most currencies are quoted in relation to the US dollar.

Spot, forward, and cross rates. Spot rates indicate the exchange rate of one currency in units of another currency immediately and "on the spot." Spot FX trades settle two business days after the trade date, with the exception of the Canadian Dollar, which is settled the next day. A large percentage of all FX market transactions are spot transactions. The following table contains data that is typical of what is provided by major trading vendors, such as Reuters. Two rates are depicted per each currency: buying price and selling price. The buying price is referred to as a "bid" rate, and the selling price as an "ask" rate.

Real Time Spot Rates from July 31, 2006				Table 5.1
Currency	Bid	Offer	Time	
EUR/USD	1.27705	1.2772	Mon Jul 31 16:04:53 2006	
USD/JPY	114.624	114.644	Mon Jul 31 16:04:45 2006	
GBP/USD	1.86802	1.86829	Mon Jul 31 16:05:00 2006	
USD/CAD	1.131	1.1314	Mon Jul 31 16:04:59 2006	
USD/CHF	1.2306	1.2309	Mon Jul 31 16:05:00 2006	
EUR/JPY	146.402	146.425	Mon Jul 31 16:04:53 2006	
EUR/GBP	0.6835	0.6837	Mon Jul 31 16:04:53 2006	
EUR/CHF	1.5719	1.5721	Mon Jul 31 16:05:00 2006	
GBP/CHF	2.29894	2.29959	Mon Jul 31 16:05:00 2006	
GBP/JPY	214.135	214.2	Mon Jul 31 16:05:00 2006	

Source: Spot rates http://www.oanda.com/

The forward exchange rate represents the rate at which a currency can be purchased in the future. Forward exchange rate dates when delivery (settlement) occurs, usually 30, 90, or 180 days from the date of the trade. Forward rates are calculated using a formula that influences the time in which settlement will take place and market expectations of fluctuations in the price of a particular currency. Forward rates are typically cheaper than spot rates. The difference between a spot rate and a forward rate is termed a *forward discount*. If a currency price is expected to rise in the future, a buyer pays a higher price, which is considered a *forward premium*. Forward rates are not quoted directly; rather, discount or premium is quoted and expressed in decimals. Forward transactions are used in hedging to protect profits of companies operating internationally.

Cross rates have to be calculated when parties are conducting a trade in currencies other than USD. For example, when customers trade EUR (Euro) against JPY (Yen), a cross rate is established based on the middle rates between EUR and USD and JPY and USD. An example of percent change calculations of cross rate using the middle rates for JPY against EUR is represented in the spot rate table presented in Table 5.1:

JPY = EUR 1, if EUR 1= USD 1.27705 and USD 1=JPY 114.624

Answer: EUR 1= 1.27705 x 114.624=JPY 146.38.

Currency swaps. There are several types of swaps; the most popular is the FX swap. An FX swap is the simultaneous purchase and sale of a currency for different delivery dates. The FX swap of currency amounts is normally fixed. The time between swaps may vary. Swaps with a far date less than a month from a near date are called short-dates swap, and swaps with far dates longer than a month are called forward swap. FX swaps are popular for several reasons. Investors use this type of swap as "an alternative to borrowing and lending in the Eurodollar and other offshore markets."[11] Another reason for FX swap popularity is the opportunity for the temporary shift of one currency into another, simultaneously avoiding the risk of exposure to daily fluctuation in exchange rates.

Futures markets. Of the futures markets that trade currencies, the most common is IMM on the Chicago Mercantile Exchange. The futures market allows smaller traders to participate in a trade. According to Swiss UBS Investment Bank, "Futures positions require a margin deposit to be posted and maintained daily. If a loss is taken on a contract, the amount is debited from the margin account after the close of trading. All contract specifications such as expiration time, face amount, and margins are determined by the exchange via the individual trading parties. Finally, the standard expiration dates for futures are each third Wednesday of March, June, September, and December."[12] The major difference between the currency futures market and the OTC market is futures settle gains and losses on a daily basis through the margin mechanism.

The global business professional is aware that the relationships that exist between currencies are volatile in terms of actual buying power of each currency in each nation. Buying power is an important principle in terms of currency trading and is related to the differences in standards of living across nations. Exchange rate theories can be used to understand these differences.

Purchasing Power Parity (PPP)

PPP is a widely accepted and cited exchange rate theory, which states that the difference in currency values between countries is related through Purchasing Power Parity (PPP). According to the theory of one price, similar goods or products in different countries should have a similar process after the conversion of currencies into the same one. If the currency of one country has more purchasing power than the currency of another country, the level of imports and exports is expected to change. Therefore, demand and supply for currency will be affected. For example, if a box of apples is cheaper in country X than in country Y, then market forces will start to buy apples in county X for use in country Y, where apples will be sold for monetary profit. This situation will call for demand of the currency of country X in order to purchase the apples and import them to country Y. PPP has an impact on exchange rates and indicates the current level of inflation of one currency against another. According to this theory, all the above factors impact exchange rates until relative purchasing powers of all currencies in the world are the same. The theory of PPP has few limitations because of the factors that directly involve the international trade; those factors include costs of transportation, government price controls, customs and tariffs costs, social perception of commodities, as well as cultural differences that will impact demand for products.

Law of one price. The "law of one price" provides the basis for PPP. In the absence of transportation and other transaction costs, competitive markets will equalize the price of an identical good in two countries when the prices are expressed in the same currency. Thus, the law of one price states that similar goods or commodities in different countries should remain at the same price after conversion of currencies according to current exchange rates. Sophisticated versions of PPP compare a large number of goods and services across nations.

However, a problem arises in that people in different countries consume very different kinds of goods and services, making it difficult to compare the purchasing power between countries. A simpler way to calculate purchasing power parity between two countries is to compare the price of a "standard" good that is in fact identical across countries, such as a hamburger.

The "Golden Arches Standard." In 1986 the British Magazine, The Economist, introduced the "Big Mac Index," which correlates the cost of a Big Mac in different countries, based on the theory of purchasing power parity and the conversion of prices using actual, current, up-to-date exchange rates. MacDonald's has opened its restaurants in more than 120 countries around the globe and uses the same ingredients in each country to produce the famous Big Mac hamburger sandwich. The Economist took the price of the Big Mac as a unit of measurement of PPP of each currency in each country a Big Mac is sold. The index displays undervaluation or overvaluation of one currency against another, regarding the price of the same Big Mac hamburger.

Table 5.2

The Economist's Big Mac Index 2005	Big Mac Price	Implied PPP of the	Under (-)/ Over (+)
	In Dollars	Dollar	Valuation against the Dollar, %
United States	3.06	-	-
Iceland	6.67	143	118
Norway	6.06	12.7	98
Switzerland	5.05	2.06	65
Denmark	4.58	9.07	50
South Africa	2.1	4.56	-31
Egypt	1.55	2.94	-49
Russia	1.48	13.7	-52
Ukraine	1.43	2.37	-53
China	1.27	3.43	-59
Qatar	0.68	0.81	-78

According to The Economist, "the cheapest burger in our [table] is in China, where it costs $1.30, compared with an average American price of $3.15. This implies that the Yuan is 59% undervalued. The index was never intended to be a precise predictor of currency movements, simply a take-away guide to whether currencies are at their "correct," long-run level. Burgernomics has an impressive record in predicting exchange rates: currencies that show up as overvalued often tend to weaken in later years, yet you must always remember the Big Mac's limitations. Burgers cannot sensibly be traded across borders, and prices are distorted by differences in taxes and the cost of nontradable inputs, such as rents."[13]

The Foreign Exchange Market is a physical and virtual institutionalized structure whereby currency of one country is exchanged to currency of another country. It is a market place where the exchange rate is determined and where transactions take place, enabling investors, banks and governments to facilitate and conduct international trade. However, the FX markets do not operate autonomous of governments. Governments have created institutions to regulate and control monetary policies.

Institutions

Central Banks and Governments are primarily the guardians of national currencies and are usually responsible for setting monetary policy and exchange rate policy. In many countries, including the U.S., the finance ministry (Treasury) sets exchange rate policy. Central banks may directly intervene in the currency market by buying or selling currency. When governments become involved in currency markets, they can either use their central bank or directly use market institutions. Government direct involvement in the FX market can be explained by an economic need, such as the establishment of hedges on foreign funding, debt conversions, and defense contracts.

Commercial banks and investment banks are generally the market makers on the foreign exchange. Traditionally, commercial banks served corporations who needed access to currency markets to conduct their international business. Commercial currency transactions cover imports, exports, remittances, and transfers.

Corporations use the FX market predominantly to facilitate their international business activities. Hedging currency exposure from the day-to-day business is known as exposure management, while hedging against balance sheet items, such as manufacturing plants abroad, is known as managing translation exposure. Coincidentally, some corporations trade currencies for profit, besides trading them for hedging purposes.

Professional money managers work on diversifying the portfolios of their clients by treating currencies as a separate asset class. Many times money managers play active roles on the FX market by establishing hedges for clients' money and lifting currency hedges—when it is deemed appropriate. International investors also depend on the FX market by purchasing foreign currency needed for investments abroad. It is not uncommon for these investments to be hedged back into the home currency of the investor.

Brokers usually facilitate a connection between two anonymous parties that are willing to trade. Successful brokers know the main sellers with the best prices of desirable currency. A broker receives the call with the request for an amount of a currency, dials the seller, negotiates the price, and only after agreement on the broker's commission, connects the seller and a buyer over the phone. However, with the proliferation of Internet trade and the Electronic Broking System (EBS), many brokers are being forced out of the FX business.

Interbank markets. The term Interbank (trade between two banks) is often used in FX terminology regarding wholesale conditions of pricing between major financial institutions, as well as to the circle of the largest banks that participate in FX trade under wholesale conditions. Banks are major market enablers on the Foreign Exchange Market—so major, in fact, that the amount of currencies being moved in just one transaction may well exceed several billion units of a currency. The pricing of such transactions is usually different from smaller transactions and is priced at wholesale. The largest players on the interbank market are Citibank, UBS Warburg, Chase Manhattan, and Deutsche Bank.[14]

Securities exchanges. Equities and securities are traded on securities exchanges. In this sense, securities refer to futures, options, stocks, bonds, treasury bills etc. When a company releases its stock for sale, owners of purchased stocks are able to make a profit from reselling stocks they hold on a security exchange market. The value of a company's stock may rise or fall in accordance with its performance, creating opportunity for acquiring profits. The two most popular products traded on security exchange markets are stocks and futures. Hence, a security exchange market is a physical market place where securities are traded for speculative monetary profit. A securities exchange is one of the safest and most popular places where companies raise money for their operations.

Stocks represent shares of equity that a company releases for sale. Anyone who has a stock of a company is considered its shareholder or part owner. If a party owns a significant amount of stock in a company, it has a powerful input in decisions regarding the present and future of the organization. The company's value on the market is determined by the amount of stock that is traded.

Bonds are an alternative way for an enterprise to raise money. A bond is a certificate with a certain monetary value. By purchasing a bond, an investor practically loans money to the company issuing the bond. A company must have enough equity or assets to guarantee the value of all bonds issued. On a corporate balance sheet, bonds appear in a column under liabilities. Bonds are classified as fixed rate bonds and floating rate bonds. Companies must pay their bond holders a return that was promised on the bond to a purchaser. Both companies and governments issue bonds. If a company needs to expand its operations and does not have enough capital for the expansion, instead of obtaining a substantial amount of credit or a loan from the bank, it issues bonds and sells them through investment banks. The yearly interest on bonds is paid monthly or quarterly; however, instead of one bank receiving the money, it is paid to the individuals or parties holding the bonds of a company.

The two most popular products that are traded on security exchange floors are stocks and futures. Futures, like currencies on the FX market, represent contracts for future delivery of a commodity. An example would be a company that produces oil-trades futures for delivery in 20, 90, and 180 days for 1000 barrels of oil. The oil producing company guarantees that the purchaser of this future will receive delivery of this product on the due date of the future. A bank, investor, or corporation may acquire this future, keeping in mind that the price of oil is on the rise and opportunity for speculative profit exists. In this case, a trader for an investment bank will purchase the oil future and then resell the future before the actual delivery date comes. The majority of futures traded on security exchange markets are traded for speculative profits.

Activities on the floor of the exchange also include speculative trading of securities. Investors purchase the securities of an organization and hope that the price of the security rises, so they can sell it for a profit. Some of the terms used in speculative trading include "bulls" and "bears." When securities turn "bulls," their values are on the rise, and when they turn "bears," their values are dropping. Stockbrokers are responsible for managing and trading securities in the securities exchanges. Investors utilize several devices to monitor the activity of their investments and performance. One of these devices is the Trade Alert, which notifies the investor of the price movement of shares he or she holds in the security exchange. This permits an investor to give instruction to his stock broker on what to sell or buy.

Several securities exchanges are in operation, most notably the Hong Kong stock exchange, New York stock exchange and the London stock exchange. Every country has its own security exchange. The first U.S. stock exchange market was founded in Philadelphia. The New York stock exchange was opened in 1792 after the traders of federal bonds and traders of New York Bank stocks agreed to operate jointly.[15] In the early part of the security exchange era, trade activity was widely unregulated. However, when companies began issuing their stocks for sale to individual investors, federal regulations mandated that annual reports would be made available for stockholders. The New York stock exchange is a voluntary association with a written constitution and by-laws, which include rules for the transaction of business and fix rates of commission to be charged by members. Seats on the exchange are limited by its constitution to 1,375 and can only be purchased from existing members. The splitting of commissions with nonmembers is prohibited and is one of the most strictly enforced rules of the exchange. The exchange itself does no business and keeps no record of transactions; it merely provides facilities for its members and regulates their conduct.[16]

Today, securities exchange commissions monitor the activities of all securities exchange markets. The Securities Exchange Commission monitors the various companies and organizations that are quoted on the security exchange and make sure they meet the requirements for being listed. The Federal Exchange Commission is the main authority issuing regulations over the American securities exchange markets. "The mission of the U.S. Securities and Exchange Commission is to protect investors, maintain fair, orderly, and efficient markets, and facilitate capital formation."[17]

Over-the-counter markets. Many innovations have evolved from the securities exchange to protect the investor, while others allow more participants in security trading. One significant innovation is Over-The-Counter Market (also called OTC market). OTC market evolved through development and growth in the information and communication technology. OTC market is a decentralized market of securities that are not listed on an exchange market. The majority of securities traded on the OTC market usually do not meet listing requirements. However, it is not uncommon to see a company that trades its securities on the OTC market, as well as on the trading floor of a security exchange. OTC participants trade over a telephone, a fax machine, or an electronic network, not a physical trading floor.

Unlike in securities exchanges, where the broker conducts trading by ordering matchmaking service on the floor on behalf of the investor, in the OTC market, trading occurs through a network of dealers. These dealers carry inventories of securities to affect the buying and selling orders of investors. In addition, they negotiate directly with one another over computer networks and telephones. In the U.S., the National Association of Securities Dealers (NASD) monitors activities of exchange markets and OTC markets. NASD is a voluntary association of securities firms formed by the Maloney Act of 1938 to regulate the affairs of securities exchange investor firms and to promote fair and ethical practices in the securities business.[18] The NASD is a self-regulated association and is the largest self-regulated securities organization in the U.S.

Eurocurrency markets. The Eurocurrency market is a money market wherein Eurocurrency is borrowed and lent by banks in Europe. The main function of the Eurocurrency market is to facilitate the international flow of capital and provide trade assistance between countries and Multinational Corporations (MNC) by allowing for more convenient borrowing. Corporations and national governments usually deposit Eurocurrency in banks away from their home countries. These banks are called Eurobanks. Despite the name, Eurocurrency and Eurobanks do not necessarily mean the currencies or the banks are European. Although the Eurodollar is the most prevalent currency, other currency held in Eurobanks includes the USD, Swiss Franks and English Sterling pound.

The first Eurocurrency markets were developed in Europe during the 1950s. Eurocurrency markets are very active in today's modern, global economy because they are able to avoid a country's domestic interest rate regulations and reserve requirements and other barriers to the free flow of capital. Eurocurrency markets play a significant role in a global economy because they allow for easier flow of money around the world. The capital deposited in Eurobanks is used by organizations and governments to finance projects all over the world.

Effect of Exchange Rates on Global Business

Exchange rates have both a positive and negative effect on global business. The most important issue in understanding the effects of exchange rates on business is its volatility. Volatility is expressed as a percentage and represents the possibility of a change in exchange rates projected over a year. One gains a better understanding of the concept of volatility by comparing it to a degree of uncertainty, expressed in numbers. The larger the degree of uncertainty of behavior for a certain currency, the higher the risk of dealing with this currency and operating business in the currency's country of origin. As an example, one should consider the case of a U.S. automotive manufacturer. If a price of the Euro goes up in respect to the U.S. Dollar, then more profit can be made from the sale of each vehicle. However, if the manufacturer is buying or manufacturing parts for its cars in Europe, the price of cars will increase or decrease relative to the fluctuation in exchange rates, potentially draining profit from the sale of each car.

Exchange rate fluctuation also has an effect on domestic production and agriculture by inciting the competitiveness of exports of domestic goods to other countries. If the price of the USD is falling, U.S. agricultural goods will be more attractive to Japanese importers than to European exporters, if the Euro is rising. Global exchange rate fluctuations affect every sector.

Currency devaluation and revaluation. Global monetary policies vary by nation. Countries with large, stable, free-market economies and strong currencies allow exchange rates to freely float and change according to market supply and demand. This type of monetary policy is termed a *floating exchange rate system.* However, nations with unstable and emerging economies and weak currencies mostly use a *fixed exchange rate system.* "Under a fixed exchange rate system, only a decision by a country's government or monetary authority can alter the official value of the currency. Governments do, occasionally, take such measures, often in response to unusual market pressures. *Devaluation,* the deliberate downward adjustment in the official exchange rate, reduces the currency's value, but a *revaluation* is an upward change in the currency's value."[19] The devaluation of one unit of a nation's domestic currency decreases in value against other currencies; thus, the Purchasing Power Parity (PPP) of the devaluated currency decreases. In turn, inflation rises and affects prices on exported commodities. Foreign companies take advantage of currency devaluation in unstable countries by buying more goods for the same amount of money and exporting the goods to other countries for resale and monetary profit. Devaluation also affects prices on commodities imported from other counties by making them more expensive than before. Devaluation is also considered a benefit to a country. The lowered currency helps the country to reduce its current trade deficit. However, a government may raise interest rates in order to control increased inflation, which may slow economic growth. Many investors consider devaluation a sign of danger and often restrict flow of their investments into countries with unstable currency.

Revaluation, on the other hand, makes the currency of a country more expensive, compared to other currencies, and has a direct inverse effect on exports and imports, respectively. Imports become cheaper because current exchange rates allow consumers to buy more foreign goods for the same amount of domestic currency. This foreign spending raises the PPP of domestic currency. Analysts often consider revaluation a sign of economic recovery and stabilization. Foreign investors are usually attracted to currency revaluation because it results in less risk.

Why stable exchange rates are desired by business. Stable exchange rates are a sign of less volatility, meaning that the risk of conducting business with a stable foreign currency is reduced. If there is less uncertainty in an exchange rate, then the opportunity to make plans for doing business operation rises. Even though there are several tools to protect a business from a high degree of volatility, entering into forward contracts can bring into play additional costs for business operations. Stable exchange rates serve as a straightening factor for a country's economy by encouraging domestic production while keeping imports and exports under control. Stable exchange rates attract investors and allow foreign capital to flow in a country. Businesses flourish under such conditions because it offers stability and lowers prices on operating costs, acquisition of raw materials, and labor costs.

Impact of unstable exchange rates on business. Unstable exchange rates are a sign of a struggling economy or an economy in crisis. Small and medium businesses usually are incapable of withstanding radical fluctuations of exchange rates, especially if an enterprise depends on purchases of imported raw parts and materials. If sudden devaluation occurs, imported parts and raw materials go up in price, making business costly. Large, stable companies, backed by significant foreign capital or foreign investors, comprise the majority of businesses capable of surviving under unstable fluctuations of exchange rates. The development of a free-market economy slows down under instability of exchange rates. Large companies take advantage of these opportunities by freely monopolizing unstable markets under such conditions.

Historical Development of the Global Monetary System

The onset of World War I sparked an overabundant supply of money, as antagonistic nations printed money at an alarming rate in order to finance their war efforts. The gold standard was violated, a trend which continued through the 1920s. However, change was on the horizon, beginning with the election of Franklin D. Roosevelt as U.S. President in 1932. Reforms instituted during this election—and the three subsequent Presidential reelections—impacted the way the world conducts financial transactions. One of Roosevelt's sweeping agendas was an effort to avoid a return to the near-fatal economic chaos of the 1930s—by no longer permitting U.S. paper currency to be redeemable in gold.[20] In fact, much of the successful recovery of Western Europe following World War II was made possible by U.S. aid.[21] The U.S. did not suffer aerial bombings on its industrial centers—unlike Europe and Japan, and was the major post-war victor capable of manufacturing much of the world's products. Furthermore, with the help of receptive governments, the establishment of the World Bank and International Monetary Fund was made possible under the United Nation (UN) backing.[22] What series of historical events led to these developments? The story begins centuries ago with the use of gold and other precious metals as a medium of exchange for cross-border trade.

The Gold Standard

Governments issued gold and other precious metals as a source of money as far back as Biblical times. When governments started issuing currency in the form of paper money, it was usually convertible into a predetermined amount of gold. This practice came to be commonly known as the "gold standard" by participating countries. In 1834, the U.S. fixed the price of gold at $20.67 per ounce and maintained this rate until 1933. Guaranteeing the convertibility of paper currency into gold was a way to maintain confidence in a country's currency value at home and overseas. The gold standard regulated the quantity and growth rate of a nation's money supply. Between 1880 and 1913, inflation in the United States averaged 0.1 percent per year. Because exchange rates were fixed, gold was directly related to the price of goods around the world; thus, the price of goods increased when the price of gold increased.[23]

1880s to World War II

Many nations backed their currencies with gold well before 1880. However, this practice became more widespread during this period; therefore, the 1880s are generally accepted as the beginning of the gold standard. Additionally, 1880 to 1914 is considered the "classical" gold standard era, because countries fixed values of their currency in gold. Prior to the onset of World War I, 1880 to 1914 was a period of dynamic economic growth, especially with regard to free trade in goods, capital, and labor. Unfortunately, during World War I, the gold standard was nonexistent because of rogue nations' abundant printing of paper currencies in order to finance their war efforts. Following World War I, a Gold Exchange Standard was reinstated, which lasted between 1925 and 1931 and permitted countries to hold gold, dollars, or pounds as reserves. The only exceptions were Great Britain and the United States, which held reserves only in gold. Great Britain departed from gold in 1931 because of massive gold and capital withdrawals. In 1932, in an attempt to move the economy out of the Great Depression, U.S. officials called for reduced government spending and an end to Prohibition. President Franklin D. Roosevelt (FDR) acted on both, because Congress granted him more legislative powers to devalue the United States dollar in an effort to manipulate inflation. FDR took the U.S. off the gold standard, and paper currency was no longer redeemable in gold. In January 1934, FDR fixed the price of gold at $35 an ounce, against the old price of $20.63, which inflated the dollar 40 percent.

Demise of the Gold Standard

The demise of the gold standard was due to a variety of circumstances. World War I and the Great Depression were two of the major contributing circumstances. The first sign of the demise of the gold standard began with the outbreak of World War I, as war financing was funded by increases in money supplies of hostile nations. It became evident that these nations' gold reserves were not capable of supporting such a rapid increase in money supply. The mid 1920s saw a return to the gold standard as currencies emerged from hyperinflation in the 1920s and 1930s. European investment from the U.S. stimulated a worldwide recovery of trade and manufacturing; nevertheless, the Versailles treaty made things worse: Germany became the sacrificial lamb, assuming all reparations as punishment for starting World War I. Hence, Germany's economic recovery was stifled as a result. Further, countries resorted to implementing restrictions, tariffs, and exchange controls in an effort to maintain momentum for economic growth.

Although the U.S. was willing to provide financial backing to Europe, it was not as eager to accept goods from Europe. Consequently, Europe and the world were at the mercy of a prosperous U.S. economy. But the U.S. lost this control when the stock market collapsed in October 1929, followed by the Great Depression of the 1930s. The U.S. notified debtor nations that the balances were due. The debtor nations responded by cutting imports in order to settle affairs with other nations. The result of this created a ripple effect worldwide. In the midst of a financial crisis, struggling nations deflated their currencies to stay steady in relation to gold, resulting in the decreased demand for their exports. In addition to notifying debtor nations that trade balances were due, the U.S. further exacerbated the situation by enacting the Smoot-Hawley Tariff Act.

The Smoot-Hawley Tariff Act of June 1930 raised U.S. tariffs to historically high levels. The original intention behind the legislation was to increase the protection afforded domestic farmers against foreign agricultural imports. Massive expansion in the agricultural production sector outside of Europe during World War I led, with the postwar recovery of European producers, to massive agricultural overproduction during the 1920s. This in turn led to declining farm prices during the second half of the decade. During the 1928 election campaign, Republican Presidential candidate Herbert Hoover pledged to help the beleaguered farmer by, among other things, raising tariff levels on agricultural products. However, once the tariff schedule revision process got started, it proved impossible to stop. Calls for increased protection flooded in from industrial sector special interest groups. And soon, a bill, primarily meant to provide relief for farmers, became a means to raise tariffs in all sectors of the economy. When the dust had settled, Congress had agreed to tariff levels that exceeded the already high rates established by the 1922 Fordney-McCumber Act. This new policy represented among the most protectionist tariffs in U.S. history.[24]

The Smoot-Hawley Tariff was more a consequence of the onset of the Great Depression than an initial cause. Though the tariff might not have caused the Depression, it certainly did not make it any better. This tariff provoked a storm of foreign retaliatory measures and came to stand as a symbol of the 'beggar-thy-neighbor' policies (policies designed to improve one's own lot at the expense of others) of the 1930s. Such policies contributed to a drastic decline in international trade. U.S. imports from Europe declined from a 1929 high of $1,334 million to just $390 million in 1932. In addition, the U.S. exports to Europe fell from $2,341 million in 1929 to $784 million in 1932. Overall, world trade declined 66 percent between 1929 and 1934. In general, the Smoot-Hawley Tariff did nothing to foster trust and cooperation among nations in either the political or economic realm during a perilous era in international relations.[25]

Unemployment, another result of this situation, was at unprecedented levels globally—nearly thirty million by some accounts. This crisis continued through World War II, and no organized system for exchange rates existed. Investment, foreign trade, and economic recovery declined because of the war. The gold standard was no longer viable in the post World War II global economy.[26]

The Bretton Woods Agreement—1944 to 1971

Following World War II, implementation of a currency exchange system for the promotion of growth in international trade that linked monies, similar to the gold exchange, received worldwide political support. In 1944, delegates from forty-four nations met in Bretton Woods, New Hampshire, to discuss the initiative. Three major events resulted: (1) the establishment of a fixed exchange rate system, (2) the International Monetary Fund, and (3) the World Bank.

At the conclusion of the Bretton Woods meeting, an exchange rate agreement was made, often referred to as the gold exchange standard. Just as before, under the gold standard, each nation was to fix its currency value in relation to gold. The United States' fixed standard was $35 per ounce, and the U.S. was the only nation capable of producing and supplying goods to the rest of the world, which resulted in goods being priced and traded in dollars. Consequently, the U.S. dollar became the reserve currency for the new gold exchange system. Trade contracts were essentially executed in dollars.[27]

Fixed Exchange Rates

Fixed exchange rates evolved from the gold standard. In order for nations to conduct cross-border trade, a fixed rate of exchange had to be established and generally maintained by intervention from governments in the foreign exchange markets. Fixed exchange rates, also known as pegged exchange rates, occur when a government or central bank ties the official exchange rate to another country's currency or the price of gold. The purpose of a fixed exchange rate system is to maintain the nation's currency value within a very narrow band. Fixed exchange rates offer the provision of greater certainty for exporters and importers, which allows governments to maintain low inflation. In other words, fixed exchange rates assist in minimizing interest rates, thus stimulating increased global trade and investment.

Establishment of the International Monetary Fund (IMF)

The International Monetary Fund (IMF) was one of the results of the Bretton Woods Agreement. The role of the IMF is to supervise the exchange rate practices of member countries and to encourage the free convertibility of any national money into the monies of other countries. In simple terms, the IMF was created to maintain order in the global monetary system. The IMF assists nations in their development through capital loans to undeveloped nations. The purpose was to achieve higher standards of living among its citizens, resulting in an increased market for more goods. The overall motivation for existence of the IMF was that the development of less-developed countries is in the interest of more developed countries.[28] While the IMF and World Bank mandate stern lending criteria for undeveloped countries, the IMF inevitably lends money to countries that are experiencing problems and meets their international payment obligation as well. The IMF conducts lending practices using the annual contributions of its 151 member nations, based on quota obligations. For example, the U.S. annual quota is $23 billion USD.

Establishment of the World Bank

The World Bank, another result of the Bretton Woods Agreement, was established to help finance economic development in poor countries. Simply put, the World Bank was created to promote general economic development. The World Bank also provides loans—in addition to technical expertise, to developing countries at more favorable terms than commercial lenders. The World Bank obtains its funding by issuing and selling bonds, and it is one of the world's major borrowers.

Demise of the Bretton Woods Agreement

With the condition and promise of the U.S. government to redeem other central banks' holdings of dollars for gold at the fixed rate of $35 per ounce, most countries settled their international business balances in U.S. dollars under the gold exchange system. However, this agreement led to persistent payment deficits with reduced U.S. gold reserves, jeopardizing confidence in the ability of the United States to maintain this standard. Americans could import more than they exported with the willing cooperation of Europe and Japan. During the 1960s, the U.S., suffering severe inflation from the deficit financing of the Vietnam War and an expanding agenda of social programs, racked up enormous budget deficits and trade deficits. The Bretton Woods system reached a crisis when it became clear that there was a run on the U.S. gold supply as foreigners sought to exchange their dollar reserves, which were convertible to gold, at the fixed price established by the Bretton Woods system. On August 15, 1971, President Richard Nixon announced that the U.S. would no longer redeem currency for gold, the final step in officially removing the U.S. from the gold standard. The system collapsed when Nixon suspended convertibility by "closing the gold window." The current monetary order, which stems from the demise of the Bretton Woods system, consists of market-determined exchange rates between floating fiat currencies, entirely lacking any commodity backing.

Floating Exchange Rates—1973 to Present

A floating exchange rate is an exchange rate that is freely determined by the interaction of supply and demand. Floating exchange rates allow nations to formulate macroeconomic policies independently of other nations. In 1971, major governments adopted a floating system, otherwise known as a floating exchange rate. The floating exchange rate is determined by the private market through supply and demand. Differences in open market supply and demand will "self correct" a floating exchange rate. For instance, if demand for the U.S. dollar is low, its value will decrease, which makes imported goods more expensive and exported goods less expensive.

Managed Float System

A managed float system is very similar to a floating exchange rate system, with one exception: the value of a currency is determined by market demand for and supply of a country's currency, with no predetermined target for the exchange rate as set by the government. Governments attempt to directly affect their exchange rates by buying or selling foreign currencies or indirectly by raising or lowering interest rates through monetary policy.

Pegged exchange rate. A fixed exchange rate, sometimes called a pegged exchange rate, is a type of exchange rate regime wherein a currency's value is matched to the value of another single currency, to a basket of other currencies, or to another measure of value, such as gold. As the reference value rises and falls, so does the currency pegged to it.[29] The adoption of a pegged exchange rate evolved at the conclusion of the Bretton Woods Agreement; hence, the U.S. dollar was pegged to gold at $35 an ounce and the value of other foreign currencies was linked directly to the U.S. dollar. For example, if one needed to buy British Sterling, the value of the Sterling would be expressed in U.S. dollars, which would be expressed in gold.

The primary reason to peg a currency is for stability, which explains why pegged rate is attractive to developing nations who want to create a stable atmosphere for foreign investment. The peg aided in the creation of global trade and monetary stability but was used only when all the major economies were part of the policy to peg. Unfortunately, the peg was discontinued in 1971 when the U.S. dollar could no longer maintain the pegged rate of $35 an ounce.[30]

Currency board. A currency board is a monetary authority for a country that operates similarly to a central bank. It has the authority to issue notes and coins; but unlike a central bank, a currency board is neither the government's bank nor is it capable of bailing out a failing bank. A currency board has the capacity to operate either independently or parallel with a central bank. Currency boards have been in existence as long as central banks and have their roots in the English Bank Act of 1844. A currency board has the capacity to issue notes and coins and the conversion of local currency into the anchor currency at a fixed rate of exchange. The anchor currency is usually a stable currency: the U.S. Dollar, Euro, or British Pound. Generally, a currency board must have 100 percent of reserve currency available and a long-term commitment to the local currency. This requires a fixed rate of exchange for the issuance of notes and coins. Since a currency board is not in the business of lending money to banks or the government—like a central bank—the only means a government has in raising capital is through taxation or borrowing.[31]

Interestingly, there is no ideal monetary authority for a nation to use regarding a central banking system or a currency board system. Executing sound economic decisions through the proper management of a nation's monetary system is the primary medium for building credibility amongst global investors.

European Monetary System—1979 to Present

As far back as World War II, a number of European nations desired a unified Europe that could compete with the economic strength of the United States. Disagreements in how this unified Europe would compete and operate under the auspices of a leading nation resulted in a contentious debate, especially between Great Britain and France. However, during the early 1980s, as European nations battled with unemployment figures in excess of 11 percent or higher throughout the region, foreign affairs became more significant in rallying support for tighter economic cooperation. Jacques Delors was appointed president of the European Economic Community (EEC) in 1985, and he became the key innovator for marshaling a plan for the European Union. One of his prior successes as finance minister in France included major economic improvement for his country by reducing inflation and cutting foreign debt. Delors set about introducing sweeping initiatives designed to expand internal trade further by convincing EEC members to pass the Single European Act (SEA) of 1987. The SEA bounded member countries to the goal of a single European market by January 1, 1993. However, not surprisingly, the major disagreement was over the European Monetary Union's management of financial unity and one common European currency—although the European Monetary Union did not yet exist. The creation of a unified European economy would require financial unity, but member countries like Great Britain and Denmark were not as eager to replace their own currency with a European currency that was yet to be tested.[32]

Exchange Rate Mechanism

The European Community established its Exchange Rate Mechanism (ERM) in 1979 and formed the initial steps for the creation of a single European currency. The purpose of the ERM was to control the exchange rates within the European Monetary System Member currencies of the ERM were fixed against each other with smaller fluctuations for change, as compared to a floating exchange rate among nonmember states. With the launch of the Euro in January 1999, the ERM has since become less significant because European Union (EU) member-states have adopted the Euro as the primary currency for the EU.

Maastricht Treaty

The SEA was a major catalyst for economic integration. The fall of the Berlin Wall and Germany's subsequent unification brought to light benefits that could be accrued through improved political cooperation. Chancellor Helmut Kohl of Germany was convinced that a more politically integrated Europe was crucial to the acceptance of a combined and larger Germany. His conviction compelled other nations to press forward toward developing a monetary union, cooperation on European affairs, and a common foreign and defense policy. Discussions were underway in the latter part of 1990 and came to a head in Maastricht, Netherlands in December 1991. These negotiations resulted in the consensus of two treaties on Economic, Monetary, and

Political Union—more commonly known as the Maastricht Treaty. The Maastricht Treaty called for the development of a European Union that utilized the existing offices of the European Community, supplemented by new intergovernmental offices on foreign and security policy, home affairs, and justice.[33]

Provisions. Maastricht arranged for additional cooperation in the creation of an economic and monetary union—in judicial and internal affairs and in foreign and defense policy. However, the ultimate achievement of the Maastricht Treaty was the Economic and Monetary Union (EMU). The agreement to adopt a single currency and central banking system for Europe has placed the Euro as a major competitor with the U.S. dollar. The Euro was launched in global financial markets for electronic use on January 1, 1999, and was subsequently accepted as the unit of exchange for all European Union (EU) nations, with the exception of Sweden, Denmark, and Great Britain. Consequently, the U.S. dollar has been on the decline against the Euro (down 27 percent) since the then twelve Euro-area countries officially issued the Euro as a form of currency for daily consumer transactions in 2002.[34]

EU membership requirements. Strict requirements exist for membership in the European Monetary Union (EMU): budget deficits within 3 percent of GDP, annual inflation to within 1.5 percent of the average of the lowest three nations, and European Monetary System (EMS) qualifications.[35]

EU membership roster and future member candidates. The European Union has made significant progress over the past decade in becoming a unified market. As of July 2007, the following nations were members:

• Austria	• Germany	• Netherlands
• Belgium	• Greece	• Poland
• Bulgaria	• Hungary	• Portugal
• Cyprus	• Ireland	• Romania
• Czech Republic	• Italy	• Slovakia
• Denmark	• Latvia	• Slovenia
• Estonia	• Lithuania	• Spain
• Finland	• Luxembourg	• Sweden
• France	• Malta	• United Kingdom

Candidate nations include Croatia, former Yugoslavia Republic of Macedonia, and Turkey.[36]

Brief Summary of Major Points

The first section of this chapter discussed the importance of global financial markets and how they play a major role in national economies through international trade. The physical and virtual structure of the foreign exchange market enables monetary systems to interlink global, financial markets, permitting the exchange of goods and services across national borders. Also discussed were the effects of exchange rates on global business and how currency de-evaluation in unstable countries affects the export of goods to other countries.

The second section of this chapter reviewed the historical developments of the European Monetary System and the multiple transitions of the gold standard to the time of the demise of the Bretton Woods agreement. Additionally, the various types of exchange rate systems were briefly discussed to include floating, managed, pegged, and fixed systems. Finally, the evolution of the European Monetary System and the creation of the European Union (EU) were examined from inauguration to the present time.

The following is a brief summary of the major points covered in this chapter:

- Global Financial Markets are physical and virtual market places that make possible the exchange of goods and services between international buyers and sellers.

- The Foreign Exchange Market (FX) is the largest Over-The-Counter (OTC) market in the world, trading twenty-four hours a day with minor breaks for weekends and holidays. The most notable FX centers are located in New York, London, Singapore, and Tokyo. Many market makers utilize the FX and include governments, Central Banks, Corporations, and Brokers. Central Banks and governments are the major safeguards for a nation's monetary fund and may intervene on a country's monetary policy by buying or selling large sums of domestic and/or foreign currency.

- Purchasing Power Parity (PPP), the widely known economic and finance theory, is based on the premise of the law of one price. According to this law, a basket of goods in one country must cost exactly the same price as a similar basket of goods in another country after conversion into the same currency. PPP theory is being used to predict fluctuation in exchange rates of currencies and inflation of economies in different countries.

- Securities Exchanges are physical market places where stocks, futures, bonds, treasury bills, and options are traded for speculative profit. Stocks and bonds are alternative ways for a company to raise money for its operations. Stocks and bonds are liabilities of a company and must be guaranteed by assets and equity. The most popular security exchange markets are located in New York, London, Tokyo, and Hong Kong.

- Global monetary systems have existed for centuries; however, the 1880s is generally accepted as the time when nations adopted a similar platform. Gold at one time was the accepted backing for a government's currency; however, when the U.S. mandated that it would no longer redeem currency for gold in 1971, a government's currency value rested on the strength of its economy.

- Floating Exchange Rates have been in place since 1971 and allow countries to formulate their macroeconomic policies independent of other nations. By comparison to a managed float system and/or pegged exchange rate, Floating Exchange Rates have proven to be a more efficient means of determining the long-term value of a currency.

- European monetary system has undergone various changes over the past century. The most lasting, however, was that of Jacques Delors, who was credited for marshaling the plan for the European Union (EU). His efforts, along with the fall of the Berlin Wall and signing of the Maastricht Treaty, have made possible the creation of the Euro and a $9 trillion economy, which has the wealth and technological capability to make itself a major unified world power.

Moving from Theory into Practice

The following summarizes a question and answer session with coauthor Joe Robinson. His answers are useful in contemplating how the global business professional can translate the theories and concepts covered in this chapter via practical answers to the questions from real life experiences.

The chapter provides reasons why the global financial markets are important to borrowers and lenders. Are these markets also important to governments as well?

Global financial markets are something that small and medium importers/exporters do not normally get in touch with on a direct basis. It is your bank or financial institution that mainly is concerned with global financial markets and their movements and trends.

However, for those companies providing products or services that are sold to governmental major projects such as highways, bridges, airports, major hospital complexes and municipalities such as waste treatment plants, water treatment plants, sewage facilities or large private complexes such as major construction sites, apartment complexes, mine projects, there may be involvement with global financial markets, or more precisely, global financial institutions that are closely involved in global financial markets. The World Bank, The African Bank, and similar global financial institutions that "bank roll" these global major projects do play a part in a company's access to participating in supplying their products or services on an export basis to the particular project.

A word of caution is needed here: The paper work to participate in the bid process on these projects is complex and the consequent time consuming efforts required in communications and meeting specification certification negate the desire of some to even bother to try to enter these large project opportunities. On the other hand, there are some small companies that have found this to be their forte and actually generate most of their revenue from these projects and thrive in this area of global business.

I think I understand how FX Markets are important to large MNCs. In what way is knowledge of FX Markets of value to the smaller global business?

The first thing you need to understand is that at any given time there are some countries that the FX makes your product or service competitive in price, and there are other countries at the same time that the FX makes your product or service not price competitive. This means that you should focus your attention and marketing and sales actions on those countries where you have a competitive price advantage due to a favorable FX.

Another thing you need to keep in mind is that you as the exporter or importer are not a bank. Do not take on the generosity of performing a bank's role. If you are a manufacturer and want to export finished product or import components, then let the banks, financial institutions, and even government organizations bear the risk and burden of FX uncertainties.

It is important, however, that you have knowledge of FX Markets and movements in order to you to search out and secure the best ways to transfer the financial risks to a bank of global instituting for a fee that is well worth the extra cost of doing global business.

I am considering taking a job in Paris, France. I currently live in Fairfax, Virginia with a base salary $USD 60,000. How much will I need to make in Paris to simply maintain the standard of living I have in Virginia?

This is a very good personal question. First you need to understand the rate or parity differentiation between the US Dollar and the French Frank. If the dollar is stronger than the French Frank, then you are lucky, as your base salary will go further to "keep you whole" during your post in Paris. If the reverse is true, then you need to do some creative financing negotiations with your company or organization.

Another thing you need to do is to ascertain the difference in the cost of living between Paris and your US resident base.

My advice is to do thorough and comprehensive research on this issue before you agree and sign up with your company or organization in order to negotiate the best financial package. Once you sign up and go overseas it becomes too late to re-negotiate what you overlooked or forgot to include in your expatriate compensation package. Be sure to compare compensation calculations, cost-of-living allowances, goods and services differential, how local (Paris and French) taxes are handled and the US taxes are handled, and most important, your major medical coverage. It is a good idea to speak with one or more expatriates to ascertain what they are receiving, what they would have done differently, and to seek their advice on what you need to do to at least keep yourself whole. Further, be sure to seek the counsel of someone who has been in a post in Paris and returned. You need to cover your return home.

There are great differences and disparities between personal expatriate compensation packages. Here are a few helpful sites that will get you started in doing your home work on this sensitive topic:

- www.expatica.com

- www.hr.com

- www.air-inc.com

- www.eiu-enumerate.com

- www.expatexchange.com

<u>Why is knowledge of exchange rates important to the global business professional and the firms they work for?</u>

An understanding about and knowledge of current foreign exchange rates are important because it directly impacts two of your most important reasons for going into global business in the first place: sales and profits. Remember, foreign exchange rates establish what your overseas customers must pay in their local currency to "buy" dollars to pay you for your goods and services.

If the foreign exchange rate negatively impacts your customer, then he has to pay more for your product. This places you in a less competitive position, and your sales may suffer as a consequence. If you are willing to reduce the dollar price of your product to offset a negative foreign exchange rate for your customers, then you may maintain you sales, but your percent of profits will decrease. Paying attention to movements in foreign exchange rates in anticipation of future forecasting and supply chain maneuvering is a good global business practice.

If you import and export, a strategy for utilizing foreign exchange rates by utilizing relevant global financial services is a wise policy. Be sure to get to know your bank and insurance companies well and the services they offer and their rates to minimize your risks and maximize your sales and profits.

<u>The chapter talks about protectionism in the early part of the twentieth century, in particular the Smoot-Hawley Act. In your view, is protectionism a problem in the twenty-first century?</u>

Protectionism still exists today but not on the scale of the twentieth century. It's all about protecting jobs. By default protectionism is practiced to cover those industries that are labor intensive. Textile and farm produce are two industries that come to mind. Other job-protecting measures revolve around emerging industries in a particular country. For example, Brazil is protective of its fledgling automotive industry. One addition area that protectionism is exercised revolves around critical or survival type industries involving national interest or national well being. Rice imports into Japan are an example. Japan must rely on sufficient quantities of rice to perpetuate its well being, so imports of rice are priced to maintain a price parity such that Japanese rice farmers will find it attractive to continue to plant and harvest this all important crop.

We will never know the full negative impact of the Smoot Hawley Tariff Act of June 1930; however, we can be sure that those countries that impose unduly high tariffs for protectionism purposes find that such policies tend to back fire. This implies that nations negatively affected by a country's protectionist tariffs will retaliate. The net result is a decrease in trade between the respective nations, and both tend to lose. This phenomenon is one of the arguments in favor of free trade that opens borders and creates economic well being for all nations.

What are some of the fastest expanding markets for U.S. exports and why?

Exports to FTA (Free Trade Agreement) nations are our fastest growing export markets. The US Trade Representative office reported to Congress on June 13, 2007 that exports to our FTA partners are growing twice as fast as our exports to non-FTA countries. FTAs implemented between 2001 and 2006 netted a $13 billion U. S. trade surplus with trade agreement partners in 2006.

Some actual examples include CAFTA-DR in 2006 where exports were up 18 percent in 2006. U. S. exports to Bahrain grew 40 percent to $491 million in 2006. U. S. exports to Chile rose over 150 percent since 2004, making the U. S. Chile's largest trading partner. The U. S. trade surplus with Australia grew to $9.6 billion with U. S. exports rising $3.6 billion to $17.8 billion in the first two years of the U.S.-Australia FTA—because U. S. exports have risen 25 percent since the agreement was implemented. U. S. exports to Jordan have risen 92 percent since the U.S.-Jordan FTA went into effect in December 2001.

Fortunately SMEs (small and medium-sized businesses) accounted for and enjoyed a significant portion of this export growth driven by FTAs.

The reasons for this favorable export growth created by FTAs is the reduction of tariffs, trimming down of nontariff barriers, decreasing time consuming and unproductive transaction costs, and enforcing intellectual property rights and greater transparency in eliminating complicated and inconsistent rules standards and business practices across FTS borders.

Key Concepts

- Global financial markets
- Monetary systems
- Foreign Exchange (FX) Market
- Bretton Woods Agreement
- Gold Standard
- Over-the-counter (OTC) market place
- Exchange rate
- International Monetary Fund (IMF)
- World Bank
- Purchasing power parity (PPP)
- Law of one price
- Interbank markets
- Securities exchanges
- Economic and Monetary Union (EMU)
- Smoot-Hawley Tariff Act

Global Business in Practice
Euro-Zone Challenges and Opportunities

When the Slovak Republic became a member of the OECD in 2000, it joined some of the world's most industrialized nations, demonstrating its attachment to basic values shared by all OECD members. It adopted OECD's instruments, practices, and policies, which have served as a powerful tool for progress.

Like accession to the OECD, joining the EU three and a half years later represented another important step towards further integration into the global economy. In both cases, accession spurred Slovakia to adopt policies that have permitted it to become more open and more competitive.

In the past few years, Slovakia has provided us with a remarkable example of a country that has not only acknowledged the need for major reform but which has moved quickly and decisively to actually implement it. The upcoming adoption of the Euro represents the next stage in Slovakia's integration into the European Union and the global economy. This integration is proceeding apace. The Slovak Republic has become an attractive location for Foreign Direct Investment not only from other European Union countries, but also worldwide. Annual foreign direct investment inflows, which amounted to only a few hundred million 10 years ago, reached two billion dollars in 2005.

Investors from outside the EU can enjoy a favorable regulatory and tax environment together with access to the world's largest internal market: the EU. Slovakia has promoted policies and institutions that strengthen its capacity for sustained economic growth and improved productivity. GDP per capita has risen to 51 percent, in PPP terms, of the EU15 average in 2005, from 44 per cent in 1998. This trend should continue, with steady convergence towards the EU average.

The gains for the Slovak economy can also be seen in the increasing importance of exports in the country's GDP, especially to Germany and the Czech Republic.

Your success in building a modern automobile industry is a perfect example of economic integration at work. It demonstrates the contribution that regional integration can make towards improved competitiveness not only within the European economy but also as a building block for competitiveness in the global economy.

Volkswagen, PSA Peugeot-Citroen and Kia all have major assembly plants here and automotive parts companies have followed, from Europe, North America and Asia. Their activities are fully integrated into the European economy.

Moreover, you are benefiting from the growing interaction between the automotive industry and its universities and training centres, creating the opportunity to move up the value-added ladder. It is not surprising that the automotive industry has become a source of pride for Slovaks. And it is not just the automotive industry. There are other interesting foreign investment plans for the future.

Slovakia's plan to adopt the Euro at the start of 2009 can only add to its potential. Meeting the conditions for adoption of the Euro will further strengthen the fundamentals of the economy. Once the Euro is adopted, you will enjoy lower interest rates, access to the very deep and liquid euro credit markets, and exchange rate stability with your major trading partners in the euro zone. The removal of exchange rate constraints and transaction costs linked to the use of a separate currency will make Slovakia even more attractive as a business location.

But capturing these benefits will depend on the development of a sound environment for business. It will depend as well on success in pursuing responsible fiscal policies and achieving a pro-competitive regulatory environment. And it will depend on sharing the benefits of growth in an equitable way.

Slovakia is clearly on the way to creating many of the conditions for success. Indeed, one can foresee that it one day could become a "Slavic tiger" ready to rival Ireland's "Celtic tiger".

Before we get to that stage, however, there is much more to be done if Slovakia is to achieve its full potential.

Employment opportunities, especially for older workers and young women, must be improved. More of the benefits of economic growth need to be shared with low-income earners. Greater competition in energy and telecommunications would bring clear benefits. More investment is needed in research and development.

More can also be done to encourage entrepreneurship. For example, it still takes too long to establish a new business in Slovakia – 25 days, compared to 2 days in Australia, 3 days in Canada and 5 days in Denmark.

Above all, improving the outcomes from the education system is critical, since what we refer to as human capital is an indispensable asset for competitiveness.[*]

---

[*] Regional Economic Conference on Euro-Zone Challenges and Opportunities
Excerpts from a speech by Angel Gurria, OECD Secretary-General Bratislava, Slovakia, 4 April 2007; http://www.oecd.org/document/7/0,3343,en_2649_201185_38362951_1_1_1_1,00.
html;

Introduction

Regional integration is the process whereby countries remove barriers to trade between themselves, but each country determines its own barriers against nonmembers.

Figure 6.1

Elements That are Addressed in the Process of Integration

- Alleviating the barriers to trade of goods and services.

- Reduction of barriers to investment.

- Easier movement of labor between members.

- Tax and monetary policies.

- Administration of the integration agreement.[1]

These agreements are designed to reduce and ultimately remove tariff and nontariff barriers to the free movement of goods, services, and factors of production between each other. Tariff barriers involve financial methods (e.g., taxes on imports) of protecting national industries from competition by foreign corporations. Nontariff barriers refer to laws and regulations affecting trade; these include barriers that governments use to ensure accountability and quality.[2] Successful *regional economic integration* is contingent upon the *integration* of national economies and multilateral links between firms and provinces of integrating countries.[3] Cooperation from geographically proximate nations forms a group with the goal of abolishing discrimination between economic units belonging to member nations. The end result promotes transactions in various economic, political, and social activities to benefit all citizens of the participating nations. Thus, the intended outcome of regional economic integration is to promote economic prosperity and stability among signatory nations.

Agreements between participating nations are managed and promoted through trading blocs. A regional trading bloc is a group of nations in a geographic region engaged in economic integration.[4] Paradoxically, the intent to form a trading bloc may range from the potential of trade creation to the desire for economic protectionism. As such, trading blocs are a notable feature of the international economy, enabling scope and scale advantages—a result of globalization. Signatory nations and their corporations exploit existing competencies, resulting in increased global competitiveness. Some established regional agreements, such as the European Union, incorporate the highest level of integration. Meanwhile, the Americas, Asia, and Africa have created trading blocs with lesser and varying levels of integration.

Currently, most industrialized and less-developed nations are participants of at least one trading bloc, since approximately one-third of all world trade agreements are organized as trading blocs.[5]

A paradox exists in that trading blocs can provide protection from global competitiveness prompted by nations outside of the bloc. The objectives behind the desire to protect the trade interests of participating regions are as follows:

- Establish some form of regional control regarding trade that fulfills the interests of nations within that region;
- Establish tariffs that protect intraregional trade from "outside" forces;
- Promote regional security and political concerns or to develop trade in such as way as to enhance the security in the region;
- Promote South-to-South trade, e.g., between Africa and Asia, and between Latin American countries;
- Promote economic and technical cooperation among developing countries;[6]

Measures that are frequently deployed to regulate the effects of global competition include the following:

- Import quotas (limiting the amount of imports into the country so that domestic consumers buy products made by their countries in their region);
- Customs delays (establishing bureaucratic formalities that slow down the ability for the imported product from abroad to enter the domestic market;
- Subsidies (government financial assistance toward sectors of the home economy so that they have an influx of capital);
- Boycotts and technical barriers;
- Bribes and voluntary restraints.[7]

While the topic of barriers to trade was discussed in Chapter 3, a review of the barriers is included because they are essential to understanding regional economic integration.

For most of the world, regional trading blocs are committed to officiate and develop trade activities for signatory nations. Trading blocs typically maintain two global, environmental, business agendas for participating nations: economic benefit and political benefit. The largest trading blocs include the European Union (EU), North American Free Trade Agreement (NAFTA), Mercado Comun del Cono Sur (MERCOSUR), and Association of Southeast Asian Nation (ASEAN). These blocs trade natural resources, healthcare, labor, and manufactured resources.

These agreements are designed to reduce and ultimately remove tariff and non-tariff barriers to the free movement of goods, services, and factors of production between each other. A major benefit is improvements in the standards of living for signatory nation citizens. The global business professional understands that these trade blocs develop over time, and generally follow a sequence of evolutionary stages.

Stages

The core element of regional economic integration is the trading bloc. These blocs serve to help integrate the economies of signatory nations. However, differences exist among the various types and levels of trading blocs. "The result is a bewildering array of regional entities, with different bodies having very different sizes, purposes, aims, depths of integration, legal foundations, and fulfillment of their stated aims."[8] Different agreements are created among different nations. Trading blocs develop in progressive stages; this is determined by the degree of economic integration, varying from the least to the greatest integration. These stages, in order of intensity of integration, are Preferential Trade Area, Free Trade Area, Custom Union, Common Market, and Economic Union.

Preferential Trade Area

Preferential Trade Areas allow preferential access to certain products from certain nations via the reduction of tariffs. The reduction does not necessarily remove tariffs entirely. An example is the Africa, Pacific, and Caribbean (ACP) pact. This pact includes nations from Africa, the Caribbean, and the Pacific Rim. The Lomé Convention of 1976 resulted in the agreement to establish a formal cooperation between the then European Community and developing ACP nations—in particular, former British, Dutch, and French colonies. The two goals of the agreement were to accomplish the following:

1. Allow most ACP agricultural and mineral exports to enter the European Community with preferential access, free of duty. This preferential access included a quota system agreed for agricultural and mineral products that were in competition with similar European products;

2. Provide $3 billion in aid and FDI from European Community to the ACP nations.

The Lomé Convention was replaced by the Cotonou Agreement in 2000, which includes the EU and seventy-seven developing nations. The goals of the Cotonou Agreement are threefold: (1) the reduction and eventual eradication of poverty in Signatory Island and land-locked nations, (2) sustainable economic development in Signatory Island and land-locked nations, and (3) the gradual integration of signatory countries into the world economy.

Free Trade Area

A free trade area offers the next stage of economic integration. Tariffs, quotas, and preferences on most (if not all) goods among members are removed, and each member can determine its own trade polices with nonmembers. Free Trade Areas are suitable in cases where economic structures in signatory nations complement one another and trade in products that do not compete with each other. The U.S.-Chile Free Trade Agreement of 2003 is an example of a Free Trade Agreement. Those in support of this agreement believe trade between the U.S. and Chile will increase as a result of the reduction in trade barriers. Those in opposition believe Chile's over-dependence on scarce, natural-resource exports will increase.

Customs Union

The next stage of regional economic integration is the Customs Union. All barriers of trade among members are removed, and a common external trade policy is adopted. Members have the same rights as in a free trade area, with the exception that they will now all have the same trade policy towards nonmembers. The purposes for establishing a customs union are twofold: to increase economic efficiency and to establish closer political and cultural ties between signatory nations. An example of a Customs Union is Mercosur, whose members include Brazil, Argentina, Uruguay, Paraguay, and Venezuela. Nations with associate member status include Bolivia, Chile, Colombia, Ecuador, and Peru. Mercosur was established in 1991 with the goal of promoting free trade and the fluid movement of goods, people, and currency among signatory nations.

Common Market

The fourth stage of regional economic integration is known as the Common market. A Common Market includes all of the elements of a Customs Union and freedom of movement of the four factors of production: goods, services, capital, and labor. The Caribbean Community and Common Market (CARICOM) is an example of a Common Market. CARICOM established an administrative arm known as The Secretariat of the Caribbean Community, which includes a Secretary General who serves as the chief executive officer. The Mission Statement of the Secretariat is to provide dynamic leadership and service, in partnership with Community Institutions and groups, towards the attainment of a viable, internationally competitive, and sustainable Community, with improved quality of life for all.

Economic Union

The final stage of regional economic integration is the Economic Union. An Economic Union is an agreement wherein nations remove all barriers to trade and the movement of labor and capital and erect a common trade policy against nonmembers. It requires that member countries harmonize their tax, monetary and fiscal policies, create a common currency, and concede a certain amount of sovereignty to the supranational organization to which they belong.[9] An example of the Economic Union is the European Union (EU).

Figure 6.2

Stages of Regional Economic Integration

- Free Trade Agreement (FTA)—Zero tariffs between member countries and reduced nontariff barriers;
- Customs Union (CU)—FTA + common external tariff;
- Common Market (CM)—Customs Union + free movement of capital and labor, some policy harmonization;
- Economic Union (EU)—Common Market + common economic policies and institutions.

Nations are free to negotiate economic integration agreements as they see fit; however, in practice, formal agreements rarely fall neatly into one of the distinct stages. This can lead to some confusion of terminology and the state of economic integration in some parts of the world. In the case of Canada, for example, the country is part of a free trade area with the United States and Mexico. However, NAFTA also includes elements of a common market in that provisions partially liberate the flow of labor and capital in the region—an element of a common market.[10]

Regardless of the stage and level of economic integration, arguments can be made regarding the purposes and outcomes of such agreements. Typically, the arguments promote the political and economic impact experienced by the person making the argument. In general, those who have been impacted in a positive manner tend to promote the idea that regional economic integration is a good thing. Likewise, those who have experienced negative outcomes tend to hold the idea that regional economic integration is not a good thing. The astute, global-business professional seeks to understand all aspects of the debate, both positive and negative.

Economic and Political Arguments Regarding Regional Economic Integration

Five basic value goals are espoused by national governments: (1) peace, (2) freedom and the absence of random violence, (3) prosperity and economic development, (4) the reduction in the incidence of poverty, and (5) democracy and a clean and healthy environment. Depending on the circumstances and their degree of development, it seems possible that regional economic integration efforts have contributed to the achievement of at least three of the basic value goals: economic prosperity, international peace, and democracy.[11] "According to its proponents, free trade helps nations take advantage of the unprecedented wealth the global economy is producing."[12] Compared to a nonparticipating nation, a participating nation in a trading bloc benefits from the established trade agreement, as a result of greater bargaining power. Consequently, the participation in a trading bloc leads to the minimization of duplication, thin spreading of resources, and wasteful competition. Some nations have benefited from a more efficient transportation system. In addition, trading blocs offer the opportunity for a greater division of labor and specialization in production.

The specialization in production and integration allows for greater prospects for technological advance and innovation. The nations' and citizens' income and wealth will increase from the freedom of transferring goods, services, labor, and capital. A growing nation results in inquiries from foreign investment. Additionally, regional integration further unites political alliances.[13] The political alliances are deepened as a result of incentives from economic growth within their own countries. These solid alliances minimize the threat of intense conflict between participating nations. The political power of these alliances can broaden trade with nonparticipating nations and different trading blocs.

Opponents of Regional Economic Integration have argued that regional economic integration agreements are dangerous because such agreements advance and establish procedures that protect participating nations from the benefits of free trade. In addition, some analysts argue that the concept of regional economic integration is relatively a new idea and the world and economists have limited data to evaluate the future economic and political benefits and limitations.

Regional Agreements

The purpose of this section is to provide an overview of established regional economic integration; it includes descriptions of agreements, lists of participating members, and major issues concerning the established agreements. The regional agreements discussed in this section include the Americas, Europe, Asia, Middle East Organizations, and African nations.

The Americas

North America is one of the largest trading blocs (NAFTA) in the world. Currently, all of Latin America, with the exception of Cuba, is governed by elected regimes, even if the depth and stability of democracy in a number of South American countries remains an open question.[14] The Americas present new opportunities for trade, investment, and services for the economic growth for the western hemisphere.

North American Free Trade Agreement—NAFTA. In 1989, Mexican President Carlos Salinas invited United States President George Bush to organize a trade agreement that would increase investment and decrease tariffs between the two nations. Furthermore, Canada joined Mexico and the United States in the negotiations. The U.S. and Canada had established a free trade agreement prior to NAFTA, called (CFTA). CFTA allowed trade of agriculture between the two nations. Canada is the United States' largest trading partner. However, CFTA was incorporated within the establishments of NAFTA. The process of the development of NAFTA resulted in several years and was signed by the presidents of Mexico, United States, and Canada in 1992.[15] Eventually, NAFTA was officially in operation on January 1, 1994. It was the first major FTA between a developing country (Mexico) and developed countries (The U.S. and Canada).[16] The country of Chile became a participating nation within NAFTA at the end of 1994.

NAFTA immediately lifted tariffs on the majority of goods produced by the signatory nations. It also calls for the gradual elimination, over a period of 15 years, of most remaining barriers to cross-border investment and to the movement of goods and services among the three countries.[17]

Figure 6.3

Important Developments of NAFTA

- The elimination of tariffs as well as import and export quotas,

- The opening of government procurement markets to companies in the other two nations,

- An increase in the opportunity to make investments in each other's country,

- An increase in the ease of travel between countries, and

- The removal of restrictions on agricultural products, auto parts, and energy goods.

The proponents of NAFTA point to the success of millions of jobs created because of the formation of NAFTA. This, however, has sparked a firestorm of debate as to whether or not these jobs have actually been created. The Office of the United States Trade Representative (USTR) has shown that the overall effect of NAFTA has been good for all member nations, especially the United States. During the period 1993–2005, trade rose from $297 billion USD to $810 billion USD. Employment opportunities rose by about 22.6 million new jobs, a 20 percent increase.[18] Industrial production in the United States rose by 49 percent, far outperforming the increase achieved during the previous twelve-year period of 1982–1993. The USTR reported that the U.S. economy experienced stronger growth during the twelve years since NAFTA'S inception than the twelve years prior. NAFTA appears to be good for the economy.[19]

NAFTA opponents posit that though one-million jobs were created through exports under NAFTA, two-million jobs were displaced as a result of imports through NAFTA. In other words, one-million jobs were displaced, mainly because of products that, prior to NAFTA, would have been created in the United States. Manufacturing jobs formerly held in the United States were lost to overseas operations. Opponents offer the following analogy: if the U.S. exported one-thousand cars, many Americans were employed to manufacture these automobiles. The converse of this is also true: if the U.S. imports the same one-thousand cars from Mexico, then the same workers will have to find employment elsewhere.[20] The evidence for and against NAFTA still needs to be weighed, as both proponents and opponents make formidable arguments for and against NAFTA.

Southern Common Market—Mercosur. Mercosur was established in 1991 with the intent of increasing the competitiveness of its five member nations' economies through the use of research on economic development.[21] Full-member nations include Argentina, Brazil, Paraguay, Uruguay, and Venezuela. Associate member nations include Bolivia, Chile, Columbia, Ecuador, and Peru. Mercosur nations combine a population of over 365 million, a GDP of over $2.97 trillion USD, and a foreign trade impact of over $120 billion USD.[22] As such, Mercosur ranks as the fifth largest economy in the world. Cooperation among trading blocs is of special interest because the EU has established an ongoing relationship with Mercosur and seeks to serves as a catalyst towards Mercosur moving to the next stage of economic development—a common market.

Andean Common Market—ANCOM. ANCOM was established in 1969 with the Agreement of Cartagena, or Andean Pact, between Bolivia, Peru, Ecuador, and Chile. The goal of the Agreement was to abolish all barriers to trade by the competition of 1980. In addition, a common external tariff would become established at the end of 1980. These establishments were to increase trade among the participating countries and capitalize on joint efforts for combining industrial resources to increase stagnant industries. In addition, a goal of common currency was to be established during the participation of this integration. However, before that period, Venezuela agreed to join in 1973, and Chile withdrew membership in 1976. During the 1980s the trading bloc had diminished and was reestablished as the ANCOM in 1996.

The ANCOM consists of a council, a General Secretariat, and a common external tariff. In 2006, Venezuela resigned its membership from ANCOM in response to the actions of Peru and Columbia establishing free trade agreements with the U.S. Venezuelan President, Hugo Chavez, said the nation's decision to leave ANCOM was irrevocable and "a strategic decision to safeguard Venezuela's national interests," adding that his country could compete with "subsidized U.S. products."[23] Additional issues confronting the Andean Community are as follows:

- The possible rejoining of Chile, which is currently affiliated with Mercosur. However, Chile and Peru have had a conflict since the nineteenth century of claiming ownership of a seaport on the coastal border of the two countries.

- Signatory nations such as Chile are promoting trade negotiations with Asia. "Chile argues that South American countries need to pool their export efforts to be able to supply the volume of products demanded by China and other Asian countries."[24]

- The establishment of an energy trade agreement between Chile and Bolivia. Chile is in need of energy and Bolivia has an excess stock. In 2006, Chile discarded import duties on most Bolivian imports.[25]

 The goal of the ANDEAN community is to establish promotion of economic and social cooperation through a free trade agreement. However, the leaders of the ANDEAN community, like Mercosur, need to combine efforts to lay aside conflicts and positively establish agreements that will lead to the growth of all the participating economies.

Caribbean Community and Common Market—CARICOM. Established with the Treaty of Chaguaramas in 1973, CARICOM's purpose is to promote economic integration and development, with a main focus in less-developed areas of the region. Signatory nations include Barbuda, Belize, Bermuda, British Virgin Islands, Dominica, Grenada, Grenadines, Guyana, Haiti, Jamaica, Montserrat, Nevis, Saint Kitts, Saint Lucia, Saint Vincent, Suriname, Tobago, and Trinidad. The Cayman Islands, the Turks, and Caicos Islands are associate members. CARICOM manages a common market and formulates policies on health, education, labor, science, technology, tourism, foreign policy, and the environment. Institutions affiliated with CARICOM include the Caribbean Court of Justice, the Caribbean Development Bank, the University of Guyana, and the University of the West Indies. The Caribbean Court of Justice was established by the organization in 2005. This organization acts as a final court of appeals and as a court of original jurisdiction for settling disputes among member countries.[26]

Central American Common Market—CACM. CACM was established in 1960 between Guatemala, El Salvador, Honduras, and Nicaragua. Costa Rica joined the organization in 1963. In 1969, the organization collapsed because of the Futbol War between Honduras and El Salvador, but it was reinstated in 1991. This five-day war (also known as the Football War or the Soccer War) was the result of political differences between Hondurans and Salvadorans, including immigration from El Salvador to Honduras. The name derives from the timing of the war, which overlapped with rioting from a series of soccer matches.[27]

CACM removed duties on most products that move between member nations, unified external tariffs, and increased trade within member nations. However, signatory nations have not been able to achieve their wider aims of stronger economic and political unification—one of the key goals of the organization. The problem stems from the organization's failure to settle trade disputes.[28] Efforts were focused on resolving political issues within the organization rather than focusing on economic integration growth. In the early 1990s, the agreement was strengthened by the addition of the Protocol to the General Treaty on Central American Economic Integration: the Guatemala Protocol.[29] The Guatemala Protocol allowed greater commercial exposure and diminished the protectionist nature of the original 1960 CACM agreement.[30]

More recently, signatory nations are working to establish an additional agreement. The new free trade agreement mirrors NAFTA. Countries such as Costa Rica, Dominican Republic, El Salvador, Guatemala, Honduras, and Nicaragua will begin trade activity with the United States—similar to the way Canada and Mexico currently trade with the United States. The new agreement will include arrangements on agriculture, automobile, and manufacturing tariffs, which will be eliminated or reduced over the next twenty years. In addition, market barriers will be eliminated or reduced. Pharmaceutical, textiles, and clothing industries will benefit from the established trade agreements.[31]

Europe (European Union—EU)

- Austria
- Belgium
- Bulgaria
- Cyprus
- Czech Republic
- Denmark
- Estonia
- Finland
- France

- Germany
- Greece
- Hungary
- Ireland
- Italy
- Latvia
- Lithuania
- Luxembourg
- Malta

- Netherlands
- Poland
- Portugal
- Romania
- Slovakia
- Slovenia
- Spain
- Sweden
- United Kingdom

The EU is an economic union of twenty-seven member states which are listed above. The following countries have applied to join and currently have candidate status: Croatia, Republic of Macedonia, and Turkey. To become a member state, a prospective country needs to fulfill political and economic preconditions known as the Copenhagen Criteria. This requires a democratic and secular government, an independent judiciary and corresponding personal freedoms.

The EU aims to enhance political, economic, and social cooperation through a process known as European Integration. Formed in 1992 by the Maastricht Treaty, the EU supersedes the European Common Market that had been in existence since 1951. The organization operates a common single market that incorporates a customs union. Included within the Common Market rules are a common agricultural policy, a common trade policy, and a common fisheries policy. The EU has also adopted a common foreign and security policy and established formal cooperation in areas of police and judicial investigation into criminal matters. People living within the EU hold EU citizenship. They can live and work in any EU country without the requirement for visas or work permits. The Schengen Agreement abolished passport and border controls within the internal-national boundaries of the EU. These measures aim to eliminate barriers to trade, investment, and the movement of labor.

Twelve of the nations have formed a single currency area, the Euro Zone, which consists of three-hundred million people. This effectively makes the Euro Zone area a true monetary and economic union. The European Central Bank (ECB) is responsible for monetary policy for the Euro and sets interest rates across the twelve participating members. All EU members are obliged to adopt the Euro as their national currency, with the exception of Great Britain and Denmark, which have been exempted under the terms of the Maastricht Treaty. Prior to acceptance into the Euro Zone, EU members must satisfy strict economic convergence criteria. This includes limits on national inflation and budgetary deficits.

The most important EU institutions include the Council of the European Union, the European Commission, the European Court Justice, The European Central Bank, and the European Parliament. The Union cannot transfer additional powers from state onto itself without member agreement through further international treaties. The European Parliament was established in the 1950s. Elections are held every five years, and all registered EU citizens are allowed to vote. The European Commission is the executive body of the EU. Consisting of twenty-five commissioners and originating from each member state and several thousand supporting civil servants, the European Commission drafts and implements legislation and enforces existing treaties. The Council of Europe contains ministers from the governments of member nations. It passes EU law on the recommendations of the European Commission and the European Parliament. The Council also approves the EU budget and seeks to coordinate the adoption of common economic, defense, and judicial policies across the EU. The European Court of Justice (ECJ) interprets European Law and adjudicates in areas of dispute. The ECJ examines and decides on claims brought by the European Commission against member states for noncompliance with EU laws or directives. Similarly, the ECJ judges claims by member states that the European Commission has exceeded its authority. The ECJ also assists national courts in the interpretation of EU law—its decisions are binding on the national courts.[32]

Asia

Asia is the world's largest continent, covering 43.6 million square miles. Home to nearly four billion inhabitants, Asia has experienced a population explosion in the last fifty years and now contains over 60 percent of the world's population.[33] Enormous differences in standards of living and life expectancy occur between the most advanced nations, such as Japan and Singapore, and its least advanced nations, such as Afghanistan and Bangladesh. Increasing attention is being paid to the rapidly growing economies of China and India, as they evolve from primarily agricultural dependence into industrial giants with regional superpower status.

South Korea, Hong Kong, Singapore, and Taiwan are known as The Four Tigers, because of high levels of prosperity and standards of living. Other nations that have developed economically are Thailand, Malaysia, Indonesia, and Vietnam. Japan is the world leader in manufacturing and consumer goods.

China's exports are high in the United States, and the country attracts foreign investment. However, China is a political risk for investors because it is divided between communism and capitalism. The major regional economic integration agreements in this region include the Association of Southeast Asia Nations, the Asia Pacific Economic Cooperation, and the South Asian Association for Economic Cooperation.

Association of Southeast Asian Nations—ASEAN. ASEAN includes Brunei Darussalam, Cambodia, Indonesia, Laos, Malaysia, Myanmar, Philippines, Singapore, Thailand, and Vietnam. The goal is to attain economic, social, and cultural aims through joint endeavors, collaboration, and assistance. They show mutual respect for the independence, sovereignty, equality, territorial integrity, and national identity of all nations. ASEAN gives every state the right to lead its existence free from external interference. The association's members also undertake to avoid interference in the internal affairs of one another and are committed to the settlement of differences or disputes by peaceful means. ASEAN includes renunciation of the threat or use of force and effective cooperation amongst members. Political and security dialog and cooperation should promote regional peace and stability by enhancing regional resilience.[34]

Asia Pacific Economic Cooperation—APEC. APEC's founding member countries include Australia, Canada, Indonesia, Japan, Malaysia, New Zealand, Philippines, Singapore, South Korea, Thailand, and the United States. In 1991 China and Hong Kong became members, followed by Mexico and Papua New Guinea in 1993, Chile in 1994, and Taiwan, Peru, Russia, and Vietnam in 1998. India is seeking APEC membership. Guam is also seeking membership, but is currently represented by the United States. At this time, the majority of nations on the coastline of the Pacific Ocean are organization members.[35]

South Asian Association for Regional Cooperation (SAARC). SAARC, the largest agreement in the world (approximately 1.47 billion people), is comprised of the following Southern Asia nations: Afghanistan, India, Pakistan, Bangladesh, Sri Lanka, Nepal, Maldives and Bhutan. Due to political and military tensions between India and Pakistan, SAARC has not been effective in integrating the economies of signatory nations. The ineffectiveness is manifested in a fear that the more integrated South Asia becomes, the greater will be India's dominance over SAARC signatory nations. SAARC currently serves as a mere platform for annual talks and meetings between its members.[36]

Middle East

The majority of economic growth and stability in the Middle East depends upon the natural resource of oil. After the September 11, 2001 attacks on U.S. soil, the Middle East gained more attention through news reports. The conflict and partnership between the Middle East regions is a concern for nations not located in the region. The natural resource of petroleum influences the worldwide economy. This region of the world is the majority producer of petroleum. Organizations have been established to evaluate the producing of the resource.

Organization of Arab Petroleum Exporting Countries—OAPEC. OAPEC was created in 1968 by Kuwait, Saudi Arabia, and Libya. Since 1968, the addition of Algeria, Bahrain, Egypt, Iraq, Qatar, Syria, Tunisia and United Arab Emirates has strengthened the economy of OAPEC. However, Tunisia has disassociated membership from the OAPEC organization. The following excerpt reveals the mission statement of OAPEC:

> OAPEC is a regional inter-governmental organization concerned with the development of the petroleum industry by fostering cooperation among its members. OAPEC contributes to the effective use of the resources of member countries through sponsoring joint ventures. The Organization is guided by the belief in the importance of building an integrated petroleum industry as a cornerstone for future economic integration amongst Arab countries.[37]

The resource of oil is valuable to the majority of industries throughout the World. This organization faces continuous pressure from these industries, as well as political conflict. History has displayed how conflicts can affect the supply and demand of oil resources, resulting in price fluctuation. OAPEC has witnessed war in the 1970s, 1990s, and the current wars in Iraq and Afghanistan. However, they have proactively invited members to discuss these issues. By May 2006, the eighth Arab Energy Conference had been implemented. Issues discussed included the following:

- To establish an Arab institutional framework for oil and energy issues in order to develop a Pan-Arab perspective,
- Coordinate relations among Arab institutions concerned with energy and development,
- Harmonize energy policies with development planning,
- Investigate present and future Arab energy requirements and the means of meeting them,
- Identify and assess existing energy resources in the Arab countries,
- To coordinate and enhance efforts to develop these resources, and

- To identify and evaluate the impact of international energy policies on the Arab countries.[38]

OAPEC has established successful committees and leaders to regulate and monitor practices within the organization. The accomplishments of OAPEC include the creation of four companies that operate with their board of directors. The Arab Maritime Petroleum Transport Company's (AMPTC) objective is to oversee entire operations related to the marine transportation of hydrocarbons. The Arab Shipbuilding and Repair Yard Company (ASRY) is responsible for repairing, building, and maintaining all types of marine transportation machinery. The Arab Petroleum Investments Corporation (APICORP) assists in financing projects related to the oil industry. The Arab Petroleum Services Company (APSCO) provides oil services by developing specialized subsidiaries of different branches of oil services. OAPEC has implemented effective measures to ensure success in different areas of supplying petroleum to nations. However, progress is continuous in the area of political conflict affiliated with oil demands.

Gulf Cooperation Council—GCC

Established in 1981, the goal of the Gulf Cooperation Council (GCC) is to create economic wealth and maintain the growth of nations affiliated with the Persian Gulf. Currently, the members include Bahrain, Oman, Kuwait, Saudi Arabia, Qatar, and the United Arab Emirates. They operate as a common union because of free trade among the participating nations and common external tariffs. In addition, by 2010, the council will possibly develop into an Economic Union. A current issue that concerns the growth of the GCC is the opportunity to conduct trade operations with China. China is interested in the free trade agreement with the GCC, as some 40 percent of China's oil consumption is imported from these six nations of the Persian Gulf.[39] Results from this agreement might have a negative impact on the energy policies in other nations, such as the U.S., Japan, Russia, and the Southeast Asian nations.

Africa

Africa, the world's second largest continent, covers 11.6 million square miles and has a population of approximately 800 million people. More than 60 percent of Africa's people depend upon agriculture, with farming being mostly of the subsistence variety.[40] Despite extensive natural resources, there are no developed countries in Africa. Many countries have low indicators for education, health, life expectancy, and nutrition. Significant manufacturing capability remains a rarity, the exception being South Africa. Africa suffers from ill-conceived national boundaries that were drawn up by the colonial powers. These boundaries often separate peoples of the same tribe or bring antagonists from different tribes into contact with each other. The result is often internal conflict or regional strife.

A major factor that inhibits success of trade is the 1,000 various languages among 750 million citizens. In addition, African history has demonstrated much political instability, which results in low foreign investment because of high risk. Against this difficult background, progress has been made to integrate regional economic activity for mutual gain. The two most notable trade organizations are the Economic Community of West African Nations and the South African Customs Union.

Economic Community of West African States—ECOWAS. ECOWAS was formed in 1975 and included fifteen nations. Through the years, there have been a few changes in its membership. The original fifteen nations were Faso, Ghana, Mali, Sierra Leone, Benin, Burkina, Cote d'Ivoire, Gambia, Guinea, Guinea-Bissau, Liberia, Mauritania, Niger, Nigeria, Senegal, and Togo. One year after the organization was founded, Cape Verde joined to increase membership to sixteen countries. In 2002, Mauritania decided to withdraw from the organization, which left fifteen countries in ECOWAS. The main objective of ECOWAS was to integrate economies and partake in shared development of economic growth.

ECOWAS has faced numerous problems in attempting to unite the region. Contributing factors include a lack of infrastructure, not having diverse economies, the existence of other organizations with the same purpose, and political instability. Member nations have tried to agree on a common currency: the ECO. The thought was that a common currency would introduce and encourage the members to join the global commerce community through free trade. The creation of this currency has been postponed several times, as member countries have been unable to meet the minimum requirements for the creation of the currency. They are still in the process of attempting to meet the minimum criteria.

Another obstacle is hunger. It is very difficult to create and sustain an economy if the individuals cannot obtain food. In 2005, a Common Agricultural Policy (CAP) was approved. The main objective of CAP was to create a sustainable food source for the member countries. In order for them to succeed in uniting ECOWAS countries, they must find a way to overcome starvation in this region.

Another issue is the need to improve the current electrical grid to create a cheaper and more reliable energy sector to produce jobs, stimulate the economy, and increase trade inside and outside of the member nations. In a related issue, a natural gas pipeline is under consideration to provide a natural gas link to Togo,

Ghana, and Nigeria.[41] The idea behind these improvements is that the provision of reliable and inexpensive energy will lead to the stimulation of the ECOWAS economies. Currently, only one-third of the citizens in the member countries have access to electricity. Finally, ECOWAS has attempted to make traveling between member nations easier through the implementation of a program that generates certificates instead of passports, so the citizens can travel more freely. The certificates will be administered by a single agency instead of each country. This will reduce costs and confusion and hopefully increase the tourism industry.

Southern African Customs Union—SACU. In 1970, an agreement between the nations of Botswana, Lesotho, Namibia, South Africa, and Swaziland was implemented as a customs union. The SACU goals are to maintain the free interchange of goods between signatory nations and provide for a common external tariff and a common excise tariff. All customs and excise collected in the common custom area are paid into South Africa's national Revenue Fund. The Revenue is shared among members according to a revenue-sharing formula as described in the agreement.[42] Since the beginning of the integration, agreements within SACU have improved economic standards. The United States has played a major role in the economic and political growth in SACU. "SACU is the United States' second largest trading partner in Africa behind Nigeria whose exports are almost exclusively petroleum products."[43] However, this trading bloc creates many issues dealing with the needs of each participant involved with the SACU. The SACU and United States consider industry, labor rights, and environmental regulations very important to the prosperity of this region.[44]

Other International Groups

Establishments of International Groups are aimed to benefit the economic and social growth of the participating parties. These groups establish committees that govern the production and issues concerning the reason for the agreement. Listed below are two examples of cooperation groups that aim at establishing organization within the petroleum industry and the social and economic benefit of conducting research. These cooperations involve countries from neighbor regions and overseas. The involvement is to benefit the global economy and the economy within the participating nations.

Organization of the Petroleum Exporting Countries—OPEC. OPEC was founded in 1960 in Baghdad. The major function is to help member countries coordinate oil production in an effort to stabilize the oil market, while achieving a reasonable return on oil investment. As a result of soaring fuel prices, OPEC has received much attention in the U.S. Consumption of oil and oil products has greatly increased, with the majority of the growth in developing countries. OPEC nations produce 34.5 million barrels of oil each day. The U.S. estimates that world consumption exceeds 85 million barrels per day.[45]

Oil prices are not set by OPEC, but the organization does have an indirect influence on price. By increasing or reducing production, OPEC nations impact price through the theory of supply and demand. Simply put, the more they produce, the cheaper the product. By producing less oil, the cost increases. This theory holds true only if demand remains unchanged or increases. Instability in the oil-producing region, along with political issues with Iran and other nations, has led to the speculation of shortages, which leads to higher prices.

The decisions made by OPEC either directly or indirectly affect the majority of consumer goods being produced, sold, or used. The world has become smaller over time because of the ability to travel. This convenience has also produced opportunities for trade. The transportation used to import and export products requires oil or gasoline, either as a primary fuel or as a lubricant. Therefore, if oil is more expensive to buy, then the cost of the actual product being carried will probably increase. The importing and exporting companies will pass the cost of transportation on to the wholesalers; the wholesalers will pass it on to the retailers; and ultimately, the customer will pay for it.

Organization for Economic Cooperation and Development—OECD. The Organization for Economic Cooperation and Development was established in 1960 as an economic counterpart to the North Atlantic Treaty Organization (NATO). Currently, the thirty members of OECD include the following:

• Australia	• Hungary	• Norway
• Austria	• Iceland	• Poland
• Belgium	• Ireland	• Portugal
• Canada	• Italy	• Slovak Republic
• Czech Republic	• Japan	• Spain
• Denmark	• Korea	• Sweden
• Finland	• Luxembourg	• Switzerland
• France	• Mexico	• Turkey
• Germany	• Netherlands	• United Kingdom
• Greece	• New Zealand	• United States

The objective of the organization is increasing economic welfare through the world by covering issues associated with social work and economic efforts within participating governments and nonparticipating governments. It focuses on areas such as macroeconomics, science and innovation, development, education, and trade. The organization reports statistics dealing with social and economic issues to better educate the governments—such as consensus.[46] For example, a study conducted by OECD reported the reading proficiency of students in the participating countries. The study found that students in Finland, Canada, and New Zealand have the highest levels of reading proficiency. Students in Brazil, Mexico, and Luxembourg have the lowest levels, and students in Norway, France, the United States, Denmark, and Switzerland are clustered in the middle.[47] The research and development by OECD demonstrates the importance of information to governments to ensure proper programs to educate, monitor, and enrich citizens' lives.

Brief Summary of Major Points

- The global economy is constantly requiring evaluation to maintain and implement positive programs to ensure stability and growth throughout the world. However, every idea has steps to produce a positive outcome.

- Regional Economic Integration is a major factor in the success of the global economy.

- Effective partnership in any organization at any level will benefit the goal and impact the outcome to benefit the countries or citizens involved.

- The most rewarding route toward the success of the partnership is through effective communication.

- Regional integration is the process whereby countries remove barriers to trade between themselves, but each country determines its own barriers against nonmembers.

- Levels of integration include Free trade area, Customs union, Common market, and Economic union.

- Economic and political arguments for and against regional economic integration are empirically inconclusive.

- The major Regional economic integration agreements cover the Americas (North American Free Trade Agreement—NAFTA; Southern Common Market—Mercosur; Andean Common Market—ANCOM; Caribbean Community and Common Market—CARICOM; and Central American Common Market—CACM), Europe (European Union—EU), Asia (Association of Southeast Asian Nations—ASEAN; Asia Pacific Economic Cooperation—APEC; South Asian Association for Regional Cooperation—SAARC); the Middle East (Organization of Arab Petroleum Exporting Countries—OAPEC; Gulf Co-operation Council—GCC), and Africa (Economic Community of West African States—ECOWAS; Southern African Customs Union—SACU)

- Other International Groups include Cartels (Organization of the Petroleum Exporting Countries—OPEC; Organization for Economic Co-operation and Development—OECD)

Moving from Theory into Practice

The following summarizes a question and answer session with coauthor Joe Robinson. His answers are useful in contemplating how the global business professional can translate the theories and concepts covered in this chapter via practical answers to the questions from real life experiences.

<u>What are some of the strongest trade blocs and which is most restrictive in terms of protectionism?</u>

It has been said that perhaps NAFTA in one of the strongest and most restrictive trade blocks. There is "free" trade within NAFTA among Canada, Mexico, and the U. S.; however, for those countries outside of NAFTA, there are protective measures in place that are certainly restrictive to open trade.

An example I ran into several years ago involved an industrial adhesive product manufactured in one of the Eastern States and exported to Mexico. A broker in California imported a cheaper competitive adhesive from China in bulk, repackaged it into smaller containers, relabeled the product, and then exported the China-produced adhesive to Mexico. When this practice was discovered, it was stopped and appropriate high tariffs and restrictive measure were put in place to prohibit this form of "outside" competition, resulting in "protection" for the indigenous members to the NAFTA protocol.

My former company designs and manufactures valve actuators in Virginia and exports them to a major valve manufacturer in Canada. The Canadian company produces the finished automated valve and exports it to the oil patch in Mexico. This trade example is "free" in movement and unhampered in duties, as well as a nonrestrictive, nontariff barrier to the benefit of all three member countries and citizens.

Another very strong trade block is the agreement between Jordan and the United States. This agreement is predicated in both economic and political roots. QIZs (Qualified Industrial Zones) are powerful economic drivers in Jordan. Products produced in these QIZs enjoy a host of "free" nonrestrictive export movements into the United States. The U. S., in turn, enjoys a reciprocal host of nonrestrictive measures in exporting into Jordan. The result is a significant growth of export trade between these two countries that results in improved economic well being for both nations.

<u>I once heard the comment that "NAFTA is supposed to be all about free trade, but nothing is free in NAFTA. I am interested in hearing your thoughts on this.</u>

NAFTA is all about free trade among the three-member nations. However, as I started in the example above, it is not "free" for outside nations, and there are restrictive and protectionist measures in place that are enforced that each member country makes on its own, regarding trade with countries outside the NAFTA membership.

For instance, I hear that there is some trade friction between Mexico and China. The result is a policy of restrictive and protectionist measures in place between Mexico and China. High duties for some commodities in Mexico on Chinese imports and vice versa are an illustration of this phenomena. Keep in mind that most of this jockeying back and forth is all protecting and sustaining jobs. This is the major driving force, and called rational for instigating protectionist and restrictive measures and creating a "not free" situation between countries' international trade. Only time will tell if free and nonrestrictive movement of goods and services among trading blocks versus restrictive measures is the best policy. I suspect that a compromise of both policies will prevail as the best long-term global trade strategy among both developed and developing nations to benefit the win-win scenario we are all striving for.

<u>The chapter lists five stages of regional economic integration. Which stage is easiest to do business with, and which stage is the most difficult?</u>

It would seem to me that the second stage to establish regional tariffs that protect intraregional trade from "outside" forces is the easiest of the five stages to do business among the block-member nations. Tariffs are finite numbers on definitive products that can be understood by all. Applying and regulating tariffs is a daily activity across borders engaged in international commerce and is easy to factor into a company's export strategy, including costing and pricing. Being able to understand and clearly define tariffs makes it easy for employees to pursue their sales and profit motives and goals from the sales force to the production staff to the administrative staff, engaged in foreign trade for their respective companies.

The stage that appears to me to be most difficult in which to conduct business is the first stage— that is to establish some form of regional control regarding trade that fulfills the interests of nations within that region. Nations have pride, and giving up local control for regional intracountry control is a sensitive and oftentimes transcends into emotional considerations. How does one nation ensure and enforce the trading block rules and regulations in another member's country without giving reciprocity to that nation? A case in point, does the U.S. FDA have the "right" or is it a "privilege" to conduct unannounced audits on Canadian and Mexican exporters of processed food products into the U.S.? Would the U.S. reciprocate by allowing Canadian and Mexican government officials free access to conduct unannounced audits of food processing factories who export to Canada and Mexico? I don't think so, but this is something to think about when evaluating the pros and cons of trading blocks.

What role do you think the U.S.-Chile FTA will play in future economic integration?

As I stated in an earlier chapter, U. S. exports to Chile have risen by over 150 percent from 2004 to 2006, making the U. S. Chile's largest trading partner. Chile has a lot of what the U. S. needs and wants, and the U. S. has a lot of what Chile needs and wants. The result of the U.S.-Chile FTA is that both countries enjoy trade with a minimum of restrictions and reduction of cumbersome and unnecessary regulations, which create an easier and more harmonious environment for both countries to continue to expand this lucrative trade with each other.

What is it like to do business in the Persian Gulf Region?

A foremost distinction in doing business in the Gulf Region is the role that religion plays in the everyday life of its citizens. The prevalence of religion is a dominant factor to recognize and understand in order to be successful in conducting and expanding one's business in the Gulf.

On an annual basis, I lead a working trade delegation to the Gulf countries. I provide a summary of the important aspects of religion, how it interacts with business practices, and an understanding of the best protocol and procedures is a pretrip dialogue with each of the members of the trade mission. You do not need to adopt another's religion, but an understanding of its importance and a respect and reverence for another person's belief goes a long way in bridging the cultural and commercial opportunities that result in a more harmonious and healthy relationship for all.

I find that doing business in the Gulf region is both fascinating and rewarding. A respect and admiration exists with the many friends I have made over the years, and I strongly recommend doing business in this part of the world. It should be considered and factored into the international marketing action plan of any global-minded company.

What is it like to do business in the Far East?

The Far East has three of the world's most populous nations: China, India, and Indonesia. It is said that both China and India may overtake the U. S. and Japan in GDP within the next thirty to forty years. Whether or not this becomes reality, the fact is that such a large market cannot be ignored if you want to become a global business player.

What is it like doing business in the Far East . . . Well, first you must realize that each country is so different from the other with their own traits, tastes, and distinction. Most would agree that Japanese and Chinese foods are different than U.S. and Mexican foods. Most would agree that the language in Thailand has no similarity to the language in Korea. In China, the individual is strong; in Japan the group is strong.

The best policy in conducting business in the Far East is to treat each country separately in its own right and to understand its distinct customs, culture, and business practices accordingly. Also, realize that high-population density is a factor that influences daily decision of governments, companies, and individuals throughout Asia. One important factor in doing business in the Far East is their desire to get to know you first before delving into initial business discussions. A little patience goes a long way in the Far East and is a good trait to develop in pursuing successful business in this part of the world.

The chapter lists five basic goals of national governments. How important are these to the global business executive and why?

Peace, absence of violence, prosperity, reduction of poverty, and a clean, healthful environment are all issues of importance to national governments. These same issues are important to the global business executive because they offer unique business opportunities.

For example, a company that provides products or services for security purposes has prospects on a global basis with almost all foreign governments. I have witnessed this first hand on my last two overseas trade missions, one to the Gulf Region and the other to the Far East.

The very same phenomenon applies to the environmental domain. Foreign governments want and will increasingly make available a cleaner and more healthful environment for its citizens. A significant increase in interest in environmental products and services is taking place through out the world. This is an exciting and promising field for any young person to enter when considering a career with a company in global marketing and business prospects.

Another foremost business prospective is the generating, transmitting, and management of all forms of electric energy. The world today is starved for electric power. In some countries, there is a definite crises created by lack of electric energy to supply residents, offices, and factories. In my opinion, the power-energy market could provide one the greatest, personally satisfying careers a young person could enter today with the long term future in mind. Couple this with a position in global commerce and the chances for advancement, travel, financial gain, and personal satisfaction are all in place for an exciting lifelong career.

NAFTA seems to be a controversial and sensitive topic for discussion. Rarely does one see a balanced discussion concerning NAFTA. Can you give us some examples of when NAFTA has helped a U.S. firm and when it has hurt a U.S. firm?

Since my Executive Briefing to the White House on NAFTA in 1993, when President Bill Clinton conducted debates on the pros an cons of adopting this powerful trade block, I have seen U.S. companies go out of business because of NAFTA, and I have seen U.S. businesses prosper because of NAFTA. I have also seen a Mexican friend who owned an electric motor factory in Mexico City go out of business because of NAFTA. I also have Mexican friends who have prospered because of NAFTA.

The only consistent thing I can truly say about NAFTA is that it is a sensitive and controversial topic. One of the most controversial subjects involves the U.S. textile industry. Most of the apparel and cut and sew factories that were in the States are mostly all gone now. A few remain, but they tend to be very small and cater to a very select market. Anyone you talk to who has an interest in this side of the textile industry will most likely tell you all the bad things they can think of about NAFTA. On the other hand, I know of several specialty fabric and yawn factories that prospered because of NAFTA. As textile companies grew in Mexico because of NAFTA, these fabric and high-tech yawn producers enjoyed increased sales and profits, and they will most likely tell you good things about NAFTA.

Another U. S. industry that was hurt by NAFTA was the furniture factories. Many of these facilities simply shut down part or all of their manufacturing facilities in the States and went to Mexico. Here again, anyone with interest tied to this industry will have negative things to say about NAFTA. On the other hand, a number of U.S. companies who produce dimensional lumber, such as Appalachian hardwood (oak, walnut, cherry, maple) prospered because of NAFTA. They lost many of their traditional U. S. furniture factories but in some cases more than made up for the domestic loss when they sold greater quantities to the Mexican based furniture factories. Today, these very same factories have again pulled stakes and relocated to China, and the Appalachian hardwood suppliers are following their customers to China. The cycle goes on. For some, the cycle is devastating. For others, the cycle is a blessing. What we do know is that NAFTA is a dynamic. As the world evolves, especially in terms of global commerce, the theories and concepts in this and similar books all will agree that change is coming at a faster and faster pace, and some will wither away, others will survive, and a few will thrive. One phrase I like to hear is "trade or fade." There are more choices for young people today to enter global commerce than at any time in the history of the planet. Those who choose wisely will be rewarded accordingly.

Key Concepts

- Regional Economic Integration
- Tariff barriers
- Non-tariff barriers
- Globalization
- Trading blocs
- Free trade area
- Customs union
- Common Market
- Economic Union
- North American Free Trade Agreement (NAFTA)
- Southern Common Market (Mercosur)
- Andean Common Market (ANCOM)
- Caribbean Community and Common Market (CARICOM)
- Central American Common Market (CACM)
- European Union (EU)
- Association of Southeast Asian Nations (ASEAN)
- Asia Pacific Economic Cooperation (APEC)
- South Asian Association for Regional Cooperation (SAARC)
- Organization of Arab Petroleum Exporting Countries (OAPEC)
- Gulf Co-operation Council (GCC)
- Economic Community of West African Nations (ECOWAS)
- South African Customs Union (SACU)
- Organization of the Petroleum Exporting Countries (OPEC)
- Organization for Economic Co-operation and Development (OECD)

Chapter 7   ENTERING GLOBAL MARKETS

Global Business in Practice
Is Your Business Ready to Enter China's Markets?

The U.S. government is increasing resources dedicated to assisting U.S. companies explore business opportunities and address challenges to doing business in China. One such initiative is the China Business Information Center (BIC). The BIC has developed the following self-diagnostic tool, which may be used to open the door to pursue export opportunities and evaluate whether a company is prepared to meet the challenges posed by China's system for regulation of international trade. The correct response for each statement should be "Yes".

* Yes	No	Readiness Statement
☐	☐	Prior export experience to at least one foreign market.
☐	☐	Commitment to developing export opportunities including top management support, designation of an internal China sales manager, sales and technical staff who are willing to travel to China often, and support staff including an interpreter or translator to facilitate communication with Chinese buyers.
☐	☐	Sufficient financial resources to actively support marketing of products in China including translation of product brochures, participation in trade shows, and organization of customer informational seminars.
☐	☐	Ability to host visits by potential buyers to conclude sales negotiations, facilitate pre-contractual equipment inspections, and provide installation training.
☐	☐	Ability to acquire and analyze Chinese market data, identify sources of competition including domestic and foreign firms, and ascertain distribution channels.
☐	☐	Ability to acquire familiarity with export logistics unique to China including negotiation of letters of credit, freight forwarders, export documentation and export licensing.
☐	☐	Ability to locate Chinese import regulations, safety certification and labeling requirements and cultural preferences to modify the product and its packaging.

Global Business in Practice
Is Your Business Ready to Enter China's Markets?

The U.S. government is increasing resources dedicated to assisting U.S. companies explore business opportunities and address challenges to doing business in China. One such initiative is the China Business Information Center (BIC). The BIC has developed the following self-diagnostic tool, which may be used to open the door to pursue export opportunities and evaluate whether a company is prepared to meet the challenges posed by China's system for regulation of international trade. The correct response for each statement should be "Yes".

*Yes	No	Readiness Statement
☐	☐	Prior export experience to at least one foreign market.
☐	☐	Commitment to developing export opportunities including top management support, designation of an internal China sales manager, sales and technical staff who are willing to travel to China often, and support staff including an interpreter or translator to facilitate communication with Chinese buyers.
☐	☐	Sufficient financial resources to actively support marketing of products in China including translation of product brochures, participation in trade shows, and organization of customer informational seminars.
☐	☐	Ability to host visits by potential buyers to conclude sales negotiations, facilitate pre-contractual equipment inspections, and provide installation training.
☐	☐	Ability to acquire and analyze Chinese market data, identify sources of competition including domestic and foreign firms, and ascertain distribution channels.
☐	☐	Ability to acquire familiarity with export logistics unique to China including negotiation of letters of credit, freight forwarders, export documentation and export licensing.
☐	☐	Ability to locate Chinese import regulations, safety certification and labeling requirements and cultural preferences to modify the product and its packaging.

☐	☐	Prepared an international marketing plan with realistic goals, China-specific marketing strategies, progress benchmarks and an exit plan.
☐	☐	Sufficient financial resources to engage the services of local attorneys or consultants to navigate China's system of international trade regulation, develop a sales contract that is enforceable in China, undertake due diligence investigations, and address problems.
☐	☐	Ability and financial resources to provide training for a Chinese sales agent or distributor in the United States, continuous guidance for conducting market research and planning sales goals.
☐	☐	Ability to establish a program for protection of intellectual property including trademark or patent registration, market monitoring, and enforcement strategy.
☐	☐	Commitment to providing domestic and foreign customers equivalent service quality, which may necessitate frequent travel to China by a technician or establishment of an equipment service and maintenance center with a Chinese partner.

* U.S. Government Export Portal (Export.Gov). Export Assessment Survey. Retrieved on September 3, 2007 from http://www.export.gov/china

Why Domestic Firms Expand into Global Markets

Numerous variables must be considered in the decision to move domestic operations and products into the global marketplace. These decision variables include the desire to increase sales and profitability and to realize cost savings and profitability as a result of a partial or whole relocation in a foreign nation. Although most firms typically choose to enter into global markets from a proactive stance, some are forced to enter the global market in a reactive stance. Such firms would rather remain domestic, but the market forces them global in order to remain profitable. Figure 7.1 depicts additional decision variables to consider for competition in global markets.

Figure 7.1

Competing in Global Markets	
Competition on Quality and Price	Overseas competitors can attack a firm's domestic market by offering higher quality and lower prices.
Competition by Counterattack	If attacked in their home market by higher quality and lower prices, the domestic firm can counterattack the overseas competitor's home market.
Realization of Additional Profits	Domestic firms often discover foreign markets to be opportunities to potentially realize higher profits than in the home market
Economies of Scale	If domestic markets become saturated, the firm may need a larger customer base to maintain economies of scale.

These factors, when combined with conditions necessary for expansion into global markets, serve as the basis to drive global expansion. The necessary conditions include (1) expanding markets, (2) gaining access to resources, (3) cutting costs, and (4) capitalizing on special features of location.

Conditions Necessary for Expansion into Global Markets

The investigation of opportunities for global expansion requires the careful consideration of various business-environment conditions. Organizations should identify their strengths and weaknesses and understand how these may apply overseas. In addition, organizations should identify the unique resources and capabilities that may be offered to them. These considerations could determine whether or not a firm's products or services in the home market extends internationally and will meet foreign demand. Organizations should research the demographics of the potential market in which they are hoping to enter to see if there is a viable market for their product. Although population growth is a great reference to start with, it is not always the key indicator of a strong potential market. The percentage increase and decrease of a population and the average life expectancy in a global market serve as indicators of the global-market potential. Usually, the most attractive markets are in nations that seem to be growing in population and increasing in economic resources.

Organizations should consider the new risks and increases in business complexity typically associated with global expansion. Depending on the make up of the firm, some may need to expand elements of their supply chain as well as manage an increased number of foreign relationships. Foreign markets may require adaptations to certain existing products, thus requiring the organization to manage multiple products and market strategies simultaneously. This can be a very difficult challenge for small firms that lack the strategic internal resources that are available to larger firms to meet the legal, financial, and trading requirements of that specific foreign nation in which business expansion is desired. The challenge for multinational corporations would be to develop a portfolio of products and marketing programs that will result in effectively reaching the global needs and wants of its market. In comparison, the challenge for smaller firms would be to identify new markets, develop a marketing niche within them, and basically fill the gaps left by the larger MNCs, with respect to competition.

A business may decide to expand by entering global markets. However, entering global markets is not necessarily an easy task or a right decision for the business. Certain conditions are necessary for successful global expansion, and a number of risks must be considered. Figure 7.2 depicts the kinds of risks that should be considered. If these potential risks are understood, taken into account, and properly planned for, then the firm can focus on primary conditions, such as the firm's managerial commitment and the motivations behind global market entry.

Figure 7.2

Market Expansion Risk Variables	
National Customer Preferences	This occurs when the firm may not understand foreign customer preferences and fail to offer "globalized" products and services.
National Business Culture	This occurs when the firm does not know how to effectively deal with foreign nationals, the direct result of failure to understand their business culture.
National Regulations	This occurs when the firm incurs unanticipated costs as the result of underestimating foreign regulations.
National Political Risks	This occurs when governments change commercial laws, devalue currency, or undergo political revolution and expropriate foreign property.
Lack of Global Experience	This occurs when the firm lacks managers with international experience.

Managerial Commitment

The decision to expand into global markets is an enormous undertaking for all areas of the organization, not just corporate executives. Successful international expansion requires total commitment from management across the organization. The planning and execution stages of global expansion typically require long hours, overseas travel, and a team attitude. Additionally, the globalization team may need to consider the cost of adding needed personnel, initial expansion expenses, and strategies for overcoming potential employee resistance to the change. Corporations will have to utilize their complete management team—from marketing to facilities—to ensure that no detail is left out. Figure 7.3 provides a series of vital questions for firms to consider when determining the commitment of their management employees.

Many corporations find that managerial commitment is not a problem. In fact, there may be much enthusiasm about the prospects of growth and professional development. However, it is important to understand that transferring current managers to run new foreign operations might not be the best strategy to pursue. Benefits accrue to firms that hire a global manager who has a proven track record and the strengths needed to lead the international expansion.

Successful global managers tend to possess experiential knowledge specific to many cultures, rather than in-depth experience in a few. They may speak only one

language fluently, but what they do have is an understanding of how to appraise and adjust to the requirements of doing business in a culture different from their own. Global managers are needed because cultures themselves are becoming less distinct.[1] Senior management must effectively communicate the importance of these benefits to other managers and gain their support. Regardless, the commitment of the firm's management team is essential to the successful growth of international operations.

Managerial Commitment Questions	Figure 7.3
<ul><li>How committed is top management to going global?</li><li>How quickly does management expect its international operations to pay off?</li><li>What in-house, international experience does the firm have (international sales experience, language skills, etc.)?</li><li>How much senior management time should be allocated to the company's global efforts?</li><li>What organizational structure is required to ensure success abroad?</li></ul>	

Motivation

Different motivating factors serve as drivers for organizations to enter the global market. Additional motivation factors include the following:[2]

- To avail the firm of international market opportunities,
- Current markets have been saturated,
- To reduce strategic risk,
- To reduce the volatility of the income stream,
- To increase net earnings,
- To seek new economies of scale and scope,
- To reduce costs through getting access to lower cost factors of production,
- To support overseas trade barriers, and
- To establish new competitive advantages.

Market entry motivation can be classified into two separate areas: (1) proactive and (2) reactive.

Proactive reasons are based on the firm's internal situation and are firm initiated, while reactive reasons are based on the firm's behavior with respect to the environment and adaptation to changes from outside the firm. Firms with proactive motivations go international because they want to, while reactive firms go international because they must.[3]

Proactive

Possibly the greatest proactive motivation for global expansion is the prospect of increased profits. The firm might see an opportunity in a foreign market that could reap greater profit margins than in their domestic market. A firm might also proactively expand internationally to give itself a strategic advantage over its competitors. The proactive motivation for smaller firms tends to relate to an exclusive product or some type of competitive or strategic technological advancement. "Firms with more than twenty-five employees export also to achieve economies of scale and to avoid losing out on foreign opportunities."[4]

Other motivators for international expansion could be that enterprises have obtained special information about promising customers or market opportunities abroad or are motivated by incentives of some sort, such as tax benefits granted by foreign governments. Since the major underlying motivation is the quest for increased profit, the need is for increased output to benefit from economies of scale and the consequent drive to expand business beyond the national boundaries.[5]

Figure 7.4

Major Proactive Motivations for International Expansion
• Quest for profit
• Competitive advantage
• Market opportunities
• Economies of scale
• Tax benefits[6]

Reactive

In contrast, some firms make the decision to enter global markets based on reactive motivations. In this case, the firm is reacting to external, environmental factors. In essence, such firms are forced to expand internationally. These situations occur when there is saturation in the domestic market and the firm must expand in order to survive financially. The firm could also be looking for ways to reduce costs, and foreign expansion could offer the firm cheaper production costs. The firm could even be reacting to tremendous pressures from competition or the political environment.

The following factors are reactive motivations for firms to expand into the global economy:[7]

- Competitive pressure
- Excess capacity
- Overproduction
- Saturated or declining home market

Regardless, the reactive firm expands as a response to other forces, not because of its own desire to globalize.

Basic Entry Considerations and Questions

As a number of organizations research, examine, identify, and evaluate potential entry opportunities into international markets, businesses must carefully consider the potential benefits, advantages, challenges, and risks involved in the efforts of competing within an international market. For years, some domestic organizations have achieved long-term success, while others have experienced failure when competing in local, regional, and national markets. As previously mentioned, the decision to expand into a global market can be intimidating. The process of international expansion may be time consuming and difficult, but it is a process that could reap great rewards for the organization. A few basic steps are essential when considering global expansion:

- Begin the global expansion campaign by preparing an international business plan to evaluate organizational needs and goals.
- Conduct foreign market research and identify international markets.
- Evaluate and select methods of distributing products overseas.
- Learn how to set prices, negotiate deals, and navigate the legal morass of exporting. Cultural, social, legal, and economic differences make exporting a challenge for business owners who have only operated in the U.S.
- Secure government and private sources of financing.
- Package and label products to comply with legal requirements of the target nation's market.[8]

Although these steps may seem simple, much time and effort must go into the implementation of each step to create an effective, successful, global expansion plan of action. A more comprehensive plan includes, but is not limited to the following:

- Secure company wide commitment.
- Define the business plan for accessing global markets.
- Determine how much is available to invest in the international expansion.
- Plan at least a two-year lead time for world market penetration.
- Build a website and implement the international plan sensibly.
- Pick a product or service to take overseas.
- Conduct market research to identify prime target markets.
- Search out the data needed to predict how the product will sell in a specific geographic location.

- Prepare the product for export.
- Find cross-border customers.
- Establish a direct or indirect method of export.
- Hire a good lawyer, a savvy banker, a knowledgeable accountant, and a seasoned logistic specialist.[9]

In addition to these considerations, three questions are especially important to international expansion: location, timing, and scale.

 Location—Which Markets to Enter?

New entrants desiring to expand and compete in foreign markets must place considerable focus on identifying potential global markets that will prove to be favorable towards the firm's profitability, performance, and financial goals. The global strategic planning process is complex and entails more factors, variables, challenges, and risks than domestic strategic planning. In formulating a global strategic entry plan, firms should research, assess, and analyze the external environments that exist in the foreign markets being considered. The global strategic planning process is an important systematic assessment and analysis approach that should be utilized by new entrants attempting to determine the direction and stability of global market considerations. Clearly, new entrants must be able to assess the direction and stability of trade practices, financial markets, social, economic, technological, environmental, political, and legal external market influences existing within potential international markets.

One of the most important questions to answer when entering the global market is that of location: What or which markets can the organization enter and be successful? Figure 7.5 depicts the business attractiveness of a location, divided among location-specific categories.

Business Attractiveness - Location		Figure 7.5
Market Existence	A market must exist for the product or service. There is no need to attempt penetrating the market if the market does not exist. The product or service must be one that foreign consumers can use, are attracted to, and can afford.	
National Attributes	The country must have attractive attributes desired by the firm. In some cases, the firm may desire to locate a local office within the foreign nation.	
Geography and Socio-Economic Attributes	This includes the attractiveness of the geography of region, the socioeconomics of the population, proximity to required resources, labor costs, costs of living, and quality of life variables.	
Openness to Global Trade	These variables include the legal system, political structure, and the business customs unique to that nation. Governments that create and promote free trade zones or other means encourage trade with other nations are deemed more attractive than locations that do not.	

Timing—When is The Best Time To Enter These Markets?

The question of timing is another important aspect. Entering the market at the right time, or the wrong time can have tremendous effects on the success or failure of the expansion. Firms must take into account the needs of the foreign market, the current economic trends, political environment, and other important factors when timing their global expansion strategy. Sometimes a move toward globalization can be timed perfectly by evaluating key indicators. Another consideration in timing a global strategy is to find the right partner. Going into business with the wrong partner can ruin the expansion efforts before they even get started. Organizations must ensure that they do not plan hurriedly or rush into foreign markets to jump on an opportunity for quick cash: "Some entrepreneurs who expanded too quickly into export markets now are struggling to survive, and some have soured on globalization completely. It takes at least three years for a company to penetrate a foreign market."[10] Organizations are well advised to exercise due diligence in terms of planning and wait until the timing is right before expanding into the global market.

Scale—Large Scale or Small Scale?

The question of the scale of expansion is a complex one, varying from organization to organization. Advances in technology, particularly in regards to the World Wide Web, allow all sizes of organizations to compete in the global economy. The global marketplace is no longer defined by corporate juggernauts but is composed of an array of organizations from large corporations to small businesses. No longer are organizations forced to set up operations on foreign soil, although many do. Small businesses can take advantage of foreign distribution companies that will take companies' products and place them in overseas markets. Small businesses can also turn to e-commerce to sell to foreign markets. Through the Internet, Business to Customer (B2C) and Business to Business (B2B) transactions can be made easily and instantaneously, without the need for brick and mortar operations. However, one must understand that combining foreign exporting and web technology does include additional costs to the firm.

Key Factors That Influence the Entry Mode Selection

Firms entering new foreign markets choose from a variety of different forms of entry: licensing and franchising, exporting (directly or through independent channels), and foreign direct investment (FDI) (joint ventures, acquisitions, mergers, and wholly owned, new ventures). Entry modes vary the degree of control the firm has over invested tangible and intangible resources and the transactions costs associated with that resource commitment.[11] The key factors that influence the entry mode selection are (1) international experience of the firm, (2) size of the market, (3) production and shipping costs, and (4) political, legal, cultural, and labor environments.

 International Experience of the Firm

A primary characteristic of the globalization of markets is the advent of the global consumer. The expectation of standardized goods and services with a corresponding level of consistency in service, quality, and performance across nations and regions signifies the trend towards global commerce. The convergence of international and domestic pricing also indicates the era of the global consumer.[12] However, technology appears to be the engine of customer globalization, fueled by increased personal contact. The result is a new level of segmentation of customer requirements, which transgresses traditional political and cultural boundaries. In response, companies must look at the world as if it were one large marketplace and segment worldwide—on the basis of commonality of preferences.[13] Market orientation is a significant contributor to the positional advantage of the company and is related to the long-term, overall firm performance. Therefore, regarding the global trends in customer preferences, global organizations should possess the capability of acquiring, interpreting, and integrating intelligence in order to identify past, present, and potential commonalities.[14] The firm should also be able to monitor the environmental changes (regulatory, economic, and sociopolitical) and estimate their impact on the commonalities present in the customer base. The successful development of a global, customer–knowledge management process will make a positive impact on the success of the company.

In a global industry, the competitive position in one country is dependent on the position present in other countries. Moreover, organizations pursuing a global strategy are facing both global and local competition. Consequently, companies have to coordinate their competitive moves on a global basis on a competitive battlefield, constituting the entire world. In addition, companies often use competitors as sources for benchmarking and best-practice transfer.[15] A key capability for firms is the competitive market knowledge process, the amount, timeliness, and accuracy of competitor intelligence constraining the ability to respond to competitive moves globally. Like customer knowledge competence, competitor knowledge competence is characterized as the knack to acquire, interpret, and integrate information regarding the global competitive environment. The competitor knowledge process is one of the global market knowledge competencies required to succeed in the global marketplace; the ability to acquire knowledge regarding global competitors may result in a significant positive impact on the performance of the company.[16]

Size of the Market

Market potential is an important variable in determining which market a firm will enter. In attractive markets, long-term profitability for a firm is expected to be provided through these investment modes.[17] A firm may sometimes choose investment modes, even if scale economies are not very large. Investment modes provide a great chance for a firm to enter, even if the economies are not significant. A company may choose investment modes since they give the greatest chance for a firm to institute a long-term market presence.

Uncertainty over current economic, political, and government policies plays a part in the investment risk in home countries. They are critical for the profitability and survival of a company's operation in the country of choice.[18] Problems can arise when changes in a country's governmental policies take place in relation to earnings, and in extreme cases, expropriation of assets. Researchers have suggested that limiting policies of foreign governments are likely to hinder inward investments.[19] While a company would be better off by not going into a country with changing policies, non-investment options might favor the firm if it does choose to enter. Market factors in target countries consist of general business environment and competitive structure of local companies.[20]

The size of the target market is an important factor when deciding on the entry mode. Small markets support entry modes that have low breakeven sales volumes, like indirect or agent exporting, licensing, and some contractual arrangements. However, markets with high sales potential are possible for entry modes with substantial breakeven sales volumes. Entry modes for high breakeven sales volumes are subsidiary exporting and equity investment in local production.

Production and Shipping Costs

A country's local production costs play an essential role in determining the profitability of the investment in production. Low production cost in a country encourages local production, and high cost goes against local manufacturing. A firm's production costs are related to energy, labor, raw materials, and other productive agents. Also, the quality and cost of an economic infrastructure has an evident bearing on the entry-mode decision. Other applicable factors include raw materials availability and experienced labor. If the raw materials or the labor is high, it is possible that the cost would be driven up. In the host country, factors might exist that could inhibit the firm's ability to transfer resources. More accurately, the host country firms often have the inability to receive and absorb its resources.[21] Certain benefits are usually achieved when a firm uses exporting strategies, such as accessing the international market more quickly. Direct market accession offers a firm low risk, gives them a simple way to initiate the process of entering a global market, and helps the firm meet demands and challenges.[22]

Exporting also has its disadvantages, such as the high cost of transportation and the potential of tariffs being placed on incoming goods. In addition, the exporter has less of a handle on the distribution of its products in the chosen country of entry, and the distributor usually gets part of the profits—either in the form of pay or adding extra to the price. The exporting mode of entry is usually used by small businesses that have a limited number of resources. If the firm thinks that it is not able to grasp a production-related advantage in the country of choice, it may choose indirect exporting if the possibility exists to generate a competitive advantage on the marketing side.

A number of firms use exporting as entry into the international market. Exporting can be a strategic alternative that helps maintain the efforts and resources, while giving the firm a chance to exploit international opportunities.[23] Exporting can become an international learning experience. Many industrial firms choose to export for their first international entry mode.[24] However, some companies succeed globally while operating primarily as exporters.[25]

Environments—Political, Legal, Cultural, Labor, etc.

A host of external environmental factors influence a firm's choice of direction, action, and ultimately, its organizational structure and internal processes.[26] External environmental factors can affect the entry of new entrants in another country, whether they are economical, social, political, cultural, or legal.

- Economic factors concern the nature and direction of the economy in which a firm operates. Because consumption patterns are affected by the relative affluence of various market segments, each firm must consider economic trends in the segments that affect its industry.

- Developed from cultural, ecological, demographic, religious, educational, and ethnic conditioning, the social factors that affect a firm involve the beliefs, values, attitudes, opinions, and lifestyles of persons in the firm's external environment. As social attitudes change, the demand for various types of clothing, books, and leisure activities change as well.

- The direction and stability of political factors are a major consideration for managers in formulating company strategy. Political factors define the legal and regulatory parameters within which firms must operate. Political constraints are placed on firms through fair-trade decisions, antitrust laws, tax programs, minimum wage, legislation, pollution and pricing policies, administrative jawboning, and many other actions aimed at protecting employees, consumers, the general public, and the environment. Since such laws and regulations are most commonly restrictive, they tend to reduce the potential profits of firms.

- To avoid obsolescence and promote innovation, a firm must be aware of technological changes that might influence the industry. Creative technological adaptations can suggest possibilities for new products, improvement in existing products, or in manufacturing and marketing techniques.[27]

Each of these variables or factors can present major challenges and risks to entrants. However, for those organizations devoted to the development and implementation of their formulated global strategic plans, whose members act responsively to address operational or consumer issues, they can eventually experience profitability and achieve their performance and financial objectives. International business managers should carefully examine, assess, and evaluate a country's organizational, social, cultural, political, judicial, market, economic, technological, and industry trends to determine whether entry into an international market is financially feasible, unfavorable, or risky.

Environmental turbulence has a significant effect on the market–knowledge–competence–performance relationship. Environmental turbulence has two dimensions: technological turbulence and market dynamism. Technological turbulence is the extent to which production/service technology in your principal market has changed over the last years.[28] Technological changes provide a firm huge opportunity in industries that are subject to high technological turbulence. In these industries, the organizations will enjoy abnormal returns from alternative opportunities, rather than those created by their market knowledge competencies. The technological turbulence will inhibit the global–market-knowledge–performance relationship. On the other hand, market dynamism is related to the rate of change of the customer preferences, market segments, and demand patterns.[29] Organizations have to adapt more rapidly to the customers changing demands in such an industry. In a dynamic global market, companies need to develop stronger knowledge competencies in the global market and focus on the global customer knowledge process and on the global responsiveness in order to succeed. Therefore, environmental turbulence is expected to have a significant role on the market, knowledge, competence, development, and utilization of the global company.

Another moderator that has been incorporated into the previous market orientation and learning frameworks is the competitive intensity present within an industry. When strong global competition is scarce, the global firm should perform well, even though it does not develop global-market-knowledge competencies or global responsiveness, because customers do not possess alternatives. However, firms with intense global competition will be forced to be quick to respond on a global scale, be able to acquire, interpret, and integrate the market knowledge, and coordinate the efforts on a global basis, in order to create higher value for their customers.

Another type of uncertainty that influences transaction costs is created by the target market environment. Environmental uncertainties are risks associated with doing business in a foreign country. The firm must feel reasonably secure in its ability to enforce contracts and manage other types of political and legal risks. If a company wants to increase control, it must commit additional resources, which could mean that the company exposes itself to other environmental risks.

Firms are better off selecting non-equity, low-investment entry modes in countries that have high environmental uncertainty. This strategy "not only avoids resource commitment, but frees entrants to change partners or renegotiate contract terms and working arrangements relatively easily as circumstances develop and change."[30] A company can keep itself flexible by following a low-resource commitment plan, allowing the firm to switch partners or exit the market altogether if the need arises.

Entry Modes

Businesses that look to expand internationally understand that other markets have to be included into the fold of its operations. These other markets could be investments in other markets outside of the company's main focus, or possibly, a company taking its product and introducing it into another area. Two types of entry modes are available into a market: low intensity or high intensity. The main difference between the two depends on how much risk and/or control an entering business is willing to take.

Low-intensity entry refers to no investment into the new market, which is optimal for businesses that may not have enough financial capital to initiate operations in a new market. However, a business can also align itself with an organization already established in the new market. Exporting and importing are great examples of low-risk (and also low control) entry modes into a new market. With no investment, a company cannot have a great amount of control, because there is no investment to be gained or lost. High-intensity entry involves making significant amounts of investment, not just financial but also with marketing, distribution, and possibly in executives.[31] Because of greater investment, businesses would have a greater amount of control over the new market entity; therefore, they would be able to influence operations in order to maximize growth potential. The key consideration is managerial control.

In the following sections, different modes of global-market entry will be discussed. These modes vary from low control to high control and also low risk to high risk. The entry modes include exporting and importing, licensing and franchising, management contracts, turnkey projects, joint ventures, and wholly owned subsidiaries.

Exporting and Importing

Businesses seeking to expand internationally can engage in the practices of exporting and importing. Exporting is the sending of goods abroad for trade or sale. Importing is the bringing in of goods from abroad to trade or sale—which may be the best option to gain a foothold. In most cases, exporting and importing requires a minimal initial investment and may allow a business to develop key relationships with export/import firms (intermediaries) that will aid in ensuring success into the new market. However, businesses must ensure that the necessary market and customer demand analyses demonstrate that exporting would be profitable, both financially and strategically. Multinational corporations (MNC) value the importance of exporting and importing. In the United States, especially, over 40 percent of exports and over 35 percent of imports occur among MNCs.[32] Firms seeking to export and import products and services to or from a foreign country may employ the services of intermediaries and facilitators.

The Importance and Use of Intermediaries

Export intermediaries are utilized to provide expertise to inexperienced exporters as they enter overseas markets. They are also contracted to assist the experienced exporter in entering markets in unfamiliar countries. Intermediaries are organizations that act as a facilitator for a potential supplier and consumer. These firms can facilitate the transfer of goods and services from a company to the consumer in a new market. Ordinarily, a business decides to use an intermediary when there is a value-added benefit. For example, the intermediary might have an extensive list of potential connections in the foreign market that would assist the business in its entry. In addition, by taking on the responsibilities of marketing, intermediaries ensure that the manufacturer's products get maximum exposure in the foreign market.

The utilization of intermediaries was originally bolstered by the Export Trading Company Act of 1982 (OECTA). OECTA created new U.S. trade incentives by promoting the export of U.S. goods and services and encouraging the formation of export trading companies and export management companies.[33] Furthermore, OECTA empowered United States banks to make equity investments in commercial ventures that qualify as export trading companies. Two types of intermediaries, export management and export trading companies, demonstrate how a business can enter into a new market with minimal investment costs.

Export management companies. A company that may not have the time and/or resources to establish an export department might consider employing the services of an export management company (EMC). Emus are independent businesses that liaison between the parent company (manufacturer) and the customer (another business, nation, or people). One of the most important advantages in using an EMC is that it can handle *all* aspects of exporting a company's product into the new market(s). An EMC would have contacts and knowledge of the designated market to make exporting successful.[34] Typically, an EMC will work with a manufacturer by either performing duties as an agent or a distributor. As an agent, the EMC facilitates the order fulfillment process between the exporter and foreign customer. As a distributor, the EMC actually buys the manufacturer's products and then sells them to the customer. An EMC functions in foreign markets just as a sales representative or exclusive wholesaler functions for a manufacturer in the United States. An EMC usually has a formal agreement with manufacturers. The primary disadvantage of using an EMC is that "a manufacturer may lose control over foreign sales. Most manufacturers are properly concerned that their product and company image be well maintained in foreign markets."[35]

Export trading companies. An export trading company transacts commercial and financial activities to facilitate exports by unaffiliated persons. These activities include distribution, shipping, warehousing, and finance. Such transactions are increasingly conducted online. An export trading company usually takes title to the goods.[36] Therefore, the terms export trading company and export management company are often used interchangeably. A special kind of export trading company is a group organized and operated by producers. These export trading companies can be organized along multiple- or single-industry lines and can also represent producers of competing products.

The advantages of utilizing intermediaries are summarized as follows:
- Intermediaries are responsible for managing all of the technical and legal issues associated with the export activities.
- Intermediaries are responsible for generating the local business clientele and maintaining the business relationship. Intermediaries usually have a network of foreign agents and distributors and can generate sales at a more rapid pace.
- Intermediaries are responsible for the distribution of the product within the host country.
- Intermediaries can be helpful in determining the credit status and worthiness of potential clientele.
- Intermediaries can determine the competitive balance within the selected host country
- Intermediaries can be helpful in training corporate staff to eventually become expert exporters in that particular market.

The disadvantages of utilizing intermediaries are summarized as follows:
- Intermediaries are independent commercial entities and are primarily interested in reaping the most profits for their business; therefore, these

companies might not be providing a plan for future growth of the contracting company within the foreign marketplace.

- Intermediaries have limited financial resources and will usually rely on the contracting company to provide immediate financial support to finance and distribute the product and or service.

- Utilizing an intermediary will usually result in the contracting company having less control of its product, distribution, and customers in the host market. This may result in smaller profit margin for the contracting company, as the intermediary is paid prior to distribution of any profits.

- Utilization of intermediaries requires a multifaceted legal relationship between the contracting company, the intermediary, and the clientele.

Finally, choosing which intermediary to use can be assisted by asking the following questions:

- What is the historical and financial history of the intermediary company?

- Does the intermediary have the proper resources to ensure the success of your export operation?

- Does the intermediary have the facilities to support your export operation and future goals?

- How long have they been in the business as an intermediary, including specifically in this foreign market?

- What is the intermediary's banking reputation in the foreign market?

- What is the reputation of the intermediary's financial officers within the business community?

Facilitators

As an organization embarks on entering a new market, whether domestic or international, problems will arise that may need amelioration. For example, one should consider a firm that wants to determine the mode of global market entry that meets the criteria of being both cost efficient and ensuring the highest instance of success. The firm may employ the services of a facilitator to assist in making this determination. A facilitator is an individual whose job is to help manage a process of information exchange. "While an expert's role is to offer advice, particularly about the content of a discussion, the facilitator's role is to help with how the discussion is proceeding."[37] Facilitators are often considered "coaches" or outside consultants brought in to help steer the firm in the right exporting direction. While this may be the end result, a facilitator's role is not to motivate employees but to make an action. Facilitators aid employees in determining what may be the best methods of making the action. Facilitators can benefit organizations in both the private and public sectors.

Private sector. The primary private sector facilitator for intermediaries, outside of export management and trading companies, are commercial banks. Commercial banks are in the business of being profitable and will assist businesses in international ventures and finance as part and parcel of their business mission. Many commercial banks employ international business experts who are knowledgeable in all areas of export finance, including, but not limited to, foreign currency exchange, correspondent relationships, funds transfer, collection of foreign debts and invoices, and foreign finance laws. Additionally, most large commercial banks either maintain local banking branches globally or have foreign representation to assist their customers within the borders of the host country. Proper intermediaries may be located via the National Association of Export Companies, one of several associations that contains a directory of export management and export trade companies, which can be utilized by United States small businesses and corporations.

Public sector. The primary public sector facilitators for intermediaries are located at both state and federal government levels. At the state level, state export assistance agencies engage in counseling sessions and sponsor conferences and trade events to educate and assist local exporters on numerous topics, including export documentation, licensing, franchising, export trading companies, market-entry in-country research, and trade policy initiatives. The International Trade Division of the Virginia Economic Development Partnership is a leading example of a public sector facilitator (http://www.exportvirginia.org). The International Trade Division provides resources, programs, and services on a global basis for the benefit of promoting economic development for those firms who employ Virginia citizens.

The United States Department of Commerce Export Centers and the United States Department of Commerce Commercial Service provide facilitating services and programs at the federal level. These facilitators have a network of approximately 1,750 trade exporters in over eighty nations to assist a global business in generating export sales and services. Export assistance centers of The United States Department of Commerce may be accessed via several Internet websites, including http://www.ita.doc.gov. Numerous other U.S. government facilitators exist, including the following:

- The United States Department of Agriculture (USDA)—The USDA acts as the primary starting point for United States companies interested in exporting agricultural products to foreign markets. The USDA, via its Foreign Agricultural Services branch, can provide United States corporations assistance in accessing foreign agricultural markets and/or accessing United States foreign agricultural programs.
- United States Small Business Administration (SBA)—Small businesses are extremely active in the foreign export market. One of the primary government facilitators for small businesses, the SBA agency will provide corporate services, which include financing, trade counseling, and commodity brokerage. The SBA will also provide prospective businessmen with "face to face" services at one of their approximately 107 locations within the United States. These services include but are not limited to the following:
    - Export Trade counseling—one of the primary methods utilized by the United States Small Business Administration in both educating and empowering small businesses within the global marketplace. This counseling is usually developed in part and parcel of larger conferences or workshops for small businesses. The counseling includes information on licensing procedures, favored nation status, trade policy initiatives, and utilization of legal counsel.
    - Export Legal Assistance Network—a nationwide directory of attorneys with experience in international trade which will usually provide an initial consultation without cost to the client.

Licensing and Franchising

Licensing and Franchising are other foreign market entry modalities. These modes can be considered indirect forms of the exporting process. Instead of exporting goods or services, a company exports technology. Technology, in this sense, is defined as the means to accomplish the goals and objectives of the organization. This includes all business function and human resource capabilities of the firm.

A license is an agreement that allows one party to use a property right in exchange for payment to the other party. The party giving the license is the licensor, while the party that gets to use the right is the licensee. A licensor does not have to invest into the foreign market because the licensee (more than likely) is established in the market. A licensee purchases the license and then afterwards pays a set fee, based on revenue, to the licensor. Similar to an alliance, the license is limited to a set period of time. Licensing enables a firm to penetrate markets that might not otherwise have been accessible because of foreign policy or laws. China serves as an example of a country that does not allow foreign countries implicit access to its market. Rather, it compels interested firms to form alliances or joint ventures in order to enable domestic firms to gain technological advancements or other resources. Through licensing, a foreign business can circumvent this policy and still obtain financial profits.

Franchising is an alternative to licensing that also does not necessitate an initial investment into a foreign market. In this case, a company sells its name, business strategies, and standard operating procedures to another party for a fee. Fees typically include an initial fee for the franchise and then a percentage of annual revenues. The franchisor usually continues to support the operation of the franchisee's business by providing advertising, accounting, training, related services, and in many instances, products needed by the franchisee.[38] The United States has the greatest number of franchisors, followed by Africa and Asia. In 2000, over $1 trillion dollars in revenue was made by U.S. franchises.[39]

A number of benefits may accrue from the use of franchising and licensing. Franchising is considered attractive to firms in that it allows entry into the international marketplace without completely needing to "reinvent the wheel" (redevelop the firm in another nation). Franchising provides an effective avenue to internationalize the business. The franchisee, or licensee, attains revenues from an established product and/or brand. Licensing allows a firm to enter a foreign market without incurring significant investment costs.

Licensing and franchising also have several drawbacks. The risks associated with licensing intellectual property and the specific portions of the contract are left to interpretation. Furthermore, after factoring in the discrepancies in international laws, it is difficult to ensure the licensee will not use the intellectual property to its advantage, after the contract has expired. Piracy can occur anywhere that licensing is used as a mode of entry and is most prevalent in countries where antipiracy laws are neither recognized nor encouraged.[40]

Management Contracts

Management contracts "represent situations where a company with experience in specific business areas or industrial sectors makes personnel available to perform general or specialized management functions for another company."[41] The duration of most management contracts is between three and five years, with renewal terms varying within individual contracts. Developing countries utilize management contracts for two primary purposes:

1. In commercial fields where technical expertise is required to manage the day-to-day operations of a corporation or government entity.

2. Within corporate circumstances where in-depth institutional knowledge or skill is a prerequisite for proper facility management to manage a facility or entity.

A management contract not only meets the current needs of the host country, but should also be used to develop and train host managers who will eventually manage the facility after the expiration of the contract. Management contracts offer the following advantages:

*   The management contractor does not utilize many of its assets to meet the contract demands.
*   The host nation provides the funds for any infrastructure associated with the project management.
*   The contractor helps to develop a local workforce in the host company, which is eventually trained to manage these fields.

The disadvantages of management contracts include the following:

*   The corporation's personnel within the host country are subject to any risks, personal and financial, associated with that country.
*   The development of host company managers eventually creates a direct competitor, not only within the country but also in other global markets.

Turnkey Projects

Turnkey projects are another mode of foreign market entry. In a Turnkey project "one client company contracts another company to build and deliver a ready to operate industrial plant or infrastructure facility, such as a power plant, a highway or a port. In such cases, the client can be a government agency."[42] Turnkey projects are common when developing with infrastructure projects or other complex subcontracting:

Turnkey projects have become quite common in recent decades, and it has become a successful mode of business operation, particularly in developing countries. Foreign banks and donors often make recommendations to developing countries on turnkey deliveries to minimize risks involved. An advantage of the turnkey project is that a single party will coordinate all the interfaces with its sub-contractors and will have all liabilities and guarantees. It also relieves the purchaser in a developing country of the responsibility of managing and coordinating the various technical and managerial aspects in a situation where there are often inadequate technical and managerial capabilities.[43]

The advantages of Turnkey projects include the following:

- Turnkey projects are helpful in the creation of the infrastructure in developing countries.
- Turnkey projects usually help to develop the contractors' capacities for subcontracting and developing managers.
- During a Turnkey project, the contractor assumes all of the responsibility of the overall project, which usually helps the client avoid any construction delays or prospective price gouging.

The disadvantages of Turnkey projects include the following:

- The Turnkey project, usually developed via bidding, can become highly political with high tendencies for bribery and illegal kickbacks.
- The Turnkey project not only creates a direct competitor to the contractor, but also builds a facility that the host contractor has designed and tested.

Joint Ventures

Joint ventures, another modality of market entry, are used as alternative-business strategic alliances for corporations in the global marketplace. A strategic alliance is a voluntary arrangement between companies involving exchange sharing, codevelopment of products, technologies, or services. Joint ventures are a "special type of alliance in which a new firm is created and owned by the alliance partners."[44] In other words, joint ventures usually involve an alliance where two or more companies contribute assets, which results in the formation of a new legal entity.

Organizations considering the use of the joint venture strategy must carefully consider the legal aspects of engaging in such a partnership. Legal counsel should be aware of the host nation's laws concerning, but not limited to, the following:

- The percentage of ownership allowed by foreign countries,
- Limitations concerning the ownership of minority shares within the host country; technology and licensing agreements, and
- Local and United States antitrust laws.[45]

When entering into a joint venture alliance, it is prudent to retain legal counsel in the U.S. and in the host foreign country, in order to be prepared for the various legal ramifications outlined above. U.S. firms should also request a business review letter from representatives of the Department of Justice when there are significant antitrust issues.

Finally, joint venture alliances are predicated on economic, social, and cultural issues. Whenever a firm enters a relationship with a foreign entity, it must be aware of the customs of the foreign partner, from both a marketing level and in developing human resource protocols.

The advantages of joint ventures include the following:

- The joint venture alliances help lessen and/or defend from the risks associated with the foreign market.
- The alliances allow a novice corporation immediate presence within a foreign country and ease the initiation process into the marketplace.
- The joint venture lessens the overhead costs of a solo operation within a foreign country.
- A joint venture allows the U.S. partner the ability to obtain foreign technology, foreign brands, and foreign managerial techniques.
- The joint venture alliances provide a tactical shield for the U.S. company because the "face" of the company is usually the foreign partner.[46]

Some of the disadvantages of the joint ventures include the following:

- The loss of managerial control in the foreign country predicated on legal ramification, minority interests, or the makeup of the entity.
- Sometimes an international manager in the alliance cannot master the sociocultural elements of the host country including, but not limited to, values, norms and beliefs, and inferior product quality.
- The U.S. company may be restricted from full ownership interests and be required to establish the alliance to enter the target market.[47]

Wholly Owned Subsidiaries

Wholly owned subsidiaries are the final entry modality to be discussed in this chapter. Wholly owned subsidiaries are market entry structures:

Where total control of the subsidiary business is a strong requisite, either for reasons such as the protection of intellectual property, because of a deeply rooted corporate culture, or because control by the headquarters is critical to the success of international marketplace activities.[48]

This market strategy is utilized when a corporate entity needs complete control over every detail of the structure within the host country. Total liability for any risks associated with the structure comes with complete control.

There are two advantages for firms deploying this entry modality: First, the parent company has complete control over every aspect of the business in the foreign market, including customer base, warehousing, distribution, accounts receivable, accounting practice, customer base, etc. Second, the wholly owned subsidiary is relatively free to establish additional subsidiary and contracting relationships with other partners in the host country. Likewise, two disadvantages exist: First, the parent company of the wholly owned subsidiary is responsible for all monetary aspects of the company; therefore, this alliance is extremely expensive. Second, the wholly owned subsidiary is liable for all aspects of the operation in the host country.

Establishment of a wholly owned subsidiary in a foreign country is a high-risk challenge for even the largest of multinational corporations. A company may control all the operations of its subsidiary, but it also bears all the costs and associated struggles to establish a share in the new market. Additionally, the strategy may lead to more efficient operations since all decisions will be made from one parent company. Taking these factors into account, a company willing to take the risks associated with this mode of market entry could find itself in a favorable position in the new market.

Brief Summary of Major Points

As business activities become increasingly global, domestic firms must be prepared to adjust and expand their operations into overseas markets in order to remain competitive. Organizations seeking to compete within the global economy face continuous threats, challenges, and pressures from competitors. Business managers must carefully examine, assess, and evaluate a country's organizational, social, cultural, political, judicial, market, economic, technological, and industry trends to determine whether entry into an international market is financially feasible or unfavorable and risky. Companies competing successfully within today's business environment realize the importance of research and development strategies and learn how to effectively implement these business plans to capitalize on market opportunities.

The thought of a company expanding globally into the international market is very exciting for a domestic firm. Whether the expansion is for greater revenue opportunities, global brand recognition, or just to have a greater market share, the survival and success of the company will be a direct result of the firm's managerial prowess. Therefore, each manager must be totally committed and have a global mindset. Each manager should have the ability to perceive both the differences and similarities between different international markets. A suggestion would be to designate an "international expansion leader" who will be put in charge to help manage this transition. Another suggestion for global managers would be to develop a hiring/retention program. This program will insure that the hiring and retaining of top international personnel takes place. Midlevel mangers, those responsible for specific departments in the company, should develop a training budget that will help them and their staff prepare for the different business environment overseas. These are just a few implications set forth for the global manager. Depending on the nature and situation of the firm, each company will have to develop its own unique plan and preparation for expanding globally.

Domestic firms expand into global markets for the following reasons:
- Strategically—many domestic firms look to capitalize on the growth potential of a foreign country's market along with its neighboring countries and seek global expansion for global brand building and awareness.
- Financially—many firms are expanding into foreign markets to increase their profits and sales, increasing their potential investors.
- Production related—some firms feel as though they must take advantage of the foreign labor market and cheaper raw materials.

Conditions necessary for expansion into global markets include the following:
- Companies should identify their strengths and weaknesses and understand how they may apply overseas. They must research the demographics of the

potential market in which they are hoping to enter. Companies need to take in consideration the new risks and increases in business complexity.

- Companies often expand globally for "motivational" reasons. They can be broken down into two types: proactive and reactive. Firms with proactive motivation will most likely go international because they want to take the initiative to be aggressive; reactive firms go international because it is a must.

Basic entry questions include the following:

- Location—which markets to enter? Initially, organizations must place considerable focus, emphasis, and thought on identifying potential global markets that will prove to be favorable towards the firm's profitability, performance, and financial goals or objectives.
- Timing—when is the best time to enter these markets? Companies must perform an assessment of the current economic trends and environmental conditions existing in expansion markets. They also must critically examine and realistically assess their own infrastructure, readiness, and exporting capabilities when attempting to determine when conditions and factors are best for entry into the expansion market.
- Scale—large scale or small scale? Business managers must carefully examine, assess, and evaluate a country's organizational, social, cultural, political, judicial, market, economic, technological and industry trends to determine whether entry into an international market is financially feasible, unfavorable, or risky.

Key factors that influence the entry mode selection include the following:

- Successful international corporations must be determined in their research and develop unique key entry strategies specifically designed to establish product differentiation and sustain a competitive advantage over competitors while capitalizing on increased sales, market shares, and profit margins. Whether economic, social, political, cultural or legal, external environment factors can affect the entry of new entrants in another country.

Entry modes include the following:

- Low intensity entry refers to no investment into the new market. High intensity entry involves making significant amounts of investment: financial, marketing, distribution, and possibly in executives.

Exporting and Importing can be defined as follows:
- Exporting is the sending of goods abroad for trade or sale.
- Importing is the bringing in of goods from abroad to trade or sale; this option may be the best method to gain a foothold.

- In most cases, exporting and importing require a minimal initial investment and may allow a business to develop key relationships with export/import firms (intermediaries) that will aid in ensuring success into the new market.

The following reveals the importance and use of intermediaries:
- Intermediaries are organizations that act as a go-between for a potential supplier and consumer. These firms can facilitate the transfer of goods and services from a company to the consumer in a new market.
- Export management Companies (EMC) are independent businesses that liaison between the parent company (manufacturer) and the customer (this could be another business, nation, or people). One of the most important advantages in using an EMC is that it can handle *all* aspects of exporting a company's product into the new market(s).
- An export trading company transacts commercial and financial activities to facilitate exports by unaffiliated persons. These activities include distribution, shipping, warehousing, and finance.

Licensing and franchising can be defined as follows:
- A license is an agreement that allows one party to use an industrial property right in exchange for payment to the other party.
- A franchise is an arrangement where one party allows another to operate an enterprise using its trademark, logo, product line, and methods of operation in return for a fee.

The following states the purpose of management contracts:
- Management contracts aid foreign businesses by allowing them to use their name on a domestic company and run the company as they would their own. These contracts, in conjunction with a franchise, will allow a parent company to be viable in foreign markets where governments have laws on foreign direct investments.

Turnkey projects:
- Turnkey means ready to begin operation. A business that is being sold as a Turnkey business would include tangibles, such as inventory and equipment, and intangibles, such as a previously established reputation and goodwill.

The following defines joint ventures (JV):
- A joint venture is when a foreign business partners with a local business partner to establish a new company that will compete in the market. The key principles of a JV are that the two combining entities contribute monetary resources and personnel—in the form of management, equipment, and other necessities.

The following defines wholly owned subsidiaries (WOS):

• A wholly owned subsidiary is a company that desires complete ownership and control when embarking on an overseas operation. The parent company maintains control over all operations and does not have to confer with any other firms in order to make decisions.

Moving from Theory into Practice

The following summarizes a question and answer session with coauthor Joe Robinson. His answers are useful in contemplating how the global business professional can translate the theories and concepts covered in this chapter via practical answers to the questions from real life experiences.

How does the global business manager put into practice and comply with export regulations?

One of the first things the savvy export manager does to insure that his global business team truly understands export transactions and best procedures to comply with pertinent regulations is provide training for staff involved in the export process. Private firms, government organizations, education institutions, and trade groups provide varying degrees of export procedures and compliance seminars and workshops. In the private sector, one of the best and most practical providers is International Business Training (IBT). They can be reached at www.i-b-t.net or by telephone at 1-800-641-0920.

I prefer the workshop format compared to the presentation or seminar approach to export procedures and compliance training. For example, workshops utilize handouts that are used and referenced during the training session rather than passing out the handouts at the end of the session. Beware of seminar sessions that are sponsored by and only use vendors (freight forwarders, attorneys, international banks, and carriers) to do all the talking and presenting. What they may actually be doing is using the seminar approach solely as a venue to generate new clients and customers—you the exporter.

Here is a tip to judge a good training session: If there is a U.S. Customs Official invited to participate or be part of the training program or to be a key note speaker then you can be reasonably assured that the training session will be unbiased and the session is put together to inform and enlighten the attendees in an open and beneficial manner.

The optimum approach to provide export training is to conduct in-house work sessions. These can be customized to your company products, policies, and type of overseas markets you want to focus on. Another approach is to utilize colleges and universities to provide your staff with export learning. International departments of state economic development agencies are a good source for this training. The U.S. Department of Commerce provides export training seminars. With so many sources for training, there is no excuse for not providing your staff with the necessary knowledge to comply with regulatory issues and to develop skills required to carry out best working procedures as you grow your sales and profits via the global market route.

Because the export process starts with the inquiry from a potential customer and the sales department is the first to respond, be sure to insist that everyone on your sales team, especially the sales person(s) directly involved in the export process, must participate in export educational sessions and workshops.

Another thing the export manager does to insure that compliance to regulations is properly carried out is to get a copy of the regulations. Then he conducts an in-house audit to ascertain what issues are compliant and where the "soft" issues are that need to be addressed and brought into line. Remember, exporting is a privilege not a right. Compliance is not something you merely take lightly but is the law so be sure you are compliant. Let me give you an example of a common noncompliant issue that is frequently found in many factories and is a high exposure problem right up front (pun intended) and that is a $25.00 fix. In the lobby or entrance of the factory you will find a guest registration book. The visitor registration book has columns for the date, visitor's name, company which you want to see, badge number if pertinent, time in and time out. If you export, you need to have a column entitled "Citizen of what country." This is a $25.00 fix. Simply go to your local office supply store and they have the proper visitor registration book for this purpose. In addition to complying with the pertinent export regulation, another important reason that this issue is sensitive and significant is that in the unlikely event you are ever audited by a government official they can only surmise that if you do not comply with this simple issue, then you must be in noncompliance with other issues. If you export, you do not want to give the perception that you do not know how to be compliant, so simply be sure your receptionist makes all visitors fill in the correct guest book properly.

<u>What outside assistance and complimentary help does the thriving global manager utilize to supplement his corporate international sales growth and increased profits?</u>

This is the thriving business domain where the know-how and expertise of the manager revolves around the clever utilization of allies and multipliers. An ally is someone who is sympathetic and supportive of your cause—namely the increase of your sales and profits. A multiplier is someone who cannot only reproduce what you need to do but can proliferate and propagate what you do.

Allies are frequently companies who produce related but not competing products. For example, if you are a world class leader in designing and manufacturing connectors for fiber optic cables, you could establish a working relationship with the maker of fiber optic cables who have already established a successful global network of sales, representatives, stocking distributors, and customers world wide that conceivably fit your international business model and commercial needs and similar aspirations. Success begets success, so utilize this approach if your product and customer mix allows this approach to utilize the ally technique. You could, for instance, ask the cable manufacturer to introduce you to overseas reps and distributors with whom he has the best success, with and you have therefore expedited the time of search and your exploration efforts to appoint a most likely successful candidate representative partner accordingly.

A multiplier is an individual or organization that enhances and elevates your own efforts. There is often a synergistic element to the relationship between the principal (you the exporter) and the multiplier. An example could be your international bank, your customs house broker, the U.S. Department of Commerce local trade specialist, your state international department, and your trade industry association—if you belong to one. For instance, I utilized the VMA (Valve Manufacturers of America) to synergize my export marketing activities. This included overseas market research to trade shows to representation based on the combined efforts of the trade association. The information and networking I gained was timely, pertinent, and practical, so I recommend this as a good technique in adopting the ally approach to enhancing your global business.

How does the successful global manager conduct and utilize international market research, and what countries are America's top five exporting countries?

The successful export manager looks for four things in actively pursuing new global markets. First is there a need for your products? Second, does the country, or more specifically, your potential customers have the money or access to the funds to pay for your products? Third, are you competitive in the country that needs and wants your product? Fourth, is the country politically stable? Answering these questions is a must for new market-entry strategy purposes.

An example might be a manufacturer of sun block windows or construction film who would do market research to determine where the sun shines the longest and strongest. Once these countries are identified, a study is conducted to make certain that the target country has adequate foreign exchange and your potential customers have access and convertibility of funds to pay for your product. Third, be sure to check if there are sufficient and adequate local manufacturers or other foreign competitors already firmly established in the target country?

Another example of a business that is receiving a lot of international attention these days is the environmental products and services industry. Careful analysis of market research is needed to pursue this growing field; however, there is caution to be followed here. Some countries that have the greatest need for environmental products and technology are either too poor to afford so-called "green" products and services or their laws and regulations and subsequent enforcement of those laws and regulations are nonexistent In this case there is the need but not the want or desire to buy your environmental products and technology. This is an unfortunate scenario but a fact of reality assessment. In order to thrive, the exporter must go where both the need and the money prevail.

What advice do you have about the foreign agent, distributor, or rep agreement?

You must remember that you are the principal. You should draft the agreement or contract and not the overseas representative.

I cannot offer legal advice because I am not a practicing attorney; however, I can provide some practical comments on this subject. First seek the counsel of a practicing international attorney with pertinent contract know-how and experience.

Next, do not take your domestic representative agreement and apply it verbatim to your overseas representation.

Next, be sure to incorporate those components into the representation agreement that are relevant to the partner and country in which you wish to engage representation. In my former company, I was custodian for thirty-eight foreign agreements. Only three of these were identical. Each agreement was a little different from the other to properly reflect the situation and business protocol in the respective country where we were doing business.

Seeking the advice and counsel of a good international contract lawyer is the best approach to take in handling foreign related agreements.

Can you give an example of a successful long term relationship?

I know of a U.S. manufacturer that has an ongoing relationship with a Japanese manufacturer. This includes cross-license manufacturing; plus, each represents the other in their respective countries, and they amicably work things out when the possibility comes up that they could compete with each other in replying to international tenders outside their own country.

Perhaps the reason for this long-term and amicable working relationship is because these two companies have learned how to communicate with each other. It has been said that communication is often the problem and also that communication is often the solution. Open and transparent communication from the top down is necessary for long-term success with an overseas partner.

Top management of both firms must set the pattern and lead by example and be willing to engage at the lower levels of the company when issues arise that require timely and forthright decisions.

One way these two companies communicate so well is when both have been invited to bid on a project. If the RFQ (Request for Quote) originates in Japan, the U.S. firm acknowledges the RFQ and favorably refers the customer to contact the Japanese side. Full details including the person, title, phone number, address, e-mail, and all pertinent information are provided. Further, the UDS side will make a positive statement regarding the amicable long-term relationship and that the Japanese factory is well positioned and the best qualified to supply the product requested in the RFQ. The same holds true if the inquiry is sent from the U.S. to the Japanese factory. The roles are simply reversed.

On a further note, if a country outside Japan and the U.S. sends an RFQ to both firms, then the two companies quickly figure out which is more competitive per related foreign exchange rates and freight costs and then decide who should be the major player in providing the offer per RFQ. As you can well imagine, effective communication is essential in conducting global business in creating long-term success in this example.

The chapter lists conditions necessary for expansion into global markets. Can you give examples of managerial motivation, from the positive and negative aspects?

Management commitment to the export process is essential. Management support is indeed crucial for export success. Management provision of funds is indispensable to export success. Further, management appointment and motivation of the export staff is a fundamental attribute for those firms who thrive the best in global commerce.

Global business is more difficult and complex than purely domestic business. Motivation from managers to those involved in the export process takes many forms. Perhaps recognition of staff is one of the most important ways a manager can provide motivation, especially on an individual basis. On the positive side, recognition seems to let the export employee know that he or she is indeed appreciated. I find this true from the largest multinational company to the smallest export firm with only a handful of employees.

On the other hand, the export staff as a group and the poor individuals who make up the export group are negatively impacted by being ignored. This is further exacerbated when necessary funds have to be constantly negotiated or begged for, or domestic issues consistently take priority over global business opportunities, no matter how small or insignificant the domestic issue. This can only yield negative feelings and contribute to demotivate those whose job is to grow your export business. Support and employee recognition are necessary components for achieving global business success.

Can you give an example of a disastrous managerial practice in terms of entering a global market?

An example that sometimes contributes to a disastrous result of a managerial practice is the employment of a so-called third country national. Wouldn't you agree that if you want to set up a liaison office in Germany that it makes sense to find and appoint a good German manager to run it for you? Who best knows the German language, how German business is conducted, and most likely has the best networking connections than a German manager for engaging in business in Germany?

I have witnessed Germans hired to run operations in Italy and Italians hired to run offices in Germany. I know first hand of Australians and South Koreans hired to run offices in Japan and Japanese hired to run offices in Hong Kong and China. Today, I receive phone calls and e-mails from Mid-East (nonSaudi) potential candidates who want to rep for American countries in Saudi Arabia, a country that I provide a lot of counseling for both the Americans and Saudis. When I ask the potential candidate what qualification he has to represent the American firm in Saudi Arabia, I mostly get the reply that "I speak Arabic."

Let me put this into perspective. Just imagine that a German firm wanted to hire a sales person to promote their product into the US. One qualification is that the salesman must live, let's say, in Atlanta. The person must speak English. The person must have a technical college degree. And finally, the person must not be an American but a third country national. In this case, suppose the German company hired a Mexican to conduct their sales activities. If you were the specifying engineer or purchasing person of an American firm and were approached by this third country national, rather than an American, how does this come across? If you perceived that the TCN was hired because the foreign firm did not trust an indigenous American, then you be the judge as to whether or not this is a disastrous managerial practice.

Please do not take this case as all encompassing. It is just an example of a scenario that could be a bad move on the part of a global manager and is not meant to be derogatory in any form. Unfortunately, what is perceived often gives shades of meaning not intended and could produce negative rather than positive results. For me, I want to do the positive thing from the beginning: I would hire a Mexican for doing my business in Mexico, an Australian for doing my business in Australia, and a Frenchman to do my business in France.

<u>What are the most attractive markets to enter in China?</u>

I asked the U.S. Department of Commerce to send me their current *Country Commercial Guide* for China in order to give the current update to this question. They sent the first page of chapter four, which lists the following commercial sectors as best opportunities for exporting to China: Agrochemicals, Air Traffic Management Equipment, Safety and Security, Automotive Components, Coal Mining Equipment, Construction Equipment, Banking Services, Education and Training, Franchising, Semiconductor Industry, machinery, Marine Industries, Oil and Gas Industries, Power Generation, Software, Travel and Tourism, Telecommunications, Water and Waste Water Treatment, and Medical Equipment.

The *Country commercial Guide* is published periodically for most countries. They are prepared in the field by our foreign trade specialists of the U.S. Department of Commerce. This is an excellent source of information, not only for ascertaining the type products a given country wants but also for analyzing many aspects of assisting you in gathering information for "Entry Level Strategy" into new overseas markets.

Whenever I lead a work trade mission overseas, I obtain the current copy of the *Country Commercial Guide* for the country we are visiting and make sure that our participants all have a complete copy for their referenced and records.

<u>Can you elaborate a bit on the practicality of using Export Management Companies? Will they continue in importance during the twenty-first century?</u>

Export Management Companies seem to have waned with the onset of e-mail, easy and inexpensive global telephone calls, readily available, international air flights, and the host of assistance, much of which is free or so very inexpensive, that companies can avail themselves in order to enter and enhance their global markets.

Also, foreign reps, agents, and distributors have a lot more to offer these days, than say, twenty-five years ago when EMS's seemed to proliferate.

Because of the necessity for immediate response and the desire for global firms to communicate directly with each other, the need for EMC's seems to be going away and not as popular as they once were.

<u>Can you give an example of the importance of timing when entering a global market?</u>

Timing is certainly an important consideration for putting together your action plan for your entry strategy. If you are maxed out in production and would have difficulty in supplying orders to a new overseas market, then it is best to wait until you have the appropriate production capacity and inventory to support your market entry.

If a political coup is predicted to be just around the corner, or if one just happened, it may be good to wait. A prime example here is a case where one of my clients was just about to locate a facility in Thailand when the military overtook the country a few months before. This appears to be a peaceful and beneficial revolution; however, the company feels, and rightly so, that it is prudent and wise to take a holding pattern until everything settles down and it appears that business and commerce are getting back to normal.

One additional example of when timing is important is if the monetary exchange rate is about to take a significant major shift. In this case, it is better to wait to enter the market if the rate will negatively affect the business; however, it is a good idea to enter a new market quickly where the monetary exchange rate is expected to positively impact the business anticipated in the new market.

Key Concepts

- Why domestic firms expand into global markets *216*
- Conditions necessary for expansion into global market: *217*
  - Managerial commitment *218*
  - Motivations *219*
- Basic entry questions: *~221*
  - Location—which markets to enter? *222*
  - Timing—when is the best time to enter these markets? *223*
  - Scale—large scale or small scale? *224*
- Key factors that influence the entry mode selection: *224*
  - International experience of the firm *224*
  - Size of the market *225*
  - Production and shipping costs *226*
  - Environments—political, legal, cultural, labor, etc. *227*
- Entry modes (include description, advantages, and disadvantages) *229*
  - Exporting and importing *229*
  - The importance and use of intermediaries *230*
- Export management companies *230*
- Export trading companies *231*
- Facilitators *232*
  - Private sector *233*
  - Public sector *233*
  - Licensing and franchising *234*
  - Management contracts *235*
  - Turnkey projects *236*
  - Joint ventures *237*
  - Wholly owned subsidiaries *238*

Chapter **8** GLOBAL OPERATIONS MANAGEMENT

Global Business in Practice

"What has been will be again, what has been done will be done again; there is nothing new under the sun."[*]

The Training Within Industry Service (TWI) was established by the United States government in 1940 during World War II to increase production output to support the Allied Forces war effort. The TWI Service was lead by the Four Horsemen, as they became known during WWII: Channing Rice Dooley, director of the TWI Service; Walter Dietz, associate director; Mike Kane, assistant director; and William Conover, assistant director. Three of the four men had met while serving in a training capacity during World War I using methods developed by Charles Allen. Charles Allen's training methodology, developed prior to World War I for shipbuilding, would become the key to the methods developed by the Four Horsemen during their TWI Service.

From Allen's four-step training method the "J" programs would evolve and have a major impact on manufacturing in the United States during the war. The "J" programs were:

- *Job Instruction*
- *Job Methods*
- *Job Relations*
- *Program Development*

These programs were incorporated into industry by a large network of trainers set-up throughout the country by the TWI Service. They focused on the interface between supervisors and employees and proved invaluable to the United States' industrial support of the war effort.[†]

Although the TWI program was abandoned at the end of the war, the instruction methods were introduced to the war-torn nations of Europe and Asia. It was especially well-received in Japan, where TWI formed the basis of the kaizen culture in industry. Kaizen, known by such names as Quality Circles in the West, was successfully harnessed by Toyota Motor Corporation in conjunction with the Lean or Just In Time principles of Taiichi Ohno.

---

[*] Ecclesiastes 1:9
[†] Source: Idea Management Training. Retrieved on September 5, 2007 from http://www.stufbang kok.net/index.php?id=2071

TWI had a direct impact on the development and use of kaizen and Standard Work at Toyota. These fundamental elements are embedded within the functional system at Toyota and Job Instruction is taught and used within Toyota today. The kaizen methodology is a direct descendant of Job Methods, and most likely Job Relations had an impact on the development and function of the Team and Group Leader structure in Toyota.

Many of the points above should look familiar to students of W. Edwards Deming. The PDCA style of the training programs, the concept of failure being on the shoulders of the instructor, and even the Job Instruction and Job Methods processes themselves. Deming lectures frequently included statements similar to the Job Relations slogan, "People Must Be Treated As Individuals."

One theory for the disappearance of TWI within the U.S. after the war is the simple fact that North American industry faced little serious competition in 1945. With no competition to an efficient industry, few saw the need to continue to improve. At the same time, foreign industries had been decimated. The defeated countries needed to establish new industry but to reject the old culture. For that purpose, TWI trainers were brought to Europe by the occupying forces there, and to Japan by Macarthur during the occupation.*

---

* Source: Training Within Industry. Retrieved on September 5, 2007 from http://www.superfactory.com/topics/twi.htm

In the fundamental sense, global business involves the buying, selling, and trading of goods and services across national borders. While many managerial aspects directly impact the profitability of a business, it is the management of business operations that determines a company's total growth potential and earning capabilities. Management involves the process of developing decisions and taking actions to direct and control the activities of employees toward the attainment of organizational goals.[1] Operations management specifically involves the management of the process and production activities that produce the goods or services. Operations managers are concerned with every aspect of the production process, including key areas, such as research and development, acquisition and distribution, inventory management, technology, transportation, manufacturing, and customer service.[2] The overall success of the business is dependent upon the efficiency and effectiveness of every function within the production process.

The rapid expansion of world markets is a mitigating factor for the globalized perspective of operations management. Taking a business to the global marketplace necessitates the development of a global operations strategy, which requires three strategic capabilities:

- Global-scale efficiency and competitiveness
- National-level responsiveness and flexibility
- Cross-market capacity to leverage on a worldwide basis[3]

Based on the extent to which these capabilities exist within the firm, operations managers are involved in the ongoing processes of strategic issues, such as planning, production, logistics, and supply chain management to maximize the business output potential. The key components in successful operations management are efficiency and effectiveness. Global organizations differ from domestic in that operations must not only efficiently move products from multiple locations but also from multiple continents.

Planning Issues

When planning an effective global business strategy, a company should consider the fundamental issues that drive production level output. These issues include, but are not limited to, the capacity of the operation, the location of the organization's facilities, the varying processes by which the products are produced, the internal layout of the facility workspace, the decision process for determining whether various components should be manufactured or purchased, and the process by which both raw material and fixed assets are selected and ultimately acquired.

| Capacity Issues | Figure 8.1 |

- Facilities location
- Location economies
- Organizational structure

Capacity

Capacity, in terms of production-oriented firms, refers to the total amount of products that can be produced by the entire operation in a given amount of time. In service-oriented firms, capacity is measured in terms of the total number of customers that can be served in a given amount of time. In either case, capacity is the metric used to measure the ability to meet customer needs. Organizations first estimate demand levels in relation to the overall capacity of their facilities and then make adjustments to meet the projected demand levels.

One should note that the capacity of a multistep production process is limited to the total output of the slowest process—also known as the operational bottleneck. Organizations identify elements of the production process that are creating constraints or bottlenecks in the overall flow of the production system. The Theory of Constraints (TOC) suggests that the greater gain will come from identifying which part of the process is a constraint to the whole, rather than focusing on increased output from an entire process. Once the constraints are identified, the organization should focus improvement energy solely in that area.[4] Thus, overall production levels will increase as a result of implementing ways to increase performance output at the source of the constraint. Another method related to improving production capacity requires the firm to focus only on key capabilities or the specific processes that an organization performs better than other organizations. This may require that some processes be outsourced to other agencies, which in turn frees up needed resources that can be dedicated to other key capabilities.

Facilities Location

Decisions must be made to determine the optimal location in which to conduct operations. The final decision concerning which nation or region in which to operate must be based on comprehensive business research. A key determinant in the facility location decision is the proximity the site has to the organization's largest customer base and suppliers.

"A company's physical settings, support services, and environmental conditions must be used effectively to add value to business objectives, strategies, and processes. This becomes increasingly important in the global business environment, as firms move towards greater flexibility to integrate new business ideas and emerging technologies in their facilities location planning strategies."[5]

Additionally, cost variables associated with a site selection must be considered in the facilities location decision: distribution channel costs, energy costs, tax costs, labor costs, raw materials costs, and so forth. Thus, facility location is one of the most important and most difficult decisions that must be made.

Many organizations are drawn overseas by the lure of diminished labor costs. Typically, facility costs are second only to labor costs, but there may be hidden facility costs associated with moving operations overseas. While lower labor costs may be attractive, other considerations may make relocation unworthy of the investment, such as the following:

- Transportation costs
- Duties on components versus those on finished goods
- Need for proximity to the market
- Foreign-exchange risk
- Economies of scale in the production process
- Technological requirements[6]

One way to reduce the risk of incurring these costs is to engage in the business arrangement known as a joint venture, where two separate entities enter into a contractual agreement to do business together. Each party provides some part of the production process, and the profits are shared between the two organizations.[7] This joint venture works especially well for organizations wanting to do business in a foreign country. A domestic firm will partner with an organization that is native to the host country, which provides assistance in dealing with the cultural and language barriers that are often present when foreign companies seek to do business overseas.[8] A caveat for those considering a joint venture is that while the joint venture may help alleviate some of the risk associated with doing business overseas, certain unavoidable problems may be encountered. For example, many third world nations that would provide the lowest labor costs have huge infrastructure shortcomings. Another shortcoming is that the political climate around the world is increasingly volatile. Terrorism is not a topic that would have raised many concerns a few decades ago, but today it is a deep concern when determining the most appropriate and profitable facility location.

Location Economies

Another key component in the decision-making process concerns the resources available within the community where the facility will be located. Companies must consider the resources available to their employees in foreign cities. In some countries, social services may be available from the local government. In other countries, the services are lacking or nonexistent. Some corporations have used their influence to improve the local services as "a way of ensuring social cohesion and a stable community, facilitating the recruitment of employees, and the safe passage of goods and people to and from company operations."[9]

Centralization vs. Decentralization

An important component of strategic planning is organizational structure planning. Strategy defines the goal or purpose of the organization, while structure defines how personnel will collectively implement the strategy.[10] One ongoing debate among strategic planners concerns deploying a centralized structure versus a decentralized structure. The difference between the two is the locus of decisions: Are decisions controlled primarily by the home office or are they allowed to be controlled in the foreign location? The debate has grown to include the argument of whether or not there should be any structure at all.

The bureaucratic hierarchy is the most common centralized organizational structure. This organizational structure has a clear chain of command, from the top down, and allows for a firm control over every aspect of the organization. Decision making is a top-down process in this form of structure. While this structure was highly successful during the twentieth century, it has grown increasingly ineffective in the twenty-first century global business model.

Organizational structures may change over time, cycling from a centralized structure to a decentralized structure and back to a centralized structure. The continual change is a result of the strengths and weaknesses of each model. A centralized structure provides control, stability, and the potential for highly effective coordination of all the organizational processes. However, it does not allow for innovative thinking, nor does it engender employee initiative for problem solving. The decentralized model, on the other hand, allows decision making authority to occur where the decisions are to be made, promoting innovation, initiative, and teamwork. When problems arise, decisions can be made immediately so production can go on. The problem with a decentralized model is the inevitability that divisional communication will break down, causing coordination efforts to become difficult and complicated.

Process

Typical processes within an organization include procurement (purchasing), distribution channels, and the following areas requiring management:

- Product and service: the management of an individual good or service such as creation, production, and marketing.

- Quality: customer satisfaction and Total Quality Management.

- Inventory: utilizing methods such as Just-In-Time, providing products and services in an efficient manner.

- Facilities: buildings, computer systems, furnishings, equipment, signage, etc.

- Configuration: various versions of products manufactured and distributed by a company (example: computer software)

- Logistics and transportation: the flow of goods or materials from suppliers throughout the organization and then to the customer.

- Human Resources: employee matters, benefits, retirement packages, safety issues, training, motivation, etc.

Thus, the process of global operations management requires making a number of interrelated decisions regarding several issues, as depicted in Figure 8.2.

Figure 8.2

Process Issues

- Standardization vs. adaptation
- Facility location
- The design and layout of a production facility
- The make or buy decision
- The selection and acquisition of raw materials
- The selection and acquisition of fixed assets

Standardization vs. Adaptation

Companies considering the possibility of expanding beyond the borders of their home countries must determine whether or not production processes and procedures will be consistent across facility locations. This standardization maintains the various aspects of the production process and ensures product uniformity. Additional cost savings accrue because machinery, training, and processes can be kept uniform across standardized production facilities. In the event of a natural disaster or economic downturn, the company can stop production at a facility in one nation while boosting production in a location that is more conducive to profitability.

Adaptation may be necessary for products that require adjustments in order to meet local market demand. For example, a company in the food industry might use a different set of suppliers that produce similar products with some subtle differences to make the item more valuable to the consumers in the local economies. Organizations that at one time focused primarily on standardized products are realizing that with expanding global markets and the reduction of trade restrictions, the potential to produce customized products exists where it might not have been possible or feasible in the past. The strategy of mass customization requires the firm to tailor mass production products to meet the expectations of the customer. Mass customization allows a producer to adapt its products to a particular group of consumers. Demand for different features or options may be based on climate, culture, or personal preference.

Facilities Layout

Once the overseas location has been selected, the design for the space to be built or modifications for a leased space is considered. Factors to be considered in the layout design include utilizing the space for the handling of materials, safety, shipping and receiving, employee movement and communication, and the possibility for future expansion. Different types of businesses adhere to different standards when determining layout design. A service-orientated business or an office would require a pleasing atmosphere for the customer or client. A manufacturing business would design a workspace that could withstand the daily effects of industrial work.

Two basic manufacturing layout designs are typically used: process or product. Process layout groups similar machines together. A company that manufactures packaged baked goods would utilize the process layout. The bakery would group all the mixers in one section and the ovens in another section of the facility. Product layout groups machines according to their roles in the production process. An assembly line would be an example of product layout. Retail locations choose between three basic layout designs: grid pattern, free-flow pattern, and self service. The grid pattern allows for premium merchandise exposure and simplifies cleaning and security issues. The free-flow pattern provides customers ease of movement and is visually appealing. The self-service layout gives customers direct access to merchandise throughout the store. A grocery store is an example of grid pattern layout. Convenience stores follow the self-service layout. Department stores usually choose the free-flow pattern. Determining the best possible layout for each business will enhance productivity and consumer purchasing.

Make or Buy Decisions

Most all products available today in the global marketplace involve input from at least one outside source. Many firms lack the required expertise and resources to supply all needed components in the production process. Thus, the need to either make or buy subcomponent parts for products is essential to business operations. Software applications are readily available to assist in the financial determination profitability of make or buy decisions. Regardless, the make or buy decision requires the firm to determine the most cost-effective approach to the production process. Factors that play into this decision include the quality, cost, and delivery timelines of a product or component.[11] The decision to buy or outsource components used in the production process from an external organization must allow for greater benefit to the organization, rather than the component being produced within the organization. Benefits might include decreased inventory and acquisition costs or shorter lead times. Those products that do not provide these benefits to the organization should be produced internally.

Selection and Acquisition of Raw Materials

Raw materials are inventory items that are used in the manufacturer's conversion process to produce components, subassemblies, or finished products.[12] The selection and acquisition of raw materials varies greatly among the business industry. Proper selection and purchase of raw materials impacts the overall quality and value of a product. Companies planning expansion overseas must conduct substantial research on the availability of the raw materials in that location. The transportation cost of materials not readily available in that region must be determined. This determination is considered in the decision as to whether or not the added transportation cost warrants that site selection. Firms involved in the refinement or distribution of raw materials are especially at-risk. The access to needed raw materials is important and substantial in the planning phase of global expansion.

The operational process of raw material selection is important to the firm's value chain. The value chain is generally considered to consist of the acquisition of raw materials, finished goods manufacturing, and distribution channels.[13] A company should examine its product and the desired characteristics and work backwards to the research and development involved in identifying and selecting the raw materials necessary to make the product. In global markets, companies selecting raw materials must consider local demand, regulatory controls, distribution channels, competition, and shelf life. Quality is also an issue. Firms must examine the quality control procedures of their suppliers to determine whether or not locally supplied raw materials meet the required standards necessary to ensure the integrity of the product. Random sampling and statistical sampling can help an organization monitor and maintain the quality of its materials.

Operations managers understand that success of the value chain depends greatly upon developing successful communication and relationships with suppliers. For example, Japanese firms develop relationships with their suppliers by investing in their organizations. Their eventual goal is to place a representative in a board position within the supplier's organization. This type of relationship is considered an interlocking directorate, which has three main benefits. The first advantage is that a company can successfully play a part in the supplier's planning process. Second, this allows the organization the opportunity to more effectively coordinate the output of raw materials to meet the needs of the manufacturing operation. Third, this approach provides for the establishment of raw material design teams that consist of representatives from a company and its suppliers. These teams can custom design the necessary raw materials needed in order to meet the company's production and quality standards. The ultimate outcome is one that saves the organization from substantial costs that can result from the use of generic or substandard raw materials.[14]

Global outsourcing and KANBAN clusters are additional means to enhance the effectiveness of the value chain—in terms of establishing processes and procedures for acquiring raw materials. Global outsourcing is effectively used by corporations to acquire raw materials from the most cost effective sources in the world. Short term contracts are established in order to ensure that future technological advances and new suppliers are not overlooked. Though the actual materials may be inexpensive, the costs associated with shipping the materials from a location on the other side of the globe may be significant. One important concept to keep in mind is that the further away the supplier, the more the shipping costs will impact the raw material acquisition decision.[15]

The KANBAN cluster, developed by Japanese companies, holds the distance between the supplier and the manufacturing hub as a key focus in the acquisition of raw materials. Continuity is an important aspect of this approach. Companies that use this method often mandate that their suppliers have a facility within a certain distance of the manufacturing facility. Any large corporation in Japan may have a network of suppliers located in the region of its production facilities. This network allows a company to experience many of the benefits considered part of Just-In-Time inventory systems. The need for large inventories of raw materials is avoided and manufacturing companies can eliminate the need for long order lead times because of the geographical proximity of suppliers. The outcome results in a reduced set of costs for inventory, shipping, and warehousing.[16]

Selection and Acquisition of Fixed Assets

Fixed assets is an accounting term that describes tangible property used in the operation of a business, such as buildings, machinery, fixtures, furniture, and equipment. These assets do not include items normally consumed in the course of business operation or production.[17] Fixed assets provide the additional benefit of tax breaks, resulting from depreciation—though real estate values generally appreciate over time. Firms investigating international expansion opportunities must determine how to achieve the right mix of fixed assets. The decision seeks to answer critical questions as to how to gain the necessary facilities and assets in a host nation. Should the firm acquire an existing company or facility? Should it build and/or purchase a new facility? Should it merge with another company to acquire its assets? Each question should be considered in terms of the advantages and disadvantages of the particular course of action. The advantages to purchasing an existing facility are manifold:

- A foreign firm can avoid many of the typical start-up problems and costs associated with building a new facility. This can provide a company with instant cash flow.

- A firm may also find that financing is somewhat easier to obtain due to the access to local capital.

- The company may also be able to avoid the exchange restrictions or controls through the exchange of stock rather than a newly purchased facility.

- In unique cases, a foreign company may also be able to purchase the facilities of a bankrupt or struggling company and avoid the expenses involved in purchasing real estate and building a new facility.[18]

On the other hand, not all circumstances permit the purchase of an existing operation. A Greenfield investment, the foreign direct investment through the establishment of new facilities, may be more practical, depending on the host nation environment. Unlike the case of an acquisition, a Greenfield Investment requires only product adaptation rather than both product and process adaptation. Product adaptation allows the firm to tailor its products to meet regional demand considerations. One possible drawback of Greenfield Investment is the high marketing costs associated with the establishment of a new organizational element.[19]

Advantages and Disadvantages for Greenfield Investments		Figure 8.3
Advantages	New links to the global market. New production and job market expansion. Influx of knowledge and technology.	
Disadvantages	MNC's tend to crowd out locally owned operations. The majority of profits are distributed back to the MNC's host country. MNC's tendency to dwindle natural resources and raw materials.	

Mergers and acquisitions (M & A), the most commonly used form of FDI to acquire fixed assets, are the transfer of existing assets from local to foreign firms. M & A's have advantages and disadvantages as well. Figure 8.4 depicts the advantages and disadvantages.

Advantages and Disadvantages for M&A		Figure 8.4
Advantages	Potential tax savings Acquisition of established resources Synergy—the reduction of duplicated offices, such as human resources	
Disadvantages	M & A's can become targets for hostile takeovers. M & A's are known to damage employee loyalty and morale. M & A managerial focus is drawn away from productivity to merger management.	

Production Issues

Productivity is the ratio of output as it relates to input—the conversion of inputs or resources into outputs of merchandise or services. Organizations have many different elements to consider when setting up international operations. Continuous improvement, delivery systems, inventory, logistics, and supply chain management are key areas to be examined by an organization's management team. The decisions made in regard to these areas will ultimately determine the success or failure of a firm's international initiatives.

Continuous Improvement

Continuous improvement, sometimes referred to as *Kaizen*, is a management technique that historically involves several incremental improvements to a process rather than a single overpowering improvement or change. The term *Kaizen,* a Japanese term, is derived from the characters (equivalent to letters) *kai*, meaning change, and *zen*, meaning good. Thus, Kaizen literally means improvement. The Japanese culture promotes the continuous search for ways to enhance every facet associated with the transformation process—converting inputs into outputs. *Kaizen* involves both management and labor in finding and eliminating waste in machinery, labor, materials, and production methods.[20]

Although many describe continuous improvement as merely a philosophy rather than a specific technique or method, it has certainly influenced all aspects of business. Continuous improvement is frequently associated with other management and production techniques, such as Total Quality Management (TQM), ISO 9000, and Just-In-Time systems.

TQM

Total Quality Management, utilized from the executive levels of the firm to the line workers, is a tool used in the managing of the total production process to generate an exceptional product or service. While numerous definitions exist, most operations managers would agree with the following:

> TQM is a people-focused management system that aims at continual increase in customer satisfaction at continually lower real cost. TQM is a total system approach (not a separate area or program) and an integral part of high-level strategy; it works horizontally across functions and departments, involves all employees, top to bottom, and extends backward and forward to include the supply chain and the customer chain. TQM stresses learning and adaptation to continual change as keys to organizational success. The foundation of total quality is philosophical: the scientific method. TQM includes systems, methods, and tools. The systems permit change; the philosophy stays the same. TQM is anchored in values that stress the dignity of the individual and the power of community action.[21]

Figure 8.5

Three Major Principles of Total Quality
• Customer Focus
• Participation and Teamwork
• Continuous Improvement and Learning

Customer focus. The philosophy of TQM is to meet and exceed the customer's expectations each and every time with minimal rework. Though each organization's TQM approach will differ, management processes that use data to detect and correct poor performance trends are essential. These processes should provide the organization with the ability to grow and continuously elevate the firm's overall performance, rather than one element of the organization.[22]

Participation and teamwork. It has long been held that people are an organization's greatest capital. TQM further supports this concept. Because employees and managers both play a large role in total quality, the entire workforce must be involved in the pursuit of the type of quality that results in customer satisfaction. Quality efforts begin and end with upper management. A mission, vision, and associated set of goals and values should be established by an organization's management team. Managers must disseminate this information to the organization's employees in a way that supports and enhances employee morale and performance. Managers must also remove various barriers that limit or prevent quality improvement. The best approach to removing these barriers is to provide workers with an environment of support and trust that encourages and rewards employees for taking on risks and correcting their own mistakes, rather than hiding them from management.[23]

TQM requires a more people-friendly approach that includes the team mentality. Teamwork stresses the importance of customer-supplier relationships and total workforce involvement, which span various functional areas. Cross-functional teams are horizontal in nature and include experts in each technical area within an organizational unit. These teams further cooperate to share information and determine best practices rather than competing for accolades. This type of environment promotes the health of the entire firm rather than a few elements.

Processes and process improvement remain the focus in an organization that practices TQM. Each and every employee of an organization should be involved in TQM planning and strategy development. Though it is often difficult for managers to hear negative reactions to current and proposed processes, it is still vital for an organization to understand that opportunities can be realized by including employees in the implementation of TQM. This involvement is essential to the success of the proposed changes.[24]

Continuous improvement and learning. Firms that deploy successful TQM initiatives believe in the importance of focusing all efforts on improving systems and processes. The firm understands that it must constantly audit and advance its capabilities. Continuous efforts to improve organizational performance will lead to the achievement of meeting or exceeding both internal and external customer requirements.

ISO 9000

Similar in theory and philosophy to TQM, ISO 9000 is a set of guidelines for quality management and quality standards, developed by the International Organization for Standardization in Geneva, Switzerland. ISO is, in actuality, a codification or assurance of quality—ISO is an internationally recognized certification system or process. In order for a firm to become ISO certified, it must first prove that it is strictly adhering to ISO standard operating procedures, which involve the inspection of production processes, maintaining equipment, training workers, testing products, and dealing with customer complaints. The benefits of an international certification are numerous to businesses, customers, governments, trade officials, developing countries, and consumers alike. The International Organization for Standardization lists the specific benefits:

- For businesses, the widespread adoption of International Standards means that suppliers can base the development of their products and services on specifications that have wide acceptance in their sectors. This, in turn, means that businesses using International Standards are increasingly free to compete in many more markets around the world.

- For customers, the worldwide compatibility of technology, which is achieved when products and services are based on International Standards, brings them an increasingly wide choice of offers, and they benefit from the effects of competition among suppliers.

- For governments, International Standards provide the technological and scientific bases underpinning health, safety, and environmental legislation.

- For trade officials negotiating the emergence of regional and global markets, International Standards create a level playing field for all competitors in those markets. The existence of divergent national or regional standards can create technical barriers to trade, even when there is political agreement to do away with restrictive import quotas and the like. International Standards are the technical means by which political trade agreements can be put into practice.

- For developing countries, International Standards that represent an international consensus on the state of the art constitute an important source of technological know-how. By defining the characteristics that products and services will be expected to meet on export markets, International Standards give developing countries a basis for making the right decisions when investing their scarce resources and thus avoid squandering them.

- For consumers, conformity of products and services to International Standards provides assurance about their quality, safety, and reliability. For everyone, International Standards can contribute to the quality of life in general by ensuring that the transport, machinery, and tools we use are safe.

- For the planet, International Standards on air, water, soil quality, and emissions of gases and radiation can contribute to efforts to preserve the environment.[25]

Just-in-Time Systems

Just-in-time production or systems is a comprehensive set of doctrines and systems founded on the philosophy that businesses should hold slight or zero inventory outside what is necessary for immediate production or distribution. The goal of this management system is eliminating waste, making best use of cost efficiency, and creating and sustaining competitive advantage. Just-in-time systems' intention is to concentrate on eradicating waste and reducing warehouse inventories; however, the high degree of coordination required to efficiently function within such a system only underscores many of the pre-existing issues, such as bottlenecks, inventory loss or spoilage, and unreliable suppliers.[26] Internet-based collaborative work tools—such as paperless pricing, ordering, restocking, shipping, and product delivery—enable any business to implement just-in-time systems. In fact, "all this facilitates just in time deliveries of parts and components and matching the production of parts and components to assembly plant requirements and production schedules, cutting out unnecessary activities and producing savings for both suppliers and manufacturers."[27]

Also known as the Toyota Production System, JIT was initially developed after WWII when the Japanese car industry was lagging far behind its U.S. competitors. The outlook for survival was calling for drastic and immediate changes. At that time, the average U.S. worker was nine times more efficient than his Japanese counterpart. Japanese industry based JIT improvements on the already existing concepts found in the U.S. factories. They recognized the importance of inventory control and based development on the elimination of waste through just-in-time and automation. Automation refers to mechanized production, where human attention is needed only when a problem occurs. Further, a number of observable production-oriented wastes were identified:

- Product defects
- Process waste

- Overproduction
- Inventory
- Waiting time
- Movement of the product through the process
- Transportation[28]

Figure 8.6

Benefits of JIT

- Better quality products
- Quality, the responsibility of every worker, not just quality control inspectors
- Reduced scrap and rework
- Reduced cycle times
- Lower setup times
- Smoother production flow
- Less inventory of raw materials, work-in-progress and finished goods
- Cost savings
- Higher productivity
- Higher worker participation
- More skilled workforce, able and willing to switch roles
- Reduced space requirements
- Improved relationships with suppliers[29]

Though it may seem like JIT should be standard operating process for all global businesses, certain problems can accrue. For instance, a depleted inventory stockpile could mean disaster for suppliers who operate in a manner that requires the storage of back up products. It could mean additional problems if the supplier is required to meet emergency demands, or if the customer base is not prepared for supply delays.[30] Additionally, environmental impacts are associated with JIT. More frequent movement of inputs and outputs may cause roads to become congested with delivery trucks, resulting in increased levels of air pollution. Moreover, many companies that decide to switch to JIT fail to address the issue of empty warehouses and trucks once used for storing inventories. These unused assets are the company's property and are an additional form of waste. Finally, JIT often fails when the relationships between suppliers and customers are not strong enough to guarantee the quality and timing needed for the system to work.[31]

Inventory

Because of the nature of their product or service, not all international firms and businesses are able to operate within the confines of a JIT system. Nonetheless, these businesses must remain vigilant in their pursuit of accurate and timely inventory control. An unnecessarily large inventory will retain money and resources which ought to be utilized in other aspects of the business. Additionally, unsold or underutilized inventory costs businesses in other ways, such as the expense incurred for storage, vulnerability to theft, and the fact that many states tax inventory separately.

The signs that a global business is experiencing inventory problems include the following:

- Inventories are mounting quicker than sales.

- Back orders are numerous.

- Customers complain that products or services are unavailable.

- Production is interrupted because of a lack of materials.

- Inventory turnover rates are slower than expected.[32]

Although the above list is abbreviated and certainly not all encompassing, it is a logical starting point to identify inventory issues.

Three main categories of inventory control emerge:

1. Inventory planning and ordering: This is approached through material requirement planning (MRP) and through the Kanban ordering system to maintain a smooth flow of inventories throughout the production process.

2. Inventory optimizations systems: Calculations are made to maintain sufficient inventories for predetermined supply chain system needs.

3. Physical inventory control: This includes all the actions needed to check the physical state of inventories throughout the process.[33]

The ABC Classification System is used to categorize inventory items and is also known as stock keeping units (SKU's). Though companies may use slightly different approaches for this classification, the basic principle lies in dividing the inventories into three categories, according to associated values. An example of category A would be where 20 percent of the company's inventory accounts for 80 percent of the profit. Category C would then represent 40 percent of SKU's with a 5 percent value, and B category would include all the items in between. This categorization system allows managers to focus on the most important items when forecasting, controlling, and scheduling inventories.[34] Once this step is approached, three types of costs must be examined: Specifically, ordering, carrying, and stockout costs must be analyzed and considered in order to implement the most suitable inventory control model.[35]

Global Logistics (Materials Management and Physical Distribution)

As a result of the trend towards globalization, logistics increasingly focuses on the global functions of materials management and physical distribution. The term logistics refers to the movement of finished products, semifinished products, components, and materials between various locations. Global logistics is a little more complex because it includes a wide range of locations, plants, warehouses, vendors, and customers that need to be managed across great distances, time zones, and cultures. Figure 8.7 depicts the key issues of global logistics.

Figure 8.7

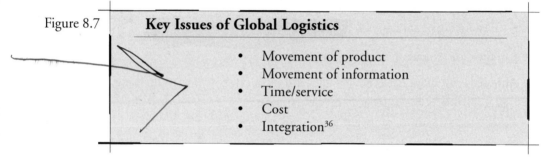

Key Issues of Global Logistics

- Movement of product
- Movement of information
- Time/service
- Cost
- Integration[36]

In principle, logistics is a fast evolving and changing field of management, attributed to the fast growth and evolution of new technologies, services, and markets. The main decisions in logistics remain unchanged and have to be addressed on both national and international levels. These decisions are made primarily on three different levels:

1. The strategic planning level
2. The network level
3. The operations level[37]

Strategic planning level decisions are the highest level of logistics decisions. The main strategic planning issues include performance objectives, the degree of vertical integration, outsourcing within the supply chain, what will be measured, and how to accomplish the measurement. These decisions are based on the existing mission and strategies of the organization. Additional considerations include customer expectations, competition, availability of financial resources, and the current logistics system.

Furthermore, related strategic level decisions exist beyond logistics that must be addressed to secure success. Such decisions include the organization's economic objectives and strategy, geographic scope of production, distribution, and marketing, along with marketing and information management objectives and strategy.[38] Though the design and development of a new product takes twelve to eighteen months to complete, on average, other factors of the supply chain network change more rapidly. Thus, it is crucial for a company to reevaluate strategic level decisions at least once a year. Some do not hesitate to do so, even if it means looking at various aspects on a monthly basis.[39]

Network level decisions include the Physical Facility Network and Communication/Information Network decisions. Based on the strategic level decisions, this set of decisions starts with determining the network strategy first. Such considerations include the degree of centralization/decentralization, degree of hierarchy, and number of echelons. After these areas are examined, the physical facilities come to the attention of the organization's management team. The type, number, location of activities, and services provided by each facility are analyzed. Finally, the communication and information network must be designed for effective flow of information along the supply chain. Therefore, the decisions must be made on the amount and type of information flow, use of information technology for transfer, processing, and storage of information.[40] It is important to remember that cost savings do not only result from looking for the cheapest method but also from looking for the most efficient method.

Operations level decisions are decisions that are rather short term and less sophisticated than the other sets of decisions. Despite this reality, these decisions are no less important. Such decisions are divided into the following categories:

- Demand Forecasting: This particular step is very important because it tells the company whether the suggested plans will be profitable. Drawing from historical data, competition analysis and market research, cost, and time restraints, a company chooses one of three main forecasting models: judgmental, intrinsic, or extrinsic.[41]

- Inventory Management: This step in logistics is very important and must be approached from the forecasted demand as well as the nature of the products. The inventory method and safety stock allowance are part of this decision. "Inventory growth may be both a cause and effect of a poorly aligned supply chain." Despite the popularity of the JIT inventory system, higher inventory, and thus warehousing costs, can offset the even higher freight costs and help improve customer service.[42]

- Production: These decisions include the movement of the inputs through the production process. Once the product design and development is planned, decisions on facility location and layout, capital equipment, work design, material, inventory, and quality management must be made in order to ensure a smooth production process.[43]

- Procurement and Supply Management: Decisions in this area include such considerations as where to purchase and what to purchase. Specifically, a company must decide how much raw material it needs. An organization must also look at the number or amount of parts, components, products, supplies, and other items needed for production. Selecting suppliers is very crucial for success because they are an important part of an organization's cost savings. The right supplier can assure timeliness and good quality. These aspects can reduce costs and are critical to a successful organization. No matter how reliable a company's suppliers are, a good quality control system must also be established.

- Transportation: Selecting a means of transportation must be based on the product's characteristics, delivery dates, and cost. The selected type of transportation can greatly affect the quality of the products. As a result of this, the cost should not be the driving factor in the decision-making process. The latest approach to transportation strategy involves the use of the internet. Software and other resources are available to assist organizations in developing an appropriate set of transportation strategies that maximize operational efficiency, cost savings, and process standardization. These tools also assist in decreasing communication time and allowing for improved information sharing.[44]

- Product Packaging: Packaging should be selected based on considerations such as the type of product and desired cost savings. The environmental impact of a product's packaging must also be considered. One popular option of environmentally friendly or "green" packaging is the use of "returnables." These are reusable containers that can be repeatedly used for refill by the supplier and in the transportation of materials. Logically speaking, this type of packaging does not work for every type of product or organization. There are a number of factors that must be considered in this area. Such considerations include the life and characteristics of the product, frequency of shipments, and quantity of shipments.[45]

- Material Handling: An appropriate means of handling material from the loading and unloading processes through the storage and production processes is selected based on the nature of the material and bundled according to the inventory and production scheduling.

- Warehousing: Decisions relating to the type, location, and layout of warehouses are critical components in global operations management. In a case of outsourcing, a company should have a thorough knowledge of the warehousing capacities in order to avoid pitfalls, such as paying higher costs for warehousing services and doubled handling charges.[46]

- Order Processing: Orders should be handled through the communication and information processing network. These networks are established to assist in guaranteeing time, cost, and quality efficiency. Other factors, such as specific customer requests, need to be considered as well.

Supply Chain Management

Supply chain management (SCM) is a major concern for managers in two significant ways. First, if properly managed, the organization may recognize a competitive advantage, ensure long-term success, and be able to make rapid and confident decisions.[47] Second, a wrong decision in the SCM design could "result in a rapid loss of expertise and competitive stature by reducing a company's leverage and splitting supplier relationships across multiple sites, businesses, and geographies."[48] The need for a dynamic SCM system is significant, as the results of a survey of global management executives has proven. Over 95 percent of those surveyed rated efficient supply chain management as "critical" to their long-term success.[49]

An efficient supply chain management system must be built on five fundamental principles:

1. Constraint management—recognize and minimize the impact of constraints.

2. Concurrent versus serial planning—plan across supply chain (synchronization).

3. Global insight—grasp the global impact of local changes.

4. Advance warning—when local changes occur, immediately notify stakeholders in terms of sales, downtime, inventory, etc.

5. Built-in business optimization—the ability to recommend operational solutions to changing business scenarios.

Each of these five fundamental principles will contribute to the overall goal of an intelligent SCM system: "to achieve maximum customer responsiveness at the least possible cost."[50] The availability of tools, such as forecasting, distribution and inventory planning, and e-commerce allow many organizational processes to be integrated across supply chains.[51] Even with these modern advances in SCM, suppliers can still effect 60 to 70 percent of an organization's cost structure, ensuring that these major concerns will remain relevant.[52]

A variety of factors can contribute to the overall success of an organization's supply chain. One factor is how efficiently the organization is able to take a customer request and turn it into a desirable service or product. Another factor is the ability to adapt to market shifts or changes in customer demand. Also, the size difference between outsourcing partners can enable or hinder an organization's ability. Finally, the level of integration between suppliers will have an influence on the effectiveness of the supply chain. Proper management of these factors may have a significant impact, as operation managers ensure that all parties work together, share information, and operate in a way that guarantees the lowest costs and the highest levels of availability throughout the chain.

Third party logistics suppliers (3PL's) play a significant role in supply chain management. In the past, 3PL's were limited to noncritical processes within an organization, such as storage, transportation, or documentation. Very few 3PL's actually had a substantial role in the overall performance or success of the supplying company. The 3PL was more or less viewed as an outside source for providing the incidentals, rather than a strategic business partner. Today, that role has changed as the result of ongoing globalization and the need for companies to manage increasingly complex supply chains. 3PL's can contribute to nearly all aspects of an organization, including purchasing, finance, marketing, and operations. The continuing integration of supplier and 3PL is having an impact in the international business community.

Brief Summary of Major Points

- *Operations management* focuses on managing the various processes needed to produce and distribute goods and/or services. These activities primarily include development, production, and distribution. The operations manager is responsible for ensuring that each process is operating with maximum efficiency, ensuring maximum potential for growth and profit.
- *Capacity.* Production capacity focuses on maximizing the productivity of the readily available plant materials and people. Rather than investing in new systems, capacity relies on planning and management to reach its desired level of effectiveness.
- *Facilities location.* This is one of the most important decisions of operations management. The location of facilities must be chosen based on the predetermined supply chain. Unlike other decisions in the organization, such as selection of suppliers or transportation that can be frequently changed based on availability of new materials, suppliers, price offers, etc., location decisions are long term, and thus, must be approached carefully.
- *Location economies.* Whenever expanding production globally, a company should be aware of the economic environment in the given country. Besides all the crucial production factors, such as availability of inputs, prices, competition, and potential demand, companies must be aware of the local laws and regulations as well. The goal is to select locations that will provide the best input selection and high potential demand.
- *Centralization vs. Decentralization Process.* Centralization means merging all the company's operations, facilities, and/or management into one location, whereas decentralization involves the spreading out of company's operations into different locations. The decision should be made based on the company's present and future needs, in order to stay cost and time efficient, flexible, objective, and well managed.
- *Standardization vs. Adaptation.* Global companies should plan production based on the knowledge of customers and competition. Standardization assumes that despite the country or culture, all people have the same needs; therefore, the same products should be sold worldwide. This is the simpler of the two approaches because it saves time and money otherwise needed for research, production, and packaging. Despite such crucial benefits, adaptation should be the preferred approach for a global company because it focuses on satisfying different customers worldwide.
- *Facilities layout.* A company must decide on the physical organization of its facilities, based on the knowledge of production requirements. The

core function is to minimize material handling costs. A facility must adhere to safety and legal requirements, such as the floor-to-ceiling height and floor loading.

- *Make or buy decisions.* Whether to outsource or produce internally is the most important decision in a supply chain. It shows the company's core competencies, as well as the investments directed towards both suppliers and a company's own internal production. These decisions take into consideration the financial standing, cost efficiency, experience, available equipment, and material.

- *Selection and acquisition of raw materials.* Acquiring the right mix of raw materials in the right quantities and at the right time and place is one of the most important decisions of the production process, because materials account for up to 80 percent of the value of the output. Companies must make sure to research, analyze, select, and negotiate potential suppliers before expanding production operations to a foreign country.

- *Selection and acquisition of fixed assets—modify existing or buy new (Greenfield Investment).* There are two alternatives for a company when expanding its operations globally: either to purchase or build a production facility. Naturally, the more affordable solution should be chosen, but a company should consider pros and cons of both alternatives to maximize the efficiency and effectiveness of an organization. For instance, though purchasing an existing facility can save money and time, building a new one eliminates the costs of production adaptation. Greenfield Investments, one form of foreign direct investment, are often met with favorable reactions from the governments of foreign host countries.

- *Continuous improvement.* Total quality management is based on the continuous improvement of all aspects of the production process, from purchasing materials, through manufacturing, and finally, to delivering finished products to customers. Employees are responsible for individual workloads in order to eliminate excessive control issues and prevent related problems. An important part of TQM is the ISO Quality System Management Standard that uses measurable objectives to determine company quality standards, as well as customer satisfaction.

- *Just-in-time systems* represent another part of TQM. Tough JIT systems evolved over fifty years ago in Japan and still serve as a basis for success in modern companies. The whole idea is based on taking steps to eliminate waste, such as product defects, process time, inventories, and human and machinery waste from the production process.

- *Inventory control* is another crucial step in eliminating costs and sustaining a smooth production process. The basic principle is to maintain sufficient inventories to satisfy demand, while avoiding overstocking and related warehousing and material spoilage costs. A tough JIT inventory model is the most commonly preferred one; however, it may not work for every organization. Inventory decisions need to be based on demand, necessary lead time forecasting, and a consideration of inventory and excess stock costs. Basically, companies need to select an inventory control model that will best fit specific production requirements.

- *Global Logistics* includes the movement of products, semifinished products, components, materials, and information worldwide. In addition to the basic concepts of logistics, global logistics has additional considerations, such as varying time zones, cultures, and currencies. There are three main levels of decision making that companies need to take into consideration. Strategic level decisions are made by top management and include the planning, fulfilling, and controlling of strategic goals. Network level decisions focus on the physical facility network and communication-information network. Operations level decisions focus on the aspects of the production process, such as demand/inventory forecasting, material handling, and warehousing.

Moving from Theory into Practice

The following summarizes a question and answer session with coauthor Joe Robinson. His answers are useful in contemplating how the global business professional can translate the theories and concepts covered in this chapter via practical answers to the questions from real life experiences.

Much has been said about the benefits of diminished labor costs overseas. Can you give an example of when this may not be a good idea?

I started answering this question by gathering details on a case involving Mexico; however, I decided to change the example to a more recent case.

It just so happened that this morning I received several e-mails involving a second shipment of medical devices recently shipped from Thailand to Japan. The medical devices are designed and owned by a U.S. company and are manufactured under license and with all due diligence having been followed in the set up of this arrangement. The financial justification for deciding to manufacture in Thailand (rather than in the USA) and shipping to other countries in Asia is to save money on the diminished labor costs involved in the manufacture as well as minor cost savings on freight charges.

Unfortunately, upon inspection of the devices, six out of one-hundred devices are being rejected due to "non-compliance to standards and cosmetic deficiencies." Because this is a new market entry it is most unfortunate that this happened. The reject rate of the very same product manufactured in the USA is zero at the customer level. The reject rate at the factory is less than one in one hundred, and the U. S. customers so far have not received any below standard products in the first year and a half of this new product.

This is clearly a case where diminished labor costs at the expense of quality and compliance to standards is not a good idea.

In determining facilities location, does the expatriate decision maker's personal considerations come into play? If so, can you provide an example?

Many young men who want to go overseas in a posting for their company may not have any strong preferences so long as the expatriate financial package and "perks" are attractive. However, in the case of the posting where the wife joins the husband, the decision as to where to go creates many personal considerations that indeed are of important concern.

Picture the scenario where the husband is dutifully working and engaged all day in his job. He is surrounded by peers, company associates, and professional clients. His wife, on the other hand, may be alone, generally inactive on a daily basis, and if she does not know the local language and is not engaged in some worthwhile activities, then she may become lonely, despondent, and even miserable.

It appears that where one goes overseas and to the extent that the wife and children are involved that personal dynamics are truly important in the expatriate decision maker's personal considerations.

What criteria do you use when considering make or buy decisions?

Some global corporations have a policy to manufacture their products exclusively in their own factory and ship on a worldwide basis. Other global corporations have a policy to exclusively buy their own products under manufacture license, while other global corporations do a combination of both practices. Each of these methods is successful. When does one company decide to buy and when does another decide to make their own product?

Generally, if a product is not covered by patents, either content or by process, but rather by the "art" of manufacturing, then that corporation may not want to divulge their trade secrets in the manufacturing process. An example of this involves two separate and unrelated manufactures that I work with in which the founders first manufactured their own production machinery to produce the product that they sell. Outsiders, especially those cognizant in the science and the art of the industry, are not allowed inside the factory to see the one-of-a-kind machine that is customized and unique to that factory and product. In this case, the company policy is to make and not buy their product.

On the opposite end of the spectrum, if a product manufacturing process is generically well known and it can be made under quality standards and there are cost savings in labor, freight, duties, and availability of raw materials to an outsource factory, then the decision to buy and drop ship most likely will be the decision of choice.

Can you elaborate a bit on the concept of KANBAN clusters?

KANBAN is a Japanese word relating to logistics and implying near-to-the-factory inventory of raw materials and components needed in the manufacturing process. The system is based on quick demand and results in minimizing both physical inventory and tying up cash flow in excess factory inventory of raw materials and components used in the manufacturing process—especially those items that are critical to the production of the finished goods.

Although this is a Japanese innovation, let me relate an example utilizing American exporters and manufacturing companies in China. The Guangdong Province in Southern China is world famous for manufacturing furniture. An American company that formulates and manufactures adhesives for the furniture industry exports their adhesives in bulk to their bonded warehouse facility located in central Guangdong Providence. Here, they repackage into smaller containers and have it ready to deliver to the numerous furniture fabricators and manufacturers practically on instant demand.

Many of these same furniture manufacturers need Appalachian hardwood in the production of the finished products. The suppliers of Appalachian hardwood, such as white and red oak, maple, walnut, and cherry in the form of dimensional lumber, send their products to central warehouse facilities for instant delivery to the surrounding furniture factories.

As you may well know, the American furniture industry migrated from the U.S. to Mexico to China. Some U.S. companies that "followed their customers" not only sustained their business but in some cases are also selling more to the Chinese factories than ever before their former U.S. domestic sales. The lesson to be learned here is that in some cases, the KANBAN concept benefits both the factories as well as the suppliers to those factories, resulting in a win-win scenario for both the seller and the buyer.

<u>Does TQM work across cultures, and can you relate this to ISO standards?</u>

Total Quality Management is a people oriented concept. It functions best when practiced as an all encompassing apparatus where company employees from factory workers to sales staff to administrative personnel to top management strive to follow the same path to achieve quality in how the overall business is conducted. The basic goal is to generate customer satisfaction on time and every time. I refer to TQM as a "thrival" method rather than a survival system. In order to work it must include everyone in the process. Further, everyone needs to have some sort of incentive to participate in the TQM system.

Those cultures who value individual contributions by respecting and acknowledging good work and performance will do best with the TQM model. Those cultures that do not recognize the individual do not do well in adopting and practicing TQM. Those cultures that exercise capitalism and entrepreneurship appear to meet the highest standards and expectations as prescribed by TQM opposed to those cultures that do not recognize the worth of the individual such as Communism and extreme socialism.

ISO is similar to TQM, but whereas TQM is more of a concept and overall operating model, ISO is more of a set of procedures that addresses specific actions and business and production behaviors, such as training, maintenance, testing, inspection, and dealing with direct customer issues, such as how to handle complaints to continuously improve all facets of the company business. A company who has ISO Certification is perceived globally to be a more attractive company to do business with than a company that does not have ISO Certification. Having ISO Certification in some cases can make the difference in being competitive and getting the order, or if you are not ISO Certified and your competitor is certified, you could find yourself losing business to some customers who make certification a requirement in order to quality for selling to them.

How important is ISO 9000 to the global business professional?

If you export to certain industries, it is essential that you be certified to ISO 9000 standards. The automotive industry is an example. The automotive industry actually has their own designation QS 9000. Exporting to the aircraft industry, the chemical industry, and petroleum industry are other examples where certification to ISO 9000 standards is a necessary requirement for doing business with customers in these industries. The best advice here is that you must follow what is expected and practiced in international protocol for your industry if you want to be successful on a global scale.

Can you provide some tips for the management of inventory?

Inventory management comes in two adaptations. One form is the inventory that you need to have in order to manufacture your own products and carry out your own business. The other is the inventory you want to manage for supplying and keeping your customers happy on a global scale.

In the first example, standard procedures such as having a relationship with more than one supplier for critical components are a good practice. Locating suppliers near your factory is another good example for inventory management. Approving and purchasing from suppliers who are ISO certified is a good idea and in some cases a necessity when your customer demands as part of the purchase agreement that your supplies must have certified quality standards and procedures built into your manufactured product.

An example of inventory management for your customers is a factory automation machine builder who needs to stock maintenance and perishable parts for immediate dispatch to his customers. If you export a lot of plasticsindustry machinery to Brazil, then you need to provide inventory management to properly service your machines for quick repair and maintenance. A local sales liaison facility is a common method for providing both the needed inventory stocking point as well as the repair technician who doubles as your salesman in the target rich market.

Another example is if you manufactured coal mining machinery and your major overseas customers are in China, you need to have an adequate inventory of components and supplies conveniently located in China to service your customers for both routine maintenance and breakdown and repair purposes. Companies who do not follow this good global type inventory management practiced often have to air freight repair components, and this creates delay and is expensive. The result is a set of unhappy customers who will leave you if your competitor provides better inventory management to avoid costly freight and unnecessary shipping delays. Good global inventory management is a skill that needs to be constantly monitored so it does not get too expensive, yet at the same time, produce the results you need to thrive as an international business player.

How has global logistics changed over the last two decades?

Speed is the one word that I would use to describe the single most noteworthy change in global logistics over the past twenty-five years. Quantum leaps in know-how, expertise, and technology have produced supply chain management techniques that were not conceivable twenty-five years ago.

Bar codes, instant communication, containerization (both marine and air), and wireless data entry from point of sale back to the original manufacturing facility have all created a global market such that even the smallest company can participate in global commerce if they have the desire, management commitment, and a quality product for sale.

In terms of transportation logistics, what should a company not do?

There are several things one should not do; yet, most international companies do them routinely. For example, it is common to utilize only one freight forwarder to handle all your transportation and logistics to multiple countries. Freight forwarders have their strong and not so strong areas of expertise and geographic connections. When I worked for my third company, we exported to 105 countries. We used one freight forwarder for Europe, another for Mexico, another for Australia, another for Israel, and yet another for Australia. I utilized the freight forwarder who could give me the best service in the country of destination where my product was being shipped. If a freight forwarder has as strong office and staff, say, in Europe, but not in Latin America, then the successful international manager will find the best freight forwarder for his product with the best connections, staff, and services for Latin America.

Do not rely solely on the FFF (Foreign Freight Forwarder) to prepare all your export documentation and paper work. It is routine to give power of attorney to a freight forwarder or custom house broker; however, if a mistake is made in the accuracy of a particular document, it is still the responsibility of the shipper (you the exporter) to comply to the corresponding regulation. The exporter is usually referred to as the shipper. Another designation is USPPI (U. S. Principal Party in Interest). Those who do best in global business are the companies who do their own paperwork and documentation in-house and rely on freight forwarders to handle and book freight scheduling and negotiate with the carriers for the best rates. Further, do not overlook the export regulation to keep your transaction records for a minimum of five years.

If you are a distant factory or a subsidiary of a large global company, do not blindly accept the parent corporation's transportation logistics company. Check it out for yourself and if you can get better service, faster deliveries, or more favorable rates—or all three—then negotiate with your parent company to switch to the more favorable transportation logistics provider.

From time to time, be sure to ascertain whether or not your freight forwarder or customs house broker continues to provide you with optimum service and favorable costs. You have to keep them on their toes or their service may slip, or they may take you for granted.

For those just starting into the global arena or for those entering a new region or country, do not rely solely on advice from friends and associates. Contact several freight forwarders or 3PL's (Third Party Logistics) who can greatly assist you by integration as well as the entire supervision and administration of all logistic steps, especially in intricate supply chain movement of your raw materials, assembly components, and your finished products. When checking out a FFF or 3PL, obtain in writing a list of their services and what they provide. Be sure you understand what they provide and analyze and compare these services and expectations, and then after careful due diligence, choose the logistics transportation firm that best suits your aggregate needs.

My company recently announced a new position, *"International Marketing and Sales Manager,"* in charge of exports. We have only exported an occasional unsolicited order. Give me advice, starting at the very beginning on what I need to consider and tell me steps to take to set up the export department and make things go smoothly in this new endeavor for my company.

Let me give you my advice in a numerical format listed in order of priority.

First be sure there is a complete commitment to this new position backed by realistic expectations of your top executive team: your CEO, CFO, and Production Manager. This is first and foremost and perhaps the most important single a factor you must consider from a personal and career point of view. Check if the creation, development, support, and expectations of the new export department all contribute to stated company goals and corporate mission statement.

Second, find out if there is a financial allocation and how much is set aside for this new department for hiring staff, travel, and administrative needs. As part of this step, run your own estimates on projected costs for setting up your business and sustenance during your start up for finances and resources to determine if adequate amounts have been provided for. If you feel that initial resources are initially inadequate, be sure to negotiate for more money and reserves at this stage because once you accept the job and find out you need more finances at a later date, it invariably becomes more difficult to request funds after-the-fact. Also be sure that funds have been projected for the distant future and not just on a first year basis. Are your short- and long-term targets realistic and are the funds available and adequate to pursue these targets? It takes time to build a successful export business, so be sure to cover this aspect of your analysis.

Third, be sure the new position manager has the authority and encouragement to hire professional and technically competent new staff with commensurate salaries and compensation packages.

Fourth, recognize the need to understand the nuts-and-bolts of operating an export department. Do you comprehend the nomenclature of the daily terms of transactions and rules of engagement in the global export process? You will be expected to understand and negotiate utilizing language such as Incoterms 2000 (ICC Official Rules for the Interpretation of Trade Terms), HTS (Harmonized Tariff Schedule, a ten-digit global product and identity descriptive code), methods of payment, such as Confirmed Irrevocable Letter of Credit or Cash Against Documents, ECCN (Export Control Classification Number), export documents such, as Pro Forma Invoice and Commercial Invoice and regulations such as when and under what circumstances you may or may not need an export license. If you or your staff directly involved in the export process, and this includes your export sales personnel, know how and when to use these terms then consider yourself lucky; however, if training is needed, there are numerous avenues to obtain this training, including world trade centers, universities, and private organizations and consultants who can help you and your staff get up to speed in this area. A refresher course in an export procedures seminar or work shop is a good idea to keep abreast of the rules and regulations as they apply to your business.

Finally, bear in mind that over 90 percent of the earth's people live outside the United States. With the acceleration of affluence and economic prosperity being developed all around the world at an all-time high, now is the best time in our planet's history to engage in a career in global commerce.

Key Concepts

- Operations Management *256*
- Capacity *257*
- Facilities location *257*
- Location economies *258*
- Centralization
- Decentralization *259*
- Improvement
- Process *259*
- Standardizations
- Adaptation *260*
- Facilities layout *261*
- Make decisions
- Buy decisions *262*
- Outsourcing
- Raw materials *262*
- Fixed assets *264*
- TQM *266*
- Continuous *267*
- ISO 9000 *268*
- Just-in-time systems *269*
- Inventory *271*
- Global logistics *272*

ENDNOTES

CHAPTER ONE

1 The World Bank. (2006). Globalization. Retrieved October 12, 2006 from http://www1.worldbank.org/economicpolicy/globalization/

2 The World Bank. (2006). Assessing Globalization. Retrieved October 12, 2006 from http://www1.worldbank.org/economicpolicy/globalization/documents/AssessingGlobalizationP1.pdf p. 1

3 Ibid. p. 2

4 Legrain, P. (2003). Cultural Globalization Is Not Americanization. The Chronicle of Higher Education. May 9, 2003. Retrieved October16, 2006 from http://chronicle.com/free/v49/i35/35b00701.htm . Para. 5

5 Castles, S. (2002). Migration and Community Formation under Conditions of Globalization. International Migration Review, 36(4), 1143-1169.

6 WTO. (2006). What is the WTO? Retrieved September 11, 2006 from http://www.wto.int/english/thewto_e/whatis_e/whatis_e.htm.

7 NACLA. (2004). NAFTA Turns Ten 1994-2004. NACLA Report on the Americas, 37, 6-8.

8 Bureau of Economic Analysis. (2006). NIPA Tables v1.1.1 – Percent Change from Preceding Period in Real Gross Domestic Product – Period 1992-A & Q to 2005-A & Q. Retrieved September 12, 2006 from https://bea.gov/bea/dn/nipaweb/.

9 Choe, J. (2006). Costly Growth: China's Environmental Woes. Harvard International Review, 27, 8-9.

10 CIA. (2006). The World Factbook – Rank Order – GDP (purchasing power parity) – 2005 Estimate. Retrieved September 12, 2006 from https://www.cia.gov/cia/publications/factbook/rankorder/2001rank.html.

11 CIA. (2006). The World Factbook – United States. Retrieved September 12, 2006 from https://www.cia.gov/cia/publications/factbook/geos/us.html.

12 Sinnett, W. (2006). Global Sourcing for Global Markets. Financial Executive, 22, 46-48.

13 International Trade Administration. (2006). U.S. Export/Import Statistics - Coal (not anthracite). Retrieved September 12, 2006 from http://www.ita.doc.gov/td/energy/coal_export_stats.htm.

14 Schlumberger. (2006). About Schlumberger. Retrieved September 16, 2006 from http://www.slb.com/content/about/.

15 Multinational Corporation. (n.d.). Reference.com. Retrieved October 16, 2006, from Reference.com website: http://www.reference.com/browse/wiki/Multinational_corporation

16 Scott, L., & Otnes, C. (1996). Something Old, Something New: Exploring the Interaction Between Ritual and Advertising. Journal of Advertising, 25, 33-39, § Conclusion, ¶ 1.

17 Moore, K. J., & Lewis, D. C. (2000). Multinational Enterprise in Ancient Phonicia. Business History, 42, 17.

18 Holy Bible (KJV). 1 Kings 5:1-18.

19 Pax Romana, Retrieved October 16, 2006 from http://www.unrv.com/early-empire/pax-romana.php

20 Woods, R. O. (2003). Harnessing the Void: How the Industrial Revolution Began in a Vaccum. Mechanical Engineering-CIME, 125, 38-41.

21 EIA. (2002). Acquisitions of U.S. Energy Assets by Foreign Investors in 2002 Remain High. Retrieved September 27, 2006 from http://tonto.eia.doe.gov/FTPROOT/financial/fdiad2002.pdf.

22 OECD. (2006). About OECD. Retrieved September 28, 2006 from http://www.oecd.org/about/0,2337,en_2649_201185_1_1_1_1_1,00.html.

23 Computer Dealer News. (2001). Integrated LAN, Video in POS System. Computer Dealer News, August 31, 2001, 17-17, 40.

24 M. Salisbury. (2006). Containerized Ocean Trade. The Journal of Commerce, 7-29, 49.

25 ISO in Brief. ISO. Retrieved October 16, 2006 from http://www.iso.org/iso/en/prods-services/otherpubs/pdf/isoinbrief_2006-en.pdf

26 Forbes Inc. (2006). The Forbes Global 2000. Retrieved September 30, 2006 from http://www.forbes.com/lists/results.jhtml?passListId=18&passYear=2005&passListType=Company&searchPar

ameter1=unset&searchParameter2=unset&result
sStart=1&resultsHowMany=100&resultsSortPro
perties=%2Bnumberfield1%2C%2Bstringfield2
&resultsSortCategoryName=rank&passKeyword
=&category1=category&category2=category&fro
mColumnClick=true&boxes=custom

27 S. Anderson & J. Cavanagh. (2000). The Rise
of Corporate Global Power. Institute for Policy
Studies. Retrieved September 29, 2006 from
http://www.ips-dc.org/downloads/Top_200.pdf.

28 D. Kruckeberg & K. Tsetsura. (2003). A
Composite Index by Country of Variables Related
to the Likelihood of the Existence of Cash for
News Coverage. Institute for Public Relations.
Published July 21, 2003.

29 R. Pierik & M. Houwerzijl. (2006). Western
Policies on Child Labor Abroad. Ethics &
International Affairs, 20-2, 193-218.

30 R. Clark. (2005). Tsunami of Cash: Too Much
Money Was Given for Tsunami Relief. Spectator,
299-9520, 18.

31 H. Levins. (2004). Demand for Arabic Linguists
Far Outweighs Supply. St. Louis Post-
Dispatch, December 13, 2004.

32. Communication Workers of America (2007).
The United States Falling Behind. Retrieved July
12, 2007 from http://www.speedmatters.org/
document-library/sourcematerials/sm_report.pdf

33. White House Live: Assistant trade representative
moore speaks befor house committee on small
business. Retrieved July 1, 2007 from http://
usfederalnews.blogspot.com/2007/06/assistant-
trade-representative-moore.html

CHAPTER TWO

1 Merriam-Webster Online Dictionary, Retrieved
September 2, 2006 from http://www.m-w.com/
dictionary/culture

2 Answers.com, Retrieved October 15, 2006 from
http://www.answers.com/topic/ethnocentrism

3 Harris, P. (2006). European Leadership in
Globalization, Retrieved October 15, 2006
from http://www.emeraldinsight.com/Insight/
ViewContentServlet?Filename=Published/
EmeraldFullTextArticle/Articles/0540960205.html

4 Answers.com, Retrieved October 15, 2006 from
http://www.answers.com/topic/polycentrism

5 Harris, P. (2006). European Leadership in
Globalization, Retrieved October 15, 2006
from http://www.emeraldinsight.com/Insight/
ViewContentServlet?Filename=Published/
EmeraldFullTextArticle/Articles/0540960205.
html

6 Ibid.

7 Penrose, John M., Rasberry, Robert W. and Myers,
Robert J. (2004). Business Communication for
Managers: An Advanced Approach. Mason, Ohio:
Thomson: South-Western p. 19.

8 Almaney, Adnan. (1974). Intercultural
Communication and the MNC Executive.
Columbia Journal of World Business. p. 23.
Retrieved July 13, 2006 from: Business Source
Premier Database.

9 Ibid. p. 25.

10 Penrose, John M., Rasberry, Robert W. and Myers,
Robert J. (2004). Business Communication for
Managers: An Advanced Approach. Mason, Ohio:
Thomson: South-Western p.21.

11 Ibid.

12 Robbins, Stephen P. (2005). Organizational
Behavior: Eleventh Edition. New Jersey: Pearson:
Prentice- Hall p. 323.

13 Ibid.

14 The Apostles Creed. Retrieved October 15,
2006 from http://www.achristiansway.20fr.com/
CHRISTIANITY.html

15 Articles of Jewish Faith. Retrieved October 15,
2006 from http://www.noahide.org.uk

16 Islam Articles of Faith. Retrieved October 15,
2006 from http://www.islam.com/artialsfaith.
htm

17 Ibid.

18 The Hindu Universe. Retrieved October 15,
2006 from http://www.hindunet.org/

19 Buddhism. Budda Dharma Education
Association. Retrieved October 15, 2006 from
http://www.buddhanet.net/

20 Our Beliefs. Western Reform Taoism.
Retrieved October 15, 2006 from http://www.
westernreformtaoism.org/ para. 3

21   About Confucianism. (2006). Retrieved October 15, 2006 from http://www.religion-cults.com/Eastern/Confucianism/confuci.htm

22   Confucius. The Great Learning. Retrieved October 15, 2006 from http://etext.library.adelaidecedu.au/mirror/classics.mit.edu/Confucius/learning.htmc

23   Shintoism. Shinto Online learning Association. Retrieved October 15, 2006 from http://www.jinja.or.jp/english/s-0.html

24   Argandona, A., (2001). Corruption: the corporate perspective. Business Ethics: A European Review, 2, pp.163-175, (p.163).

25   USINFO Trade and Economics. Report Underpins View of Corruption as Obstacle to Development (2006), Retrieved October 15, 2006 from http://usinfo.state.gov/xarchives/display.html?p=washfile-english&y=2006&m=November&x=20061107120940SAikceinawz0.6615412. (para.2)

26   Ibid.

27   Transparency International USA (2006), Retrieved October 15, 2006 from http://www.transparency-usa.org/

28   Transparency International USA Toolkit (2006), Retrieved October 15, 2006 from http://www.transparency-usa.org/toolkit.html

29   U.S. department of Justice. Foreign Corrupt Practices Act Anti-bribery Provisions (2006), Retrieved October 15, 2006 from http://www.usdoj.gov/criminal/fraud/fcpa/dojdocb.htm

30   Attitude. (2006). Retrieved July 24, 2006 from http://dictionary.reference.com/browse/attitude.

31   Merriam-Webster Online Dictionary, Retrieved September 15, 2006 from http://www.m-w.com/dictionary/attitudes

32   Doing Business. (2006). Retrieved July 23, 2006 from http://www.frommers.com/destinations/southamerica/1010027590.html.

33   France. (2003). Retrieved July 29, 2006 from http://www.cyborlink.com/besite/france.htm.

34   United Arab Emirates. (2003). Retrieved July 29, 2006 from http://www.cyborlink.com/besite/uae.htm.

35   Italy. (2003). Retrieved July 29, 2006 from http://www.cyborlink.com/besite/italy.htm.

36   Mexico. (2003). Retrieved July 29, 2006 from http://www.cyborlink.com/besite/mexico.htm.

37   Women in Society. Retrieved July 29, 2006 from http://countrystudies.us/germany/91.htm.

38   Role of Women. Retrieved July 29, 2006 from http://countrystudies.us/iran/53.htm.

39   Role of Women. Retrieved July 29, 2006 from http://countrystudies.us/mexico/60.htm.

40   Social Class. Retrieved July 29, 2006 from http://countrystudies.us/iran/48.htm.

41   Mooney, L. A., Knox, D., & Schacht, C. (2000). Understanding social problems (2nd ed.). Cincinnati, OH: Wadsworth.. pp. 5-9.

42   McCrae, Robert R. (2004) Personality and Culture Revisted: Linking Traits and Dimensions of Culture Retrieved August 18, 2006 from http://ccr.sagepub.com/cgi/content/abstract/38/1/52

43   McCrae, Robert R. (2004) Personality and Culture Revisted: Linking Traits and Dimensions of Culture Retrieved August 18, 2006 from http://ccr.sagepub.com/cgi/content/abstract/38/1/52

44   Hofstede, Geert, Cultures and Organizations: Software of the Mind, 1997. Retrieved October 15, 2006 from http://www.geert-hofstede.com/

45   Trompenaars, F. and C. Hampden-Turner (1993). Seven Cultures of Capitalism. Doubleday Press.

46   Ibid.

CHAPTER THREE

1   Brandly, M. (2002) A Primer on Trade. Retrieved on July 24, 2006 from http://www.mises.org/story/1084

2   U.S. Department of Commerce International Trade Administration (2006, July) Promoting Trade and Investment. Retrieved on July 19, 2006 from http://www.trade.gov/promotingtrade/index.asp

3   National Center for Policy Analysis (2003) Benefits of Subsidies to New Businesses. Retrieved on July 24, 2006 from http://www.ncpa.org/sub/dpd/?page=article&Article_ID=4183

4   Spivey, M. (2006, July) The Export – Import Bank. Retrieved on July 19, 2006 from http://www.ita.doc.gov/exportamerica/FederalScoop/FS_EXIMBank.htm

5   el-Kaissi, Kamal (2006, January) Export Financing Institutions: The New Economic Player. Retrieved on July 19, 2006 from http://english.daralhayat.com/business/07-2006 Article-20060701-29d9fe69-c0a8-10ed-0186-f41e7d64627c/story.html

6   Foreign Trade Zone Resource Center (2006) A Brief History of the U.S. Foreign-Trade Zones Program. Retrieved on July 20, 2006 from http://foreign-trade-zone.com/history.htm

7   Ibid, para. 2

8   Young, R. (2006) International Trade Protection Methods. Retrieved on July 22, 2006 from http://www.bized.ac.uk/learn/economics/international/trade/notes.htm#Heading219, para. 5.

9   Moffat, M. (2006) Why are Tariffs Preferable to Quotas? Retrieved on July 22, 2006 from http://economics.about.com/cs/taxpolicy/a/tariffs_quotas.htm

10 Portman, R. (2006, March) U.S., EU File Trade Case over China's Tax on Imported Auto Parts. Local content requirement for cars, higher tariff violate WTO commitments. Retrieved on July 25, 2006 from http://usinfo.state.gov/eap/Archive/2006/Mar/30-612145.html

11 Regibeau, P., Rockett, K. (2003, June) Administrative Delays as Barriers to Trade. Retrieved on July 23, 2006 from http://www.essex.ac.uk/economics/discussion-papers/papers-text/dp557.pdf

12 Reguras, F., Naim, T., Chen J. (2006) 2006 Update to Granting Stock Options in China. Retrieve on July 25, 2006 from http://www.fenwick.com/docstore/Publications/Corporate/2006_Update_Stock_Options_China.pdf

13 France-Presse, A. (2006, May) China Says it Will Loosen Currency Controls. Retrieved on July 25, 2006 from http://www.industryweek.com/ReadArticle.aspx?ArticleID=12065

14 Court and its Procedure (2007). Retrieved on August 20, 2007 from http://www.judiciary.gov.bt/html/court/trial.php

15 United Nations Conference on Trade and Develpoment (2000). The Standardization of Law and Its Effect on Developing Economies. Retrieved on August 20, 2007 from http://www.unctad.org/en/docs/pogdsmdpbg24d4.en.pdf

16 WTO (2006) Intellectual Property: Protection and Enforcement, para. 6. Retrieved on July 25, 2006 from http://www.wto.org/english/thewto_e/whatis_e/tif_e/agrm7_e.htm

17 WTO (2006) What are Intellectual Property Rights? para. 1. Retrieved on July 25, 2006 from http://www.wto.org/english/tratop_e/trips_e/intel1_e.htm, para. 1

18 Ibid., para. 3

19 WIPO (2006) Summary of the Berne Convention for the Protection of Literary and Artistic Works, para. 6. Retrieved on July 25, 2006 from http://www.wipo.int/treaties/en/ip/berne/summary_berne.html, para. 3

20 Ibid, para. 4

21 Frey, Donald E. (1998). Individualist Economic Values and Self-Interest: The Problem in the Puritan Ethic. *Journal of Business Ethics*. Oct 1998 Part 2, Vol. 17 Issue 14, p1573-1580, 8p. Retrieved July 6, 2006 from: http://www.springerlink.com/(xy1bh5y5qrv4xt551uzham45)/app/home/contribution.asp?referrer=parent&backto=issue,6,11;journal,181,342;linkingpublicationresults,1:100281,1

22 Sun, Tao; Horn, Marty; Merritt, Dennis. (2004). Values and lifestyles of individualists and collectivists: a study on Chinese, Japanese, British and US consumers. *Journal of Consumer Marketing*, 2004, Vol. 21 Issue 5, p318-331, 14p. Retrieved July 6, 2006 from: http://www.emeraldinsight.com.ezproxy.liberty.edu:2048/Insight/viewContentItem.do?contentType=Article&contentId=856508

23 Morris, Michael H.; Davis Duane L.; Allene, Jeffrey W. (1994). Fostering Corporate Entrepreneurship: Cross-cultural Comparisons of the Importance of Individualism versus Collectivism (paragraph 6). *Journal of International Business Studies*, 1994, Vol. 25 Issue 1, p65-89, 25p, 6 charts, 1 graph. Retrieved July 6, 2006 from: http://www.palgrave-journals.com/jibs/journal/v25/n1/abs/8490849a.html

24 Ibid, (paragraph 7)

25 Ibid, (Table 1)

26 Ibid, (Table 2)

27 Economic reconstruction in Cuba. U.S. Department of State Dispatch; 6/1/92, Vol. 3 Issue 22, p436, 3p. Retrieved July 17, 2006 from: http://www.findarticles.com/p/articles/mi_m1584/is_n22_v3/ai_12493749

28 Ibid

29 The economy: Economic policy. Country Profile. Cuba. 2004. *The Economist Intelligence Unit Limited 2004* p24-25, 3p.

30 The New Dictionary of Cultural Literacy, Third Edition, 2002. http://www.bartleby.com/59/18/marketeconom.html

31 The economy: Economic policy. Country Profile. Russia, 2005. *The Economist Intelligence Unit Limited 2005* p34-36, 3p.

32 Ibid

33 The World Fact Book. *Developed Countries.* CIA. Retrieved from: https://www.cia.gov/cia/publications/factbook/appendix/appendix-b.html

34 Yamada, Bundo. (Oct. 20, 1990). DEV Centre WP 28: Internationalization Strategies of Japanese electronics Companies:Implications for Asian Newly Industrializing Economies (NIEs). Retrieved July 18, 2006 from: http://www.oecd.org/searchResult/0,2665,en_2649_201185_1_1_1_1_1,00.html

35 Fraser, Simon; Wresch, William. (2005). National Competitive Advantage in E-Commerce Efforts: A Report from Five Caribbean Nations. *Perspectives on Global Development & Technology.* Vol. 4 Issue 1, p27-44, 18p. Retrieved July 18, 2006 from: http://www.springerlink.com/(0zjor3jzmt5x23bqmfy05e55)/app/home/contribution

36 UNDP (2006). *Human Development Report 2006: Power, poverty and the global water crisis.* http://hdr.undp.org/hdr2006/

37 Stephenson, K. Arinaitwe. (March, 2006). Factors Constraining the Growth and Survival of Small Scale Businesses. A *Developing Countries* Analysis. *Journal of American Academy of Business, Cambridge.* Vol. 8 Issue 2, p167-178, 12p.

38 Ibid., p. 168

39 Ibid.

40 Craig, Ben. (4/1/2005). The Growing Significance of Purchasing Power Parity. *Economic Commentary.* P1-4, 4p, 2 graphs. Retrieved July 18, 2006 from: http://ideas.repec.org/a/fip/fedcec/y2005iapr1.html

41 Ibid.

42 UNDP (2006). *Beyond Scarcity: Power, poverty and the global water crisis.* http://hdr.undp.org/hdr2006/pdfs/report/HDR_2006_Tables.pdf

43 Barth, Steve. (Jul98). Risky business. *World Trade.* Vol. 11 Issue 7, p38, 6p, 1 chart, 5c.

44 Miceli, T.J., Sirmans, C.F. & Turnbull, G. K. (Feb2003). Land Ownership Risk and Urban Development. *Journal of Regional Science.* Vol. 43 Issue 1, p73-94, 22p. Retrieved July 21, 2006 from: http://papers.ssrn.com/sol3/papers.cfm?abstract_id=388549

45 Matz, Leonard. (Feb/Mar 2005). Measuring Operations Risk: Are We Taxiing Down the Wrong Runways? *Bank Accounting & Finance.* Vol. 18 Issue 2, p3-47, 5p. (page 3) Retrieved July 21,2006 from: http://www.kamakuraco.com/Docs/BAF_18-02_Matz.pdf

46 A Merton approach to transfer risk. *Risk.* Sep 2005, Vol. 18 Issue 9, p110-114, 5p. (abstract). Retrieved July 21, 2006 from: http://www.asiarisk.com.hk/public/showPage.html?page=58113

47 Court and its Procedure (2007). Retrieved on August 20, 2007 from http://www.judiciary.gov.bt/html/court/trial.php

48 Leiken, Robert S. (Winter96/97). Controlling the global corruption epidemic. *Foreign Policy.* Issue 105, p55, 19p, 1bw. (paragraph 1)

49 Strodes, James. (Dec97). ...Begins at home. *World Trade.* Vol. 10 Issue 12, p24, 2p, 1 cartoon, 1c.

50 Leiken, Robert S. (Winter96/97). Controlling the global corruption epidemic. *Foreign Policy.* Issue 105, p55, 19p, 1bw.

51 Hamra, Wayne. (Oct2000). Bribery in International Business Transactions and the OECD Convention: Benefits and Limitations. *Business Economics.* Vol. 35 Issue 4, p33, 14p, 1 diagram. (paragraph 6). Retrieved July 22,2006 from: http://www.allbusiness.com/periodicals/article/686469-1.html

52 Ibid.

53 Hoxter, Curtis J. (7/20/2000). Military in some Latin American countries is upsetting the

democratic process. *Caribbean business.* Vol. 28 Issue 28, p12, 1/2p.

54 Ibid.

55 Praying to make their kingdom nicer. *Economist.* 1/11/2003. Vol. 366 Issue 8306, p37-38, 2p, 1c. Retrieved July 22, 2006 from: http://www.economist.com/world/africa/displayStory.cfm?story_id=1525180

56 Ibid.

57 Bosnia Peace Operation: Pace of Implementing Dayton Accelerated as International Involvement Increased. *GAO Reports.* 6/5/1998. p1, 206p. Retrieved July 22, 2006 from: http://www.gao.gov/archive/1998/ns98138.pdf

58 Ibid.

59 Ibid.

60 Lenain, Patrick; Bonturi, Marcos; Koen, Vincent. (May2002). The fallout from terrorism. *OECD Observer.* Issue 231/232, p9, 2p, 1c. Retrieved July 22, 2006 from: http://www.findarticles.com/p/articles/mi_qa3648/is_200205/ai_n9059363

61 Robin, Raizel. (3/17/2003). Worst-case Scenario. *Canadian Business.* Vol. 76 Issue 5, p29, 1p, 1 diagram.

62 Ibid, p. 30.

63 Dunning, John H. (Jul98). An overview of relations with national governments. *New Political Economy.* Vol. 3 issue 2, p280, 5p. Retrieved July 24, 2006 from: http://www.npe-journal.group.shef.ac.uk/Vols_1-4.htm

64 Ibid.

CHAPTER FOUR

1 Promoting Trade and Investment. U.S. Department of Commerce International Trade Administration. (¶ 2) Retrieved July 8, 2006 from: http://trade.gov/promotingtrade/index.asp

2 Ministry of Foreign Affairs of Denmark. Trade Growth and Development. (¶ 1) Retrieved July 24, 2006 From: http://www.um.dk/en/menu/DevelopmentPolicy/DanishDevelopmentPolicy/Tradegrowthanddevelopment/

3 Bush, George W. Radio Address by the President to the Nation. July 21, 2001. (¶ 3) Retrieved July 8, 2006 form: http://www.whitehouse.gov/news/releases/2001/07/20010721.html\

4 Stelzer, I. Competition: The Secret weapon that keeps progress going. London Sunday Times. (¶ 2) Retrieved July 29, 2006 form the World Wide Web: http://business.timesonline.co.uk/article/0,,8209-2199739,00.html

5 Stelzer, I. Competition: The Secret weapon that keeps progress going. London Sunday Times. (¶ 2) Retrieved July 29, 2006 form the World Wide Web: http://business.timesonline.co.uk/article/0,,8209-2199739,00.html

6 Drucker, Peter F. (2005). Trading places. *The National Interest,* p101(7). Retrieved July 29, from: 2006, http://www.findarticles.com/p/articles/mi_m2751/is_79/ai_n13502257

7 U.S. Congress. (1776). Declaration of Independence. Retrieved July 16, 2006, from National Archives Web Site: http://www.archives.gov/national-archives-experience/charters/declaration_transcript.html

8 Smith, Adam. (1776). An Inquiry into the Nature and Causes of the Wealth of Nations. Library of Economics and Liberty, Book 4, (Chap. 2, ¶ 12.) Retrieved July 17, 2006 from the World Wide Web: http://www.econlib.org/library/Smith/smWN12.html

9 Ricardo, David (1821). On the Principles of Political Economy and Taxation. London: John Murray. Third edition.

10 Olin, Bertil. (1933). *Interregional and International Trade.* Cambridge: Harvard University Press.

11 Reeve, T., (2002). *Factor Endowments and Industrial Structure.* Publication number 731. (p. 5). Retrieved July 22 from Federal Reserve Web Site: http://www.federalreserve.gov/pubs/ifdp/2002/731/ifdp731.pdf

12 Vernon, R. (1966). "International Investment and International Trade in the Product Life Cycle," Quarterly Journal of Economics, 80:190-207.

13 World Trade Organization. (2006) *World Trade Report 2006.* (p. 60). Retrieved July 17, 2006 from World Trade Organization Web Site: http://www.wto.org/english/res_e/booksp_e/anrep_e/wtr06-2c_e.pdf

14 Porter, Michael. (1990). The competitive advantage of nations. New York: Basic Books.

15 Ibid.

16   *Principles of the Trading System.* (n.d.). (Principles Section ¶ 1.) Retrieved July 25, 2006 from http://www.wto.org/english/thewto_e/whatis_e/tif_e/fact2_e.htm

17   Merriam-Webster Online. (2005). Retrieved July 25, 2006 from http://www.m-w.com/dictionary/system

18   *The GATT Years: from Havana to Marrakesh.* (n.d.) (GATT: 'provisional' for almost half a century Section, ¶ 4.) Retrieved July 17, 2006 from World Trade Organization Web Site: http://www.wto.org/english/thewto_e/whatis_e/tif_e/fact4_e.htm

19   *What is the World Trade Organization?* (n.d.) (Did GATT succeed? Section, ¶ 5) Retrieved July 17, 2006 from World Trade Organization Web Site: http://www.wto.org/english/thewto_e/whatis_e/tif_e/fact1_e.htm

20   *What is the World Trade Organization?* (n.d.) (Above all, it's a negotiating forum Section ¶ 2.) Retrieved July 17, 2006 from World Trade Organization Web Site: http://www.wto.org/english/thewto_e/whatis_e/tif_e/fact1_e.htm

21   *Principles of the Trading System.* (n.d). (Principles Sections ¶ 1-8.) Retrieved July 25, 2006 from http://www.wto.org/english/thewto_e/whatis_e/tif_e/fact2_e.htm

22   *Principles of the Trading System.* (n.d). (Principles Sections ¶ 9-18.) Retrieved July 25, 2006 from http://www.wto.org/english/thewto_e/whatis_e/tif_e/fact2_e.htm

23   Reason, T. America For Sale. CFO Magazine Copyright 2006 economist.com. February 2006. (¶ 3) Retrieved July 29, 2006 from the world wide web: http://www.cfo.com/article.cfm/5435380/c_5461573?f=insidecfo

24   Winning Investments. Foreign Direct Investment Magazine. Published June 5, 2006. Retrieved August 19, 2006 from: http://www.fdimagazine.com/news/fullstory.php/aid/1646/Winning__Investments.html

25   Irwin, D. A., & American Enterprise Institute for Public Policy Research. (1996). *Three Simple Principles of Trade Policy.* Washington, DC: American Enterprise Institute. Retrieved October

4, 2006, from Questia database: http://www.questia.com/PM.qst?a=o&d=97673215

26   Balance of trade. (2006, September 30). In *Wikipedia, The Free Encyclopedia.* Retrieved 07:12, October 3, 2006 from http://en.wikipedia.org/w/index.php?title=Balance_of_trade&oldid=78697689

27   Foreign Direct Investment. (n.d.) (Foreign Direct Investment Section, ¶ 1) Retrieved July 17, 2006 from World Bank Web Site: http://rru.worldbank.org/Themes/ForeignDirectInvestment /?gclid=CNu539astYYCFSsuGgodxDT3OQ

28   Trade and Foreign Direct Investment. (1996) (FDI and employment in the host country Section, ¶ 12) Retrieved July 17, 2006 from World Trade Organization Web Site: http://www.wto.org/English/news_e/pres96_e/pr057_e.htm

29   Chandra, A., Fealey, T., Rau, P. (2006). National barriers to global competitiveness: the case of the IT industry in India. [Electronic Version] Competitiveness Review. 16(1), p. 12. Retrieved on July 26, 2006 from http://search.epnet.com.ezproxy.liberty.edu:2048/login.aspx?direct=truc&db=buh&an=21416807

30   Leong, K., (1998). Managing global operations: focus on expatriates-Mary Blonigen, the Scots company. *Production operations management.* The Ohio State University Fisher College of Business. Retrieved October 4, 2006, from http://www.decisionsciences.org/decisionline/Vol29/29_4/pom_29_4.pdf#search=%22expatriates%22

31   China set to restrict foreign property investment. China Daily Retrieved July 29, 2006 from: http://www.chinadaily.com.cn/china/2006-07/17/content_642827.htm

32   *Foreign Direct Investment (FDI).* (n.d.) (¶ 2) Retrieved July 17, 2006 from United Nations Conference on Trade and Development Web Site: http://www.unctad.org/Templates/Page.asp?intItemID=3146&lang=1

33   Foreign Ownership of Property in Mexico. Blue Road Runner.com (¶ 1) Retrieved August 19, 2006 from: http://www.blueroadrunner.com/ownprop.htm

34 Brown Field Investments (2006). *The free dictionary from Farlex.* Investopedia.com. Retrieved October 6, 2006, from http://financial-dictionary. thefreedictionary.com/Green+Field+Investment

35 Trade and Foreign Direct Investment. (1996) (FDI and employment in the host country Section, (¶ 4) Retrieved July 17, 2006 from World Trade Organization Web Site: http://www.wto. org/English/news_e/pres96_e/pr057_e.htm

36 Labyrinth of Incentives. Foreign Direct Investment Magazine. Published December 2, 2002. (¶ 7) Retrieved August 19, 2006 from the World Wide Web: http://www.fdimagazine. com/news/fullstory.php/aid/187/Labyrinth_of_ incentivesUnited_States.html

37 Labyrinth of Incentives. Foreign Direct Investment Magazine. Published December 2, 2002. (¶ 7) Retrieved August 19, 2006 from the World Wide Web: http://www.fdimagazine. com/news/fullstory.php/aid/187/Labyrinth_of_ incentivesUnited_States.html

38 Berniker, M. Dell Affirms Commitment to India. Internet News Bureau. Retrieved (¶ 21) August 19, 2006 from the world wide web: http://www. internetnews.com/ent-news/article.php/3113721

CHAPTER FIVE

1 Boyes, William and Melvin, Michael. (1991). Markets, Demand and Supply, and the Price System. *Economics.* (p. 56) Boston, MA: Houghton.

2 Ibid., p. 165

3 Schwartz, A. J., (1993). Money Supply. Retrieved July 9, 2006 from http://www.econlib.org/library/ Enc/MoneySupply.html

4 Ruffin, R. J. and Gregory. (1988). Productivity and Cost. In Ruffin, R. J. and Gregory, P. R. (4th Ed.), *Principles of Economics.* (p. 265). Glenview, IL: Scott, Foresman.

5 Ruffin, R. J. and Gregory. (1988). Demand and Supply. In Ruffin, R. J. and Gregory, P. R. (4th Ed.), *Principles of Economics.* (p. 124-25). Glenview, IL: Scott, Foresman.

6 Kapoor, J. R...et al. (1994). Banking Services. Kapoor, J. R...et al. (3rd Ed.), *Personal Finance.* (p. 189). Boston, MA: Irwin.

7 Samuelson, P. A. and Nordhaus, W. D. (1998) Uncertainty and Game Theory. In Samuelson, P. A. and Nordhaus, W. D. (16th Ed.), *Economics.* (p. 204). New York: Irwin/McGraw-Hill.

8 Bank for International Settlements. (2005). Press release March 17, 2005 Triennial Central Bank Survey of Foreign Exchange and Derivatives Market Activities. p. 9 Retrieved July 7, 2006, from http://www.bis.org/publ/rpfx05.htm

9 Bank for International Settlements. (2005). Press release March 17, 2005 Triennial Central Bank Survey of Foreign Exchange and Derivatives Market Activities. p. 15 Retrieved July 7, 2006, from http://www.bis.org/publ/rpfx05.htm

10 Ibid.

11 Cross, S.Y. (1998). *The Foreign Exchange Market in the United States.* Federal Reserve Bank of New York: NY FRBNY p. 41.

12 UBS Investment Bank (2004). *Foreign Exchange and Money Market Transactions.* Zurich: UBS AG.

13 Fast food and strong currencies. *The Economist,* June 9 2005. Page 1. Retrieved July 26, 2006 from http://www.economist.com/markets/ bigmac/displayStory.cfm?story_id=5389856

14 Bedell, D (1999).*Citibank the winner again but Deutsche snaps at its heels.* Corporate Finance, Euromoney Publications.

15 Jost, K. (1997). The stock market. Retrieved August 13, 2006, from http://library.cqpress. com/cqresearcher/cqresrre1997050200.

16 Boeckel, R. (1930). *Stock exchanges and security speculation.* Retrieved August 13, 2006, from http://library.cqpress.com/cqresearcher/ cqresrre1930020100

17 (2006). The Investor's Advocate: How the SEC Protects Investors, Maintains Market Integrity, and Facilitates Capital Formation. Para. 1 Retrieved August 13, 2006, from http://www.sec. gov/about/whatwedo.shtml

18 Report Persuant to Section 21(a) of the Securities Exchange Act of 1934 Regarding the NASD and the NASDAQ Market. Retrieved August 13, 2006, from http://www.sec.gov/litigation/ investreport/nd21a-report.txt

19   (2006). Currency Devaluation and Revaluation. Para. 1 Retrieved August 13, 2006, from http://www.newyorkfed.org/aboutthefed/fedpoint/fed38.html

20   Borlan, Bruce. (1994). The Great Depression and the New Deal. In Nash, G. B…et al. (3rd Ed.), *The American People.* (p. 824). New York: HarperCollins.

21   Roberts, J.M. (1995). The Shaping of a New World. In Roberts, J.M. (3rd Ed.), *History of the World.* (p. 936). London: Penguin

22   Perry, Marvin…et al. (1989). International Relations in an Age of Superpowers. Perry, Marvin…et al. (3rd Ed.), *Western Civilization.* (p. 826-27). Boston: Houghton

23   Bordo, M. D., (1993). Gold Standard. Retrieved July 9, 2006, from http://www.econlib.org/library/Enc/GoldStandard.html

24   U.S. Department of State. Smoot-Hawley Tariff. Para. 1 Retrieved October 15, 2006, from http://www.state.gov/r/pa/ho/time/id/17606.htm

25   Idid, Para. 2

26   Roberts, J.M. (1995). The Shaping of a New World. In Roberts, J.M. (3rd Ed.), *History of the World.* (p. 878-80). London: Penguin

27   Boyes, William and Melvin, Michael. (1991). Markets, Demand and Supply, and the Price System. *Economics.* (p. 1005) Boston, MA: Houghton.

28   De George, R. T. (1995). Famine, Natural Resources, and International Obligations. In De George, R. T. (4th Ed.), *Business Ethics.* (p. 550). Englewood Cliffs, NJ: Prentice Hall.

29   Boyes, William and Melvin, Michael. (1991). Markets, Demand and Supply, and the Price System. *Economics.* (p. 1015) Boston, MA: Houghton.

30   Heakal, R., (2003). Floating and Fixed Exchange Rates. Retrieved July 18, 2006, from http://www.investopedia.com/articles/03/020603.asp

31   Heakal, R., (2003). What is a Currency Board? Retrieved August 12, 2006, from http://www.investopedia.com/articles/03/020603.asp

32   Eichengreen, B. (1992). European Economic Community. Retrieved July 10, 2006, from http://www.econlib.org/library/Enc/EuropeanEconomicCommunity.html

33   Wegs, J.R. and Ladrech, R. (1996). European Unity. In Wegs, J.R. and Ladrech, R. (4th Ed.), *Europe Sine 1945.* (p. 154-156). Boston: Bedford/St. Martin's

34   CIA The World Factbook, European Union. Retrieved July 10, 2006, from http://www.cia.gov/cia/publications/factbook/geos/ee.html

35   Wegs, J.R. and Ladrech, R. (1996). European Unity. In Wegs, J.R. and Ladrech, R. (4th Ed.), *Europe Sine 1945.* (p. 154). Boston: Bedford/St. Martin's

36   Europa. Retrieved on 1 July 2007, from http://europa.eu/abc/european_countries/index_en.htm

CHAPTER SIX

1   Hufbauer, G. C., Schott, J. J. (1994). *Western Hemisphere Economic Integration.* Washington DC. Institue for International Economics.

2   Shaffer, Ellen R., Waitzkin, Howard, Brenner, Joseph, Jasso-Aguilar, Rebeca,(2005). Global Trade and Public Health. American Journal of Public Health, 00900036, Vol. 95, Issue 1 (§ Trade Rules ¶ 1 p.23-24)

3   Mwase, Ngila (1995). Economic integration for development in eastern and southern Africa. Round Table Vol. 36, Issue 1 (§Economic integration: theoretical overview ¶2)

4   *Regional Economic Integration*, (n.d.). Retrieved July 7, 2006, from http://www.accd.edu/sac/mgt/ibus/1305090/Chapter%208%Lecture.htm

5   Haftel, Yoram Z. (2004). From the Outside Looking in: The effect of Trading Blocs on Trade Disputes in GATT/WTO. International Studies Quarterly, Vol. 48 Issue 1 (¶ 2 p.121)

6   UC Atlas of Global Inequality (2006). Regional Trade Blocs: The role and function of regional trade blocs. (§ General Debates on Trade Blocs ¶4) Retrieved September 1, 2006 from http://ucatlas.ucsc.edu/trade/subtheme_trade_blocs.php

7   Ibid. § General Debates on Trade Blocs ¶5

8   Kirkham, Richard, Cardwell, Paul James (2006). The European Union: A Role Model for Regional

Governance. European Public Law. Vol 12 Issue 3 (§The Case for Regional Governance ¶ 1,2 p.405)

9 Yap, J. (2005). Economic integration and regional cooperation in East Asia. Retrieved on July 8, 2006, from http://www.eaber.org/intranet/documents/22/711/PIDS_Yap_05.pdf

10 Stages of Economic Integration: From Autarky to Economic Union (2006) Government of Canada. Retrieved on July 8, 2006, from http://dsp-psd.communication.gc.ca/Collection-R/LoPBdP/inbrief/prb0249-e.htm

11 Mahant, E. (2000) Regional Economic Integration -Bringing Values Back In. Retrieved on September 1, 2006 from http://www.apfpress.com/book2/pdf_files/3.pdf

12 Arnold, Dennis (2006). Free Trade Agreements and Southeast Asia. Journal of Contemporary Asia. Vol. 36, Issue 2 (p. 195 ¶ 2)

13 Mwase, Ngila (1995). Economic integration for development in eastern and southern Africa. Round Table Vol. 36, Issue 1 (§Regional integration benefits ¶2)

14 Seligson, Mitchell A. (1999). Popular Support for regional economic integration in Latin America. Journal of Latin American Studies Vol. 31 Issue 1 (p. 130 ¶1)

15 Goss, Brian Michael (2001). All of our Kids Get Better Jobs Tomorrow: The North American Free Trade Agreement in the New York Times. Journalism and Communication Monographs. Vol. 3 Issue 1 (p.4 ¶1)

16 Hufbauer, Gary C., Wong, Yee (2003). Security and the Economy in the North American Context: The Road Ahead for NAFTA. Canada – United States Law Journal Vol. 29(¶1 p. 53)

17 U.S. Customs and Border Protection (2006). North American Trade Agreement (NAFTA). (§NAFTA ¶ 1) Retrieved on September 1, 2006 from http://www.cbp.gov/xp/cgov/import/international_agreements/free_trade/nafta/

18 USTR. 2006. NAFTA: A Strong Record of Success. Retrieved 7/18/06 from http://www.ustr.gov/assets/Document_Library/Fact_Sheets/2006/asset_upload_file242_9156.pdf

19 Ibid.

20 Ratner, D., Scott R. E. (2005). NAFTA's Cautionary Tale: Recent History Suggests CAFTA could lead to further U.S. job displacement. (¶ 10). Retrieved from http://www.epi.org/content.cfm/ib214

21 Mercosur Economic Research Network Website. Retrieved on July 6th, 2006 from http://www.redmercosur.org.uy/Index03/objectives03.htm

22 Profile: Mercosur-Common Market of the South(2007). Retrieved on July 5, 2007 from http://news.bbc.co.uk/1/hi/world/americas/5195834.stm

23 Venezuela announces exit from Andean trade blocPeople's Daily Online. Retrieved on July 6th, 2006 from http://english.peopledaily.com.cn/200604/24/eng20060424_260673.html. Para. 4

24 (2006). Pisco sour. Economist, 00130613, Vol. 380, Issue 8492 ¶5

25 Ibid. ¶6

26 Glossary – Venezuela. Library of Congress. Retrieved September 30, 2006 from: http://lcweb2.loc.gov/frd/cs/venezuela/ve_glos.html

27 El Salvador Soccer War. Global Security. Retrieved September 30, 2006 from: http://www.globalsecurity.org/military/world/war/elsalvador.htm

28 Caribbean Community and Common Market. The Columbia Electronic Encyclopedia, 6th ed. Columbia University Press. Retrieved from Infoplease: http://www.infoplease.com/ce6/history/A0810434.html

29 Stout, James V, Ugaz-Pereda, Julieta (1996). Western Hemisphere Trading Blocs and Tariff Barriers for U.S. Agricultural Exports. Economic Research Service/USDA.p.138 § CACM ¶ 1. Retrieved September 30, 2006 from http://www.ers.usda.gov/publications/aer771/aer771q.pdf

30 Ibid. p.139 § CACM ¶ 3,4.

31 (2006). The Central American Free Trade Agreement (CAFTA). World Almanac & Book of Facts, 00841382, 2006 § Trade and Transportation

32 EUPOPA – The EU at a Glance. § Euro-jargon. Retrieved from http://europa.eu/abc/eurojargon/index_en.htm

33   Geographica – The Complete Illustrated Atlas of the World, 2005 Edition, p.145. Milsons Point, Australia: Random House

34   Association of South East Nations. Retrieved September 30, 2006 from http://www.aseansec. org/64.htm

35   Asia-Pacific Economic Cooperation. Retrieved September 30, 2006 from http://www.apec.org/

36   South Asian Association for Regional Cooperation. Retrieved September 30, 2006 from http://www. saarc-sec.org/main.php

37   (2006). Organization of Arab Petroleum Exporting Countries. §OAPEC Establishment ¶1Retreived September 30, 2006 from http:// www.oapecorg.org/About.htm

38   Ibid. §OAPEC Monthly Bulletin

39   Iran Press News (2006). China and Persian Gulf Council sign free trade agreement. Retrieved October 4, 2006 from http://www.iranpressnews. com/english/source/014925.html

40   Geographica – The Complete Illustrated Atlas of the World, 2005 Edition, p.313. Milsons Point, Australia: Random House

41   West Afica. (2005, February). New African. i437 p24(1)

42   (2004). Department of Foreign Affairs – Republic of South Africa. §History ¶3

43   Langton, Danielle (2005). CRS Report for Congress. United States-Southern African Customs Union (SACU) Free Trade Agreement Negotiations: Background and Potential Issues Retrieved October 6, 2006 from http://www.nationalaglawcenter.org/ assets/crs/RS21387.pdf#search=%22Southern%20 African%20Customs%20Union%E2%80%94SA CU.%20%22. p. 2, para. 2.

44   Ibid.

45   OPEC & World Supply. (2005, December 26). APS Review Oil Market Trends. v65 i26 p0

46   Organization for Economic Co-Operation and Development. Retrieved October 6, 2006 from http://www.oecd.org/about/0,2337,en_2649_ 201185_1_1_1_1_1,00.html

47   Reviews (2003). New OEDC report offers insights into adolescents' reading performance. Reading Today Vol. 20 Issue 4 ¶3

CHAPTER SEVEN

1   Henricks, M. (1997). From a distance. *Entrepreneur magazine* (§ Beyond Bicultural, ¶ 3). Retrieved July 22, 2006 from http://www.entrepreneur.com/ article/0,4621,227655-7,00.html

2   Koch, A.J. (2001). Selecting overseas markets and entry modes: Two decision processes or one? *Marketing Intelligence and Planning*, 19, p. 6.

3   Heriot, K.C., Poff, J.K. (n.d.). Costs of developing a foreign market for a small business: The market & non-market barriers to exporting by small firms, pp. 2-3. Retrieved July 22, 2006 from http://www. sbaer.uca.edu/research/icsb/2005/092.pdf

4   Palmetto Consulting. (2004). Costs of developing a foreign market for a small business: The market and nonmarket barriers to exporting by small firms (p. 8). Retrieved August 11, 2006 from http://www.sba.gov/advo/research/rs241tot.pdf

5   United Nations Industrial Development Organization. (2006). Alliances and Joint Ventures: Patterns of internationalization for developing country enterprises (pg. 19). Retrieved August 11, 2006 from http://www.unido.org/file-storage/download/?file_id=53677

6   United Nations Industrial Development Organization. (2006). Alliances and Joint Ventures: Patterns of internationalization for developing country enterprises (pg. 19). Retrieved August 11, 2006 from http://www.unido.org/file-storage/download/?file_id=53677

7   Ibid. p. 19

8   Entrepreneur magazine. (2005). How to take your company global (§ Going Global, ¶ 1). Retrieved July 23, 2006 from http://www.entrepreneur. com/article/0,4621,312297-2,00.html

9   Delaney, L. (2004). 20 factors to consider before going global. *Entrepreneur magazin.e* Retrieved August 11, 2006 from http://www.entrepreneur. com/article/0,4621,319156,00.html

10   Kurlantzick, J. (2003). Stay Home? *Entrepreneur magazine* (§ New Strategies, ¶ 1). Retrieved July 24, 2006 from http://www.entrepreneur.com/ article/0,4621,305948-3,00.html

11   Anderson, E., and Gatignon, H. (1986). *Modes of Foreign Entry: A Transaction Cost Analysis and*

Propositions. Journal of International Business Studies, pgs. 1-26

12   Levitt, T. (1983). The globalization of markets. *Harvard Business Review.*

13   Hult, G. T. M., & Ketchen, D. J. (2001). Does market orientation matter? A test of the relationship between positional advantage and performance. *Strategic Management Journal.*

14   Huber, G. P. (1991). Organizational learning: The contributing processes and the literature. Organization Science.

15   Drew, S. A. W. (1997). From knowledge to action: The impact of benchmarking on organizational performance. *Long Range Planning.*

16   Javorski, B. J., & Kohli, A. K. (1993). Market orientation: Antecedents and consequences. *Journal of Marketing.*

17   Pan, Y. & Tse, D. (2000). The Hierarchical Model of Market Entry Modes. *Journal of International Business Studies.*

18   Zacharakis, A. (1997). Entrepreneurial Entry into Foreign Markets: A Transaction Cost Perspective. *Entrepreneurship Theory & Practice.*

19   Osland, G. E., C. R. Taylor and Zou Shao Ming (2001), "Selecting International Modes of Entry and Expansion", Marketing Intelligence and Planning.

20   Keillor, B., Davila, V., Hult, G. T., (2001). Market entry strategies and influence factors: A Multiindustry/Multiproduct investigation, *Marketing Management Journal.*

21   Eriksson, K., Johansson, J., Majkgard, A., & Sharma, D. D. (1997). Experiential knowledge and the cost in the internationalization process. *Journal of International Business Studies.*

22   Hitt, M. A., Hoskisson, R. E., & Kim, H. (1997). International diversification: Effects on innovation and firm performance in product-diversified firms. *Academy of Management Journal.*

23   Czinkota, M. (1982). Export development strategies: US promotion policies. New York: Praeger.

24   Peng, M. W., Hill, C. W. L., Wang, D. Y. L., (2000). Schumpeterian dynamics versus Williamsonian considerations: A test of export intermediary performance, *Journal of Management Studies.*

25   Luostarinen, R., Welch, L., (1990). International Business Operations, Kyriiri Oy, Helsinki.

26   Pearce II, John A., Robinson Jr., Richard B. (2003). *Strategic Management: Formulation, Implementation, and Control..* 8th ed. pg. 57. New York: McGraw-Hill/Irwin.

27   Ibid. pp. 58-60.

28   Narver, J. C., & Slater, S. F. (1990). The effect of a marketing orientation on business profitability. *Journal of Marketing.*

29   Erramilli, M.K., Agarwal, S., and S-S. Kim "Are Firm-Specific Advantages Location-Specific Too?" *Journal of International Business Studies.*

30   Zou, S., & Cavusgil, S. T. (2002). The GMS: A broad conceptualization of global marketing strategy and its effects on firm performance. *Journal of Marketing.*

31   Arnold, David. (2003). Strategies for Entering and Developing International Markets. *Financial Times* (Oct 2003), Chapter 2, ¶ 1. Retrieved from http://www.phptr.com/articles/article.asp?p=101588&rl=1

32   Novicevic, Milorad M. and Harvey, Michael. (2003). Export-import relationships in a global organization: a relational contracting analysis on subsidiary behavior. *International Marketing Review.* Volume 21, No. 4/5. pp. 378-392. Retrieved from http://www.emeraldinsight.com/10.1108/02651330410547090.

33   Hester, S. (1985) Export trading companies: A marketing vehicle for small textile and apparel firms, Journal of small business management, Vol. 23.

34   Joyner, Nelson T. (N.d.). How to Find and Use an Export Management Company. ¶1. Retrieved from http://www.fita.org/aotm/0499.html.

35   USA Trade (2005) Developing an export strategy, (Electronic Version) Retrieved July 13, 2006 from www.usatrade.com., Chapter 4, .p.4.

36   Power Home Biz (2006), Export definitions. (Electronic Version) Retrieved July 13, 2006 from www.powerhomebiz.com/vol7/export.htm, p.1.

37   Bascal, Robert. (1997). The Role of the Facilitator: Understanding What Facilitators Really DO! ¶ 3. Retrieved from http://www.iaf-world.org/i4a/pages/Index.cfm?pageid=3291.

38   USA Trade (2005) Developing an export strategy, (Electronic Version) Retrieved July 13, 2006 from Developing an Export Strategy, USA Trade.gov, 2005, Chapter 6, p.3.

39   Hoffman, Richard C. and Preble, John F. (2004). Global franchising: current status and future challenges. *Journal of Services Marketing*. Volume 18, No. 2 (2004). pp 101-113. Retrieved from http://www.emeraldinsight.com/10.1108/08876 040410528700.

40   Prusaitus, S (2005). International marketing theory and practices: An investigation of marketing communications in the film industry in latin america. , Florida State University, p. 25.

41   UNIDO (2004) Alliances and joint ventures: Patterns of internationalization for developing country enterprises, Unido Series, p. 13.

42   Ibid. p. 14.

43   Kock, S (2003) Project business as a distinct entry mode: A conceptual discussion, IMP Conference, Logano, Switzerland, p11.

44   Kemp, R.G.M. (2004) Managing interdependence for joint venture success: An empirical study of dutch international joint ventures. Gronigen Press, p.216.

45   USA Trade (2005) Developing an export strategy, (Electronic Version) Retrieved July 13, 2006 from Developing an Export Strategy , USA Trade.gov, 2005, Chapter 6, p.4.

46   Gulati, R (1998) Alliances and networks. Strategic management journals, v. 19, p. 293-317.

47   Ibid.

48   UNIDO (2004) Alliances and joint ventures: Patterns of internationalization for developing country enterprises, Unido Series p. 18, 2004.

CHAPTER EIGHT

1   Jones, G. & George, J. (2003). Contemporary Management (3rd ed.). New York: McGraw-Hill Companies. p.615.

2   Bruner, R., et. al. (1998). The Portable MBA (4th ed.). New Jersey: John Wiley & Sons, Inc. p.128.

3   Bartlett, C. & Ghoshal, S. (1989). Managing Across Borders: The Transnational Solution. Massachusetts: Harvard Business School Press. p.32

4   Blocher, E., Chen, K., Cokins, G., & Lin, T. (2005). Cost Management. New York: McGraw-Hill. p.387.

5   Alexander, K. (2002). Business the Ultimate Resource. Massachusetts: Perseus Publishing. p.179.

6   Caslione, J. & Thomas, A. (2002). Global Manifest Destiny. Illinois: Dearborn Trade Publishing. p.155.

7   Ibid., p.157.

8   Ibid., p.158.

9   Grayson, D. & Hodges, A. (2002). Everybody's Business. New York: DK Publishing, Inc. p.39

10   Eccles, R. & Nohria, N. (1992). Beyond the Hype – Rediscovering the Essence of Management. Boston: Harvard Business School Press. p. 117.

11   Heizer, J. , & Render, B. (1999). Operations management (5th ed., p. 209). New Jersey: Prentice-Hall.

12   Inman, R. A. (2006) Business Reference. Encyclopedia of Management - Comp-De. (§ Inventory Types, ¶ 21). Retrieved July 15, 2006 from: http://www.referenceforbusiness.com/ management/Int-Loc/Inventory-Types.html

13   Fitzpatrick, W. M. , & Burke, D. R. (2000). Virtual partnering for transactional and relational competitive advantage (¶ 3). Global Competitiveness. Retrieved July 23, 2006, from http://www.allbusiness.com/periodicals/ article/719310-1.html

14   Fitzpatrick, W. M. , & Burke, D. R. (2000). Virtual partnering for transactional and relational competitive advantage (¶ 14). Global Competitiveness. Retrieved July 23, 2006, from http://www.allbusiness.com/periodicals/ article/719310-1.html

15   Ibid., (¶ 15).

16   Ibid., (¶ 16).

17   Fixed Assets. (n.d.). Bitpipe. Retrieved August 16, 2006 from: http://www.bitpipe.com/tlist/Fixed-Assets.html

18   Daniels, J. D. , & Radebaugh, L. H. (1998). International business: Environments and operations (8th ed., pp. 352-353). United States: Addison Wesley Longman.

19   Gorg, H. (n.d.). Analysing foreign market entry:

The choice between Greenfield investment and acquisitions (p. 4). Retrieved July 23, 2006, from http://www.tcd.ie/Economics/TEP/1998/981.pdf#search='Greenfield%20investment'

20 Inman, R. A. (2006) Business Reference. Encyclopedia of Management - Comp-De. (§ Continuous Improvement). Retrieved July 20, 2006 from: http://www.referenceforbusiness.com/management/Comp-De/Continuous-Improvement.html

21 Evans, J. R., & Lindsay, W. M. (1999). The management and control of quality (4th ed., p. 118). Cincinnati: South-Western College Publishing.

22 Kline, J.J. (1992). Total quality management in local government.Government Finance Review (¶ 5). Retrieved June 16, 2006 from http://www.allbusiness.com/periodicals/article/337928-1.html

23 Frednell, L.D., & Robbins, T.L. (1995). Modeling the role of total quality management in the customer focused organization (¶ 3). Journal of Managerial Issues. Retrieved June 16, 2006 from http://www.allbusiness.com/periodicals/article/534858-1.html

24 Briggs, S., & Keogh, W. (1999). Integrating human resorce strategy and strategic palnning to achieve business excellence (¶ 18). Total Quality Management, pS447. Retrieved June 16, 2006 from Infotrac database.

25 International Organization for Standardization. Overview of the ISO System. (§ How ISO Standards Benefit Society, ¶ 1-4). Retrieved July 19, 2006 from http://www.iso.ch/iso/en/aboutiso/introduction/index.html

26 Blocher, E.J., Chen, K. H., Cokins, G., Lin, T. W. (2005). Cost Management: A Strategic Emphasis (3rd ed., p 14). NY: McGraw Hill/Irwin.

27 Thompson, A. A., Strickland III, A. J., and Gamble, J. E., ((2006) Crafting & Executing Strategy. (15th ed. p 139). NY: McGraw Hill/Irwin

28 Beasley, J. E. (n.d.). Just in Time (JIT). Retrieved July 5, 2006 from: http://people.brunel.ac.uk/~mastjjb/jeb/or/jit.html

29 Ibid.

30 BBC. (2001, September 25). Just-in-Time Manufacturing. Retrieved July 5, 2006 from: http://www.bbc.co.uk/dna/h2g2/A593769

31 Ibid.

32 Norman, J. (1998). Entrepreneur.com. Business Start-ups. How to Manage Inventory. Retrieved July 24, 2006 from: http://www.entrpreneur.com/article/0,4621,229017-1,00.html

33 Donovan, R., M. & Co. (n.d.) Inventory Control: Improving the Bottom Line. Retrieved July 15, 2006 from: http://www.rmdonovan.com/inventory_control.htm

34 McLeavey, D. W. & Narasimhan S. L. (1985). Production Planning And Inventory Control. Massachusetts: Allyn and Bacon, Inc.

35 Moyer, McGuigan & Kretlow. (2006). Contemporary Financial Management. (10th ed.). Thomson, South-Western; Ohio.

36 Craig, T. (1996, June). Global Logistics. Information is a Key Ingredient.Retrieved July 13, 2006 from: http://www.ltdmgmt.com/mag/art3.htm

37 Langevin, A. & Riopel, D. (2005). Logistics Systems: Design and Optimization. New York; Springer Science & Business Media.

38 Ibid.

39 Buelow, D. M. (2001, November). Eight Symptoms of Poorly Optimized Distribution Networks. Retrieved July 10, 2006 from: http://www.supplychainbrain.com/archives/11.01.opinion.htm?adcode=30

40 Langevin, A. & Riopel, D. (2005). Logistics Systems: Design and Optimization. York; Springer Science & Business Media.

41 Ruch, W. A., Harold, E.F., Wieters, C. D. (1992). Fundamentals of Production/Operations Management. (5th edition). St. Paul, MN: West Publishing Company.

42 Buelow, D. M. (2001, November). Eight Symptoms of Poorly Optimized Distribution Networks. (§5-High levels of invetory). Retrieved July 10, 2006 from: http://www.supplychainbrain.com/archives/11.01.opinion.htm?adcode=30

43 Ruch, W. A., Harold, E.F., Wieters, C. D. (1992). Fundamentals of Production/Operations

Management. (5th edition). St. Paul, MN: West Publishing Company.

44 Sanderson, T. (2001, December). Developing an Internet Transportation Management Strategy. Retrieved July 10, 2006 from: http://www.supplychainbrain.com/archives/12.01.opinion.htm?adcode=30

45 Meachum, M. (1997, April). Returnable Packaging: Logistics Providers Hel Make It a Green-Green Solution. Retrieved July 10, 2006 from: http://www.supplychainbrain.com/archives/4.97.logistics.htm?adcode=90

46 Buelow, D. M. (2001, November). Eight Symptoms of Poorly Optimized Distribution Networks. Retrieved July 10, 2006 from: http://www.supplychainbrain.com/archives/11.01.opinion.htm?adcode=30

47 Kelton, K. (1998, Fall). A Business Case for Enhancing Supply Chain in the Metals Industry Information Systems Management, Vol. 15 (4): 72-76. Retrieved July 7, 2006 from: http://www.ism-journal.com/Contents1998.html

48 Rogers, S. (2004, April). Supply Management: Six Elements of Superior Design. Supply Chain Management Review. (¶ 4). Retrieved July 5, 2006 from: http://www.manufacturing.net/scm/index.asp?layout=articlePrint&articleID=CA412838

49 Kelton, K. (1998, Fall). A Business Case for Enhancing Supply Chain in the Metals Industry Information Systems Management, Vol. 15 (4): 72-76. Retrieved July 7, 2006 from: http://www.ism-journal.com/Contents1998.html

50 Ibid. ¶pg. 15

51 Ibid

52 Rogers, S. (2004, April). Supply Management: Six Elements of Superior Design. Supply Chain Management Review. Retrieved July 5, 2006 from: http://www.manufacturing.net/scm/index.asp?layout=articlePrint&articleID=CA412838

INDEX

W